I0799785

UnCORKED!

Kentucky Sports Legend
Corky Withrow

Sherrill Williams

&

Charles Thurman

AP™
Acclaim Press
— Your Next Great Book —

Acclaim Press
— Your Next Great Book —

P.O. Box 238
Morley, MO 63767
(573) 472-9800
www.acclaimpress.com

Book Design: Devon Burroughs
Cover Design: M. Frene Melton

Copyright © 2016, Sherrill Williams and Charles Thurman
All Rights Reserved.

No part of this book shall be reproduced or transmitted in any form or by any means, electronic or mechanical, including photocopying, recording or by an information or retrieval system, except in the case of brief quotations embodied in articles and reviews, without the prior written consent of the publisher. The scanning, uploading, and distribution of this book via the Internet or via any other means without permission of the publisher is illegal and punishable by law.

Library of Congress Control Number: 2016900196
ISBN-13: 978-1-942613-32-9
ISBN-10: 1-942613-32-6

First Printing 2016
Printed in the United States of America
10 9 8 7 6 5 4 3 2 1

This publication was produced using available information.
The publisher regrets it cannot assume responsibility for errors or omissions.

Contents

Foreword 4

Preface 6

Acknowledgments 8

Chapter 1: The Cowlicked Boy from Old Turd Creek 13

Chapter 2: Daddy, Won't You Take Us to Muhlenberg County? 17

Chapter 3: Say It Ain't So, Roy Settles! 23

Chapter 4: Great Expectations and a Whole Lot of Hope 31

Chapter 5: Eastward, Tourney-Bound, Loadin' Up, and Truckin'! 39

Chapter 6: Much A-Do About Corky... and a Little A-Don't 48

Chapter 7: The King and I 64

Chapter 8: The Bloody Butler County Kerfuffle of '56 75

Chapter 9: Ebb Tide 91

Chapter 10: To Be An Actor, Or More Likely, Not to Be 98

Chapter 11: With a Fist Full of Dollars 104

Chapter 12: Corky Goes to College 112

Chapter 13: Waycross to Wellsville 161

Chapter 14: Corky's Got a Ticket to Ride 174

Chapter 15: The Miserable Misfits of Mobile Bay 187

Chapter 16: A Bus Load of Spam, Billy Graham, and the Southside Bar and Grill 191

Chapter 17: Dead Goats and Armed Guards 202

Chapter 18: If Ya Ain't Strikin' out, Ya Ain't Swingin' the Bat 214

Chapter 19: Rejection, Readjustment, Reality 262

Chapter 20: Is There Life After Baseball? 277

Epilogue 281

About the Authors 283

Index 284

Foreword

It seems to be happening more and more. As time catches up to us all, it also claims its share of legendary sports history. It's really the fault of no one in particular that former greats, with their stories, slip through the proverbial cracks of the ages, never to be heard from again.

Writer Sherrill Williams has made sure this didn't happen to one of Kentucky's great two-sport athletes from the mid '50s. It was an era when high school basketball, more often than not, was the only game in town.

Central City's Corky Withrow was as big as it got. From the time he was fifteen years old, he was a man among boys, at least on the basketball court in this western Kentucky coal town. His name took on rock star status, even to the point of upstaging two other local boys of notoriety, Don and Phil Everly.

Williams takes us back to the days when high school basketball was of high importance. Central City was a town of hard-working men, risking their lives to haul coal from beneath the Muhlenberg County soil. Their pleasure in life usually meant cramming into the Central City gym to see a 6'3" raw-boned, rough and tumble teenager play basketball.

With scores of colleges in a tug-of-war to recruit him, almost out of nowhere Corky surprised many by inking a professional baseball contract. In doing so, he broke the hearts of Central City fans who had hopes of seeing him play basketball for Coach Adolph Rupp at the University of Kentucky.

Withrow opens up to writer Williams with unglamorous and gut-wrenching stories of almost a decade of baseball struggles in an effort to get to the "bigs." He finally did it!

By this time Corky was twenty-eight and had seen it all, beyond his years. That's what pressure, travel, and not knowing what was next do to a man... especially a man playing in professional sports, raising a family, and questioning his very own future.

What a story.

—Gary P. West, Author

Preface

Little boys have big dreams... especially in rural Kentucky. Almost without exception, little boys growing up in a small town during the early '50s had common dreams and aspirations.

In an era long before cable television, most winter nights in sleepy hometowns were spent watching local high school basketball teams play in loud, musty, crowded gymnasiums. It was on this stage that gangly teenage boys became heroes to starry-eyed kids. They dreamed of wearing those school colors, carrying on oftentimes modest tradition, and having an entire community cheer wildly as they battled their mirror images from the adjoining county or community. It was a scenario played out over and over, year after year; it was, in short, a ritual—a right of passage if you will—to manhood. As these starry-eyed little boys grew and experienced the thrill of playing for their beloved high school, most could only imagine Coach Rupp might see in them that special gift and ask them to play for the University of Kentucky.

Fast forward to dusty, hot summer days when those same little boys would find a vacant lot, choose teams, and play baseball 'til supper time. Some even had organized leagues with actual uniforms and rubber cleats, bases that were not cardboard boxes, and bats with big leaguer's names on them. On these sweaty battlefields little boys became Babe Ruth, Whitey Ford, Pee Wee Reese, and Stan Musial. As those long summer days drifted into sultry summer nights, many kids knew exactly where to turn the AM dial on the family radio to hear the real big leaguers play baseball.

Raymond "Corky" Withrow was an average kid who dreamed these dreams like all the other little boys of his time—with one exception. His dreams came true! Corky's incredible life's journey is strewn with both heartbreak and triumph. This amazing man, who today seems as "regular" as you and me, was a star that shone brighter than he could have ever imagined. In high school he was "The Man" for the Golden Tide of Central City High School and Coach Rupp's prized recruit for the Wildcats. Later he was tapped as the player to replace Stan Musial in the St. Louis Cardinals' outfield.

Corky lived every dream any little boy could have. Amidst the glory and accolades life happens, and dreams sometimes come with crushing disappointments. Even as a High School All-American Basketball player, one of the top five prep stars in the nation, he was buried in the shadow of THE basketball player in Kentucky, "King" Kelly Coleman of Wayland High School. Through it all, Corky met each challenge and turned them into opportunities. Yet, even after this roller coaster life, Corky is a fun-loving, kind, and gentle man whom I proudly call my friend. I know you'll enjoy Sherrill's insight into Corky's amazing life, taking from it that, even against all odds, dreams can and do come true.

—Rick Whobrey
Former Executive Director
Kentucky High School Basketball Hall of Fame

Acknowledgments

A project of this magnitude isn't one accomplished without the advice, assistance, and critical oversight of others. My sincere thanks is offered to the following, most of whom have been with Corky and me every step along this joyful journey. Their roles cannot be overstated.

First, thanks to Gary West. Your advice, experience, expertise, and constructive criticism have proven invaluable.

Thanks also to my long-time friend and North Hardin teaching comrade, Ron Bevars. Your knowledge and insight into the history of Kentucky High School Basketball are unequalled, and our many trips across the state in pursuit of that history are valued. As for your wife, Susan, may this book address her inquiry of several years ago, that question being: "Who in the Hell is Corky Withrow?!!"

Rick Whobrey...Your assistance in this, as well as with other projects we have taken on, has made it more fun than anyone deserves to have. May there be many more. To Kim, your wife, also go thanks. Without her grammatical scrutiny, the number of errors would, no doubt, be off the charts. The ones that remain are mine alone.

To the guys in Floyd County—Jerry Fultz and "King" Kelly Coleman—I offer thanks as well! As you know, our journey with Corky began with you two in Sonora and Wayland several years ago.

Mark Stone and Richard Deavers, publishers of the Central City *Times-Argus*, can't be overlooked, either, as they not only allowed the use of their valuable archives, but offered information via their vast and unequalled knowledge of Central City history.

Equally important, as both background material and a fact-check of greatest value, was Gary West's 2006 biography, *King Kelly*

Coleman: Kentucky's Greatest Basketball Legend, and Tom Wallace's 2015 comprehensive look at Central City High's basketball history, one titled *Golden Glory: The History of Central City Basketball.* Of no less value has been Jeff Bridgeman's *Encyclopedia of Kentucky High School Basketball.* It is an unparalleled storehouse of Kentucky high school basketball material.

UnCORKED!

Kentucky Sports Legend

Corky Withrow

Chapter 1

The Cowlicked Boy from Old Turd Creek

This story—one chronicling the life and athletic career of Raymond "Corky" Withrow—doesn't begin in Muhlenberg County, Kentucky, nor does it begin in the Bluegrass State at all. Instead, we must travel 300 miles east to Highcoal, a coal mining camp deep in the mountains of Boone County, West Virginia. Here, in this remote, isolated, and rough and tumble pocket of the Mountaineer State, Corky was born on Nov. 28, 1937, the second of three children born to Otis Earl and Flo Eva Allison Withrow.

Otis Earl Withrow (1914-2007) was a native of the Equality community of Ohio County, Kentucky, a rural area not far from the Green River, and only a dozen or so miles north of the Muhlenberg County town of Central City. A coal miner more by necessity than choice, Otis had moved to Highcoal sometime between 1935 and '37, taking with him Flo Eva, his wife, and Roy Duane, their son. Roy, their first child, had been born in Muhlenberg County on the 24th of February, 1935.

Corky isn't sure how his father acquired the job in Highcoal, but the fact that Corky's grandfather, Etsel Lee Withrow, was a miner there, too, would surely provide the answer. Etsel Lee, born in Ohio County in 1886, had died from injuries suffered when struck by an ambulance in Highcoal in 1941, only three years after the death of his wife, Cleopatra Brown Withrow, in June of '38. "Cleo," too, was a native Ohio Countian, having been born there in 1891. Corky, being so young at the time of their deaths, has no memories of these paternal grandparents.

There wasn't much to brag about in Highcoal—"one road in, and one road out," according to Corky—and it was a "company town." That company was Anchor Coal.

Here, the Withrows settled into a narrow, wooden-sided, shotgun-style house, one built by the coal company sometime around 1900. The house, like most there, contained four rooms—two bedrooms upstairs, a kitchen, and living room downstairs. There were about 200 people in Highcoal at that time, and most of the houses—except those for company officials and the camp's doctor—were equipped much the same. There was a coal burning stove, of course, and electricity... but no indoor plumbing. Drinking water was drawn from a hand-pump located at the foot of a steep path leading up to the mountaintop camp, and "wash-water" came from a nearby stream. Like everything else in Highcoal, the Withrows' dwelling was owned by Anchor Coal, with the monthly rent of $15, and the coal and electricity bill, all deducted from Otis's pay. "Cut over the payroll," they called this.

It was here, in this carbon copy house, Corky first saw morning's light. Otis and Flo Eva named their second born Raymond Wallace, but Otis tagged him "Corky," the same name as his favorite Sunday "funny papers" cartoon character. Cartoon Corky had a cowlick in his hair; so did Raymond. The nickname stuck.

There would be a third child born to Otis and Flo Eva. This child, a blonde and curly-haired daughter, was born in Highcoal on the 25th of November, 1940. They named her Peggy Sue.

Life and work in a coal camp was difficult, and even dangerous, but Corky remembers little from this time and place. He does recall an odorous, foul-smelling creek, however, this one meandering through town and very near their house. Mapmakers labeled this stream the "Seng," but the locals called it "Turd Creek." Corky and Roy, as little boys are apt to do, played along its banks, sometimes snatching minnows and crawdads from its turbid waters.

There was also an old man, Mr. Stitts, who owned and managed just about everything in Highcoal, including the coal company, the company store, the pool room, and even the camp's baseball team and its uniforms. Otis was probably Highcoal's best ballplayer, and the team photo that survives is a treasured reminder of good times the family experienced there. In the front row of the photo, near Otis, sits plump Mr. Stitts, the team's owner, coach, and manager.

"Dad," Corky says of Otis, "was a fairly big man... somewhat rough, with huge hands. In his younger days he was a great baseball player—a catcher—and might have played at some level of professional ball had he been given the opportunity. But that never happened."

Corky also has dim, dingy, and faded recollections of Stitts's pool room, but still ones clear enough to recall times he was allowed to accompany his Dad when Otis wanted to shoot pool, play cards, catch up on the local news, or down a couple of beers with friends. He fondly recalls the times with his father at Stitts's thriving establishment, but Flo Eva, had she known, would never have approved.

"Both of my parents worked hard and were good providers of the material things our family needed, but Dad wasn't one to spend a great deal of time around the house," Corky says. "He was a coal miner, a Greyhound Bus driver (Central City to Louisville), and then a Muhlenberg County sheriff's deputy. All these jobs required long hours." Corky's mother held a steady job, too, working several years as a cashier for a Central City grocery.

It's clear Corky holds his father in highest esteem, revering him as one who loved his family, worked hard, and was highly-respected by all who knew him. "Dad was my hero," beams Corky. "He could be tough as he needed to be, but always put the needs of his family above those of his own. My brother and I had happy, good childhoods because of him, and Dad lived a long and useful life. He was ninety-three when he passed away in 2007."

Making up for his father's scarcity was Corky's mother, Flo Eva. She was a petite woman, but one who set the rules in her household and for her kids. "It was best," Corky assures, "that her authority was never questioned. Mom absolutely ruled the roost with an iron fist, and we didn't ever want to make her mad. Dad called her 'Lightning.'" Like her husband Otis, Flo Eva lived a long and useful life, passing away in an Owensboro nursing home at age ninety-seven in 2012.

Flo Eva Allison, a native of Todd County, Kentucky, was born in 1915. Her parents, Atlas and Maud Keeling Allison, moved the family to the Cleaton community of Muhlenberg County in the

1920s, but Corky is unclear exactly when. He has only vague memories of his Grandfather Allison, but does recall him being "a little fellow with a great big chew of tobacco in his mouth," and one, it seems, "content to 'eek out a living on his small farm."

Otis, according to family lore, first met Flo Eva at a barn dance near Cleaton in 1933 or '34. With fiddle, guitar, and mandolin music pleasantly echoing through the surrounding countryside, the two promenaded and do-se-doed the night away. It is likely some of the rowdier sorts had slipped in some strong Kentucky brew for this occasion—produced locally, of course—and it's possible Otis took a nip or two that night. "Dad drank a little," Corky confirms, "but wasn't ever anything close to being much of a drinker." If Flo Eva objected to his drinking even a little that evening, we'll never know, but she was attracted to Otis, and he was attracted to her. Courtship and marriage followed. So did baby Roy and the move to West Virginia.

Corky isn't sure exactly when his family returned to Muhlenberg County, but does know it was prior to the fall of 1944, the year of his enrollment at Central City Graded. He also knows the reason for their return: "Anchor mine played out, and Dad lost his job."

Chapter 2

Daddy, Won't You Take Us to Muhlenberg County?

With their return to Kentucky, Otis and Flo Eva soon bought a house in Central City. This house, located on Resevoir Avenue, was purchased for the sum of $1,700 and came with a monthly payment of $17. It would prove to be the only house his parents would ever own, although not one they could enjoy immediately.

Otis found steady work, but not locally. Instead, the work was in a Hammond, Indiana, steel mill, 330 miles north of Central City. His brother-in-law and sister, Halford and Juanita Withrow Walls, lived in Hammond, and this, Corky figures, would surely account for his father finding work there. Renting an apartment, but hoping soon to return to Central City, Otis and Flo Eva continued making the payments on their house.

Corky can recall games of wiffle ball played with his father and brother in the backyard of their apartment building in Hammond, and there was also an unforgettable trip the family made to Chicago that summer, one taken to watch the Cubs play ball against the St. Louis Cardinals at Wrigley Field. This would be the first time he and Roy had been to a big league park and game.

Corky's Uncle Halford and Aunt Juanita also had tickets that day, but had driven to Chicago separately, and with seats in the stadium a good distance from those of the Withrows. As a result of this separation, as well as their desire to explore the nooks and crannies of Wrigley Field, Corky and Roy spent much of their time trampling to-and-fro from their seats to those of their uncle and aunt.

But with game's end, the boys were nowhere to be found. Otis and Flo Eva, assuming their sons had decided to ride home with the Walls, started back to Hammond without them. The Walls, assuming the boys were returning with their parents, did the same. Both couples were wrong.

Not once thinking to ask for help from Wrigley employees, Roy and Corky combed the stadium in search of family, but with no success. After considerable time searching inside the park, they took their search to the sidewalks outside, again with failed results. Now, recognizing their search efforts were futile, the two took seats on a wooden bench next to a newspaper and magazine stand.

After a half hour or thereabout, and realizing they'd probably been left behind, Roy and Corky took action. "We decided we'd hitch a ride back to Hammond," Corky laughs. "Roy was nine and I was six, and there we were... hitching a ride on Lakeshore Drive in northern Chicago!"

Shortly, after walking only a few blocks distance, a man in a white Chevrolet convertible—one with top down—pulled over to inquire. After hearing the boys' story, and then requesting they get in his car, this Good Samaritan drove the pair to a nearby police station. "We were pretty scared waiting for Dad and Mom to come back and get us," Corky admits, "but they didn't say much about it on the way home."

A little over nineteen years later—Sept. 24, 1963—Corky returned to Wrigley, but this time as an outfielder for the St. Louis Cardinals. As the team bus drove along the street outside the ballpark, and while staring out the bus window, Corky noticed the same newspaper stand and bench where he and Roy sat, pondering their options years earlier. "It was," Corky describes, "like an episode from *The Twilight Zone*."

The Withrows' stay in Indiana proved to be short. After eight months, as hoped, they were returning to their home in Central City. Otis had found another job, this time with the Crescent Coal Company in Muhlenberg County.

The house at 424 Resevoir Avenue would be Corky's home throughout his elementary, high school, and college days. Here he grew to manhood, and here he shared mostly good times with his family. But there were also those less frequent difficult times, and even one of a truly tragic nature, this involving his five year old sister, Peggy Sue.

For most every school-aged child, the most exciting day during any school year is the final one before dismissal for Christmas break. Christmas parties with candies, cookies, and brightly-decorated presents make for a festive mood, and the two-week vacation that follows is eagerly anticipated.

Such was the case for Corky and Roy Withrow on this December day in 1944. The five-block walk home from school was filled with excitement, but little could they have known what fate awaited their family during the weeks ahead. Corky, unable to tell this story without tearing up, explains:

> "The closer we got to home that day, the more I noticed people in their yards. I probably didn't think too much about it at the time, but I can still see neighbors standing along the street to our house. Junior Howerton, a neighborhood friend, ran up and told us that Peggy Sue had been badly burned. We ran to our house, and I can still see her pink, chenille dress laying in the grass outside the backdoor. It was charred."

Becoming even more emotional, Corky pauses, but insists on continuing:

> "She was a sweet little blonde-headed girl... only four... and had gotten too close to the open grate of the fireplace. She was at home with a babysitter, but the sitter couldn't get her burning dress off fast enough. They rushed Peggy Sue to the hospital in Greenville, but she lived only twenty-one more days. That whole time she was heavily bandaged, and in horrible pain. I can still see nurses sprinkling water over the gauze on her ribs. I don't think they'd do that today. My mother was with her the whole time, and I can't describe how awful it was to watch my parents go through something like that. I think that's why my mother became so protective of Roy and me, and it probably even changed the relationship between Dad and Mom... some

for the good, and some for the bad. My mother was with her when she died, and right before she passed away, Peggy Sue whispered something to Mom I've never forgotten."

The words that Peggy Sue whispered—"I think I'm going to fly away"—were her last. Corky can still picture his sister in her casket in the front room of their house on Resevoir. "It was," weeps Corky, "like an old-time wake."

Peggy Sue was buried in Rose Hill Cemetery, and Corky still can't gaze at her gravestone without tears. That stone tells, with beautiful simplicity, the tragic story of a life too short:

PEGGY SUE WITHROW
Born Nov. 25, 1940, Died Jan. 15, 1945
"Our Darling"

After Corky finished this story, he added a comment, one concerning something still haunting him. "Roy and I would heat up marbles in that fireplace and then hand them to Peggy Sue. They would be too hot to hold, and she'd throw them down. We thought that was funny then."

In the early 1940s—the timeframe during which Otis and Flo Eva brought their three children to Muhlenberg County—Central City was a town of about 3,000 hard-working, mostly middle class folks. Since coal was the predominant industry in this region, many of these folks depended on it for their economic well-being, either directly or indirectly.

The town is located thirty-three miles south of Owensboro, and eighty miles north of Nashville, Tennessee. A few miles north of town is a horseshoe bend in the mostly north-south flowing Green River. Traveling twenty or so miles west, one arrives in Madisonville. Eight miles south is Greenville, the seat of government for the county of Muhlenberg.

Central City's history can be traced back to 1826, the year Charles Morehead built "Morehead's Horse Mill" on this site. For most of the next half-century, nothing much happened here, except for the activities of his steam-powered gristmill.

In 1870 things began to change when the newly-formed Elizabethtown and Paducah Railroad constructed its tracks near the site of the old mill. Soon after, in 1871, a post office was established and given the name Owensboro Junction. Two years later the village was deemed large enough to be incorporated by the state, and the name was changed to Stroud City after a local landowner, John Stroud.

As the town grew, the duPont Central Coal and Iron Company was beginning its operations in the area, as the town, and much of the county, sat above a generous supply of #9 bituminous coal located beneath its bedrock. Soon the city was re-incorporated, and with this, became Central City.

With the large amount of coal production, soon the town and region began to develop as a regional hub for both the Illinois Central Railroad and the Louisville and Nashville Railroad. With this came train yards, roundhouses, and an elevated railroad station.

Today, though much has changed above ground, a number of old underground mining shafts still crisscross beneath the city. In the surrounding area are thousands of acres of reclaimed land where surface mining was once heavily engaged, a practice later lamented by singer/songwriter John Prine:

> "And Daddy won't you take me back to Muhlenberg County, / Down by the Green River where Paradise lay. / I'm sorry my son, but you're too late in asking, / Mr. Peabody's coal train has hauled it away." ("Paradise" by John Prine)

Along with its coal production, the county would also gain a reputation as a Kentucky musical hotbed. Much of the early notoriety is owed to a handful of gifted musicians who developed a distinct finger-thumb style of guitar-picking. One was Ike Everly who, with wife Margaret Embry Everly, traveled the region as a popular singing and guitar-picking duo.

There were also Ike's fellow musicians and guitar legends, Mose Rager, Kennedy Jones, and Merle Travis. Travis (1917-1983) became equally famous as a songwriter. His works included "Sixteen Tons," "Dark as a Dungeon," and several other coal-themed songs. Clearly, his music was influenced by the coal and those who mined it.

It is also worth noting, a few miles east of Central City and along HWY 62 is the small community of Rosine in Ohio County. On Jerusaleum Ridge, overlooking Rosine, is the birthplace and childhood home of Bill Monroe, "The Father of Bluegrass Music." Across the hollow—"High on a hill and above the town"—lived Monroe's fiddle-playing "Uncle Pen."

Of course, any mention of Muhlenberg musicians would be incomplete without the names of Don and Phil Everly. These brothers, sons of Margaret and Ike, are true pioneers of rock-n-roll and are considered among the all-time greats in the music industry.

Contrary to what some may think, the brothers spent relatively few of their years in Kentucky, although Don was born in the Brownie community of Muhlenberg County in 1937. Phil, who died in 2014, was born in Chicago in 1939. Still, though, they had relatives here, and summer visits were frequent.

Actor James Best, a first cousin of Don and Phil, was born in Powderly, a community near Central City. Best made several television appearances on *The Andy Griffith Show* as a guitar player with the hipster band Freddy Fleet and His Band with The Beat, and then followed this as Roscoe P. Coaltrane, the bumbling deputy on *The Dukes of Hazard*. Best's mother, Margaret Everly Guy, was Ike Everly's sister. James Best died in early 2015.

Corky recalls seeing the Everlys—Don and Phil—around town, but only when they were young boys. "They would come in the D & W Cafe with their parents," he recalls, "and they would be in cowboy outfits... with cap pistols and all that. They weren't big celebrities then, and it seems like, for some reason, their family would always come in the D & W."

This was the Muhlenberg County of the 1940s and '50s, a time and place where Corky and Roy were raised by Otis and Flo Eva. Here, the two learned to play ball, hunted and fished, were baptized at the First Baptist Church, and explored the hills and "hollers" as well as the sidewalks and playgrounds of Central City. It was, indeed, life at its best in a small Kentucky town!

Chapter 3

Say It Ain't So, Roy Settles!

In the fall of 1952, Corky began his high school career as a freshman at Central City High. When school began in early September, he was fourteen years old, but would turn fifteen in November, about the same time basketball season would begin.

Central City was a basketball school with a long and successful history in the sport. Most of the earliest success can be credited to Coach George Taylor, but his successor, Delmas Gish, would continue to add to the Golden Tide basketball legacy.

George Taylor took the helm at Central City in the fall of 1925, and in the next seventeen years guided the Tide to 438 victories with only 105 defeats. During this span he had only one losing campaign ('25-'26), and took the Tide to eight Sweet 16s, including one stretch of five in a row.

Delmas Gish continued this winning tradition after taking the program over during the 1942-43 season. Gish, a former Tide player, had coached at McHenry High in Ohio County before returning to his alma mater to assist Taylor. When Taylor stepped down, Gish was the logical choice to take his place.

In his first ten seasons at the helm prior to Corky's varsity arrival, Coach Gish amassed a 246-69 record. The '52 Tide squad's 19-13 record represented the most losses for a Gish-coached team, but even that was respectable in the eyes of most coaches. Now, with the Corky Withrow Era about to begin, Delmas Gish's success would skyrocket even higher.

With no football, basketball was king at Central City. Golden Tide students had few other fall activities competing for their time, so basketball was eagerly awaited not only by the students, but the town's general population as well. It was almost as if the arrival of basketball in November marked the real start of the school year.

The decade of the 1950s was a magical time in America's history, at least enough, so it seems, that a certain mystique evolving from that time remains with us even today. Following the Second World War, and with the dawning of the "Atomic Age," the "Fabulous Fifties" proved to be the nation's last gasp of innocence before the turmoil and upheaval of the rebellion-laden sixties. In many areas—especially sports—it was truly a "Golden Age."

This decade brought many changes, of course, and among these was a new form of music called "rock-n-roll." Corky liked this music when it first hit the airwaves, but claims he, like most of his pals, paid only minor attention. "It wasn't that big a deal at Central City," he concludes. "I guess we just weren't much for dancing."

A check of the top hits of '52-'53 clearly confirms his freshman year was still pre-rock-n-roll. "That's Amore" by Dean Martin, "Don't Let The Stars Get In Your Eyes" by Perry Como, "How Much Is That Doggie In The Window?" by Patti Page, and "Your Cheatin' Heart" by Hank Williams could hardly be classified in this new genre of music, but with groups like Bill Haley and The Comets, the Drifters, and the Orioles experimenting with new material and musical techniques, things were about to change.

There was also a device that was beginning to make its way into the homes across America. That device, still in its infancy, was television, and for families affording such a luxury, evenings could be filled watching now-classic shows, such as *I Love Lucy, The Red Skelton Show, The Life Of Riley, The Adventures Of Ozzie And Harriet, Mr. Peepers, Our Miss Brooks, The Jackie Gleason Show, Cavalcade of Stars*, and several others. Unlike today, families would gather around the one set, usually in the "living room," and watch the shows together. Imagine that!

Since sports events were rarely shown on television then, the local high school games had little competition in most rural Kentucky communities. Smoke-filled, musty-smelling gymnasiums were packed on game nights, as basketball was literally "the only game in town," and most families could easily afford the 25 cent student admission price, 50 cents for adults!

Corky's first experience in organized basketball had been a couple of years earlier as a 7th grader at Central City Jr. High in 1950-51. In a game against Owensboro Catholic Jr. High, he scored his first two points as a reserve player on a B-team roster that, he calculates, "included myself and about forty-four others." All had aspirations to one day play for Coach Gish's varsity squad at Central City High.

His first significant amount of playing time came a few games later, in Central City's "old" gymnasium, when the B-teamers faced the Jr. High team from Drakesboro. After the eighth and ninth graders built a 37-point lead by the end of the third quarter, Coach Gish gave Corky his first opportunity for extended action.

He didn't disappoint. Basket after basket followed, while his coach and teammates looked on. When the final horn sounded, Corky had totaled 17 in just one quarter of play. These points, coming on eight of eight from the field, and one for one at the foul-stripe, represented, at least to him, the perfect game. "I knew I could play after that," he will tell you. His coach, Delmas Gish, knew it, too.

Good things quickly came to Corky! At practice the following day he was issued a jersey—a real jersey to replace the white tee shirt that he and most of the other B-team reserves wore. But to him, this jersey was much more than just a uniform. It served as a clear indication he had arrived!

The following season, Corky's eighth grade year, would find him on Central City's varsity roster, but his playing time was limited to a couple of minutes in the team's second game of the season. In this game, against Dunmor, he scored no points, but picked up a foul in the team's 47-46 loss. It is of some interest to note this game was only the second to be played in the school's new 2,500-seat Memorial Gymnasium.

Although his initial varsity action was of little note, Corky's years of dreaming were starting to come true. He was wearing the Black and Gold.

When varsity basketball started in the Fall of his freshman year, Corky was not only on the Tide roster, but was soon penciled in as a starter for the opening game. This marked the first time Coach Gish started a freshman in a varsity game and, as far as Corky knows, there would never be another. Corky, with one exception, would start every game during his four years of high school ball.

This new season would find the Tide a team of youth and inexperience, but not without talent. Corky, the roster's lone freshman, would handle one forward spot while Bobby Don Millard, a junior, would take the other. The guard duties would be handled by Larry Ray and Roy "D.D." Withrow, both juniors. Experience would come from 6'4" senior pivot, Dick Wolfe. Filling the reserve roles would be Billy Lee Robinson, Eddie Houston, Junior Howerton, Bobby Mercer, Stanley Ruby, and Charles Owen Gray.

Most of these were returnees from the previous season's 19-13 squad that advanced to the 1952 4th Region semis before losing to Breckinridge County 42-40, but, with the exception of Wolfe, had seen only limited playing time in reserve roles. Despite this inexperience, excitement was high when the team took the court on opening night. Corky recalls: "It's hard to describe my feelings when I walked on the court that night. This was all I had ever wanted to do as a boy, and I hadn't really looked beyond playing for the Golden Tide. In my mind this was as good as it would ever get, and I never dreamed there could be anything better. Here I was now... starting for the Golden Tide!"

As exciting as the school day and evening had been, the results were not what he had anticipated. In his first high school game of a four year career that would end with only twenty losses, the Tide, on their home court, lost to Bremen 53-52. It was a disappointing start to the season, and for Corky, a high school career.

Dick Wolfe led the Tide that night, scoring 14. Roy Withrow had 13, and Bobby Don Millard, 12. Corky, initiating a scoring career that would eventually total 3,136 points, had only one field goal for two points... indeed, an inauspicious and disappointing beginning.

Things improved, though, and the Tide began a short winning streak. The team's first win was over Muhlenberg Central 79-34.

Roy scored 20, and Corky's 18 marked his first respectable scoring effort as a high schooler, as well as being an early indicator of great things to come.

Graham fell next (54-43), followed by Calhoun (76-37), and Drakesboro (79-45), but the winning streak ended with a 52-48 home court loss to Dunmor. Corky scored some in these games, but was yet to prove himself to be a major offensive threat on a nightly basis.

Central City returned to their winning ways by defeating Hughes-Kirk 48-42, and then crushing Bremen 68-45. The Tide now faced their biggest rival, the Greenville Blackhawks. This game proved no contest, however, and the Tide rolled to a 46-31 win. But it is worth noting that Greenville also had a talented freshman on their varsity roster. Roger Newman was his name, and although not on the court for this game, he, like Corky, would quickly develop into one of Kentucky's all-time greatest high school cagers.

With school dismissed for Christmas break, the Central City Invitational Tournament came next. The Tide defeated Drakesboro 68-40 in the opening round, and then gained a measure of early season revenge by defeating Dunmor 64-58 in the title tilt.

The Tide followed their CCIT championship with a 60-53 victory over the Rebels of Louisville Atherton. Charlie Tyra, Atherton's 6'8" all-state performer, had 20 in this game, but so did the Tide's Dick Wolfe.

This was followed with a 65-50 victory over Muhlenberg Central, but the Tide's seven game win streak came to a halt with a loss to visiting London High, 59-54, in the next. This loss was their third of the season, all coming on their home court. The Tide's record now stood at 11-3.

Greenville's Blackhawks, Owensboro Catholic's Aces, Owensboro Senior's Red Devils, and Bowling Green's Purples bowed to the Tide in the next four, but the Purples gave them a mighty tussle before succumbing 55-52. With the four wins the Tide's record climbed to 15-3, but what followed next would prove the most humbling of their experiences that season.

This began with a 68-64 loss at Hughes-Kirk and was followed with an 80-73 loss to Ralph Dorsey's Caverna Colonels and their all-stater, Kenny Sidwell.

The next game, at the Sportscenter in Owensboro, resulted in a hand-wringing 51-50 victory over Daviess County, but was followed with another home court loss, this time to Paducah Tilghman's Blue Tornado 53-51.

Madisonville was the next opponent, and again the Tide lost. The final score was 66-50, with most of the damage coming from the Maroons' all-stater Jimmy Mitchell and his 33 points.

With a 16-7 record, and a demoralizing three losses in their last four games, the Tide traveled to Louisville to face Male. What transpired here was, in Corky's opinion, "absolutely the worst defeat of my entire athletic career." In totally humiliating fashion, Kenny Kuhn, Male's outstanding three-sport athlete, in only his sophomore season, poured in 37 points to lead his team to a 94-49 thrashing of the Golden Tide. "We left there with our tails between our legs," Corky acknowledges.

Kuhn was not only a basketball star, but was equally gifted as a baseball and football player. By graduation he had earned first team all-state basketball honors three times and would be signed as a $100,000 "bonus-baby" by the Cleveland Indians. An arm injury would end his career, however.

After the loss to Male, and while still in the locker room, the team was told by Gish of his decision to step down as their coach. It was certainly shocking news, and the team felt their poor performance in the last few games was the cause. Gish accepted most of the blame for this, however, claiming he failed to properly prepare and motivate the team. "Mr. Gish," explains Corky, "was not one to say much during a game. He believed if a team had been properly prepared for an opponent during the weekly practice, there was little coaching needed once the game began." Corky, after briefly pausing, added," Mr. Gish didn't ever talk much at all, and seldom ever smiled or joked. But that didn't mean he wasn't a wonderful, caring person. He was definitely that."

Fearing Gish meant what he said, the team went to him with an appeal the following school day. "We asked him to stay as our coach and promised not to lose any more games if he would," says Corky. Gish, after quietly listening to his boys' appeal, agreed to those terms. With his promise to remain, the team's efforts had paid off. Coach Gish was back on board, and the squad prepared to finish the season with renewed effort.

Drakesboro was the first of three remaining games. The Tide swept them aside 53-44. Owensboro fell next, 61-52, and in the final game the Tide defeated Calhoun 65-60. Now, with a record of 19-8, the Tide prepared for the 16th District Tournament at Muhlenberg Central in Powderly.

Central City's 1953 district tournament run found them opening with a 57-49 win over Drakesboro's Cardinals. Corky's 16 led the Tide.

Greenville came next, and the Tide, in a foul-plagued, hard-fought game, won 52-48. This game marked the first time Corky faced the Blackhawks' Roger Newman on the hardwood. Although Corky's team won the game, Roger outscored him 9-4.

Central City won the 16th district crown by defeating Dunmor 65-58 in the championship game. Dick Wolfe led the Tide with 22, Roy Withrow scored 14, and Corky eight. With a 22-8 record now, regional play was only days away.

The 1953 4th Region Tournament, held in Morgantown, proved to be a chance for the Tide to avenge their semi-final loss to Breckinridge County the previous season. Several of this current squad had been on that Tide team and were eager for another opportunity to earn a trip to the Sweet 16. The games proved competitive, but in the end, and with everything on the line, a ref's whistle would play the deciding role.

In the opening round Cromwell beat Hawesville by two in overtime. The next two games found Breckinridge County defeating McHenry by ten, followed by Central City's heart-pounding 58-56 victory over Morgantown. The final game of this round resulted with Dunmor defeating Leitchfield by two.

The semi-finals found Breckinridge County squeaking past Cromwell 51-48, while Central City followed with a bit more comfortable 71-63 victory over Dunmor. With this win, the final was set. It would pit Breckinridge County against the Golden Tide of Central City.

Breckinridge County was coached by Truman Layton "T.L." Plain. The Bearcats had an all-state performer, Carlos Irwin, and if the Tide was going to win, they would have to slow the big center down.

On Saturday night, March 14, 1953, the gym at Morgantown was packed. The game was close throughout. In the final seconds Central City led 66-65, but Corky, having fouled out with four minutes remaining, could only watch from the bench. "We were leading by one when Roy Settles, the ref, comes from out of the blue and makes a chicken s—t call on Bobby Don," Corky fumes. "Nobody knew why, since Bobby Don was behind the guy he supposedly fouled. Mr. Gish got irate. It was the only time I ever saw him lose control of his temper, and the only time I ever heard him use a cussword. But he sure did give Settles an earful that night."

Corky, six decades later, still grumbles when describing the final few minutes of that game and is quick to point out that Coach Gish, via KHSAA channels, prevented Roy Settles from calling any future games involving a Golden Tide team. "I doubt that Roy Settles ever set foot in Central City again after that game," Corky laughs.

Settle's phantom call sent Carlos Irwin to the foul line for two shots. He connected on both, giving the Bearcats a one point lead. The Tide, unable to answer, fell to the Bearcats for the second time in two years. The final score was 67-66.

With all things considered, it had been a successful season. The team had a bumpy ride at times, and the one point loss in the regional finals would not be easy to forget. But the team had managed to finish with a respectable 24-9 record, and more importantly, still had their coach.

Corky finished his freshman season with 309 points in thirty-three games. A 9.4 scoring average for a freshman was pretty good, and although rebounds were usually not charted then, this was where he excelled.

But now, with basketball over, it was no surprise that Corky's thoughts turned to spring, and for him that meant baseball.

Chapter 4

Great Expectations and a Whole Lot of Hope

The 1953-54 basketball season, Corky's sophomore campaign, would begin with high expectations. Locals were already comparing the team to the powerful '45 Tide crew that finished as runner-up in the state, and most of these expectations were based on the fact that Coach Gish had lost only one starter, Dick Wolfe, from the previous squad, but would be replacing him with a talented 6'2" senior transfer from Drakesboro High named H.L. "Hub" Hope.

Hub Hope was a rugged, hard-nosed forward who had averaged 13.2 points per game during his junior season at Drakesboro. Corky claims to know but little concerning the reason for Hub's decision to transfer, but does recall the assertions, accusations, and rumors that spread across the region that summer, fall, and throughout the basketball season.

"Lots of people thought Mr. Gish had something to do with getting Hub to transfer, but that's not true," Corky emphatically states. "He wouldn't do that, and I know that for a fact." However, Corky won't rule out the likelihood that someone else was involved in Hub's recruitment.

Regardless of what transpired, most opposing fans, especially those from Drakesboro, thought the whole thing smelled of foulplay. Hub, Coach Gish, and the entire Tide team would hear plenty from these opposing fans when the season started that fall.

Even Ted Sanford, the KHSAA Commissioner, investigated Hope's transfer. "First we'd get word Hub was eligible, then ineligible... and then eligible again," groans Corky. "One day he'd be at practice... the next he wouldn't. It went on like that for several weeks and became a real distraction."

Sanford eventually ruled Hope eligible, but, as expected, rival fans in Muhlenberg County continued to voice their disapproval. "Other schools and fans didn't want to believe it, but Mr. Gish was just as surprised as anyone when Hub moved to Central City," Corky explains. "We, and especially Hub, heard several nasty comments that season, but nothing ever seemed to bother him much. He was just a steady, strong 'ol country boy who did what was needed, workman-like, and never seemed to get shook or rattled."

Corky isn't sure why Hub left Drakesboro but does know he moved in with Carl Simmons, a relative living across the street near the school. "I think Hub just wanted to play on a good team during his senior year," says Corky, "and since he had family that close, why not transfer?" His transfer proved a beneficial and timely one for Central City, as Hub, according to Corky, "fit the team like a glove... definitely the missing piece of the puzzle for us that season."

Roger Newman, former Greenville star, remembers Hope and all the controversy surrounding his transfer. "Central City probably was recruiting some," Roger laughs. "They always seemed to come up with a new player whenever they needed one," he added, tongue-in-cheek.

When asked about Hub's contributions that season, Corky was quick to mention rebounding. "Hub was about 6'2", real strong, and a tough 'ol raw-boned country bumpkin. He could rebound with the best and had the sharpest elbows I ever saw. He didn't mind using them, either!"

Corky adds that Hub, from the time of his graduation until now, hasn't been seen or heard from by his teammates. "He just vanished. We have no idea what happened to him... no phone calls, visits, letters, reunions... nothing! It's like he just dropped off the face of the earth."

Hub truly may have been the missing puzzle piece that season, but he was only one of several outstanding performers on the Tide roster. First, there was plenty of front court talent to go with Hope. There was Corky, with both rebounding and scoring abilities, and Bobby Don Millard, a poised senior possessing outstanding athleticism and finesse, as well as being a savvy ball-handler. It would be Bobby Don who would also provide the needed on-court leadership that season.

The Tide backcourt was equally blessed with skilled and seasoned performers. At the starting guard positions would be Larry Ray and Roy Withrow, both seniors. When added together, the five projected starters would be returning with a combined total of 53 points per game from the previous season. Billy Lee Robinson, a defensive trouble-shooter, would fill the reserve guard role.

A pre-season incident almost cost the services of guard Larry Ray, however. Larry, according to Corky, had been dismissed from the squad for smoking. After asking for a second chance from Coach Gish, he was given his day in court—this held in the gym, and in front of his Tide teammates.

After assembling the team on the gym bleachers, Gish informed his players that Larry Ray's basketball future was in their hands, and not his. With his message delivered, Gish walked out. The humbled Ray now pleaded his case before a jury of his peers, in this case, his teammates. With their positive verdict delivered, Larry was allowed to return. It is probable, Corky feels, that Coach Gish was pretty sure how the jury's vote would go that day.

Coming off the bench for the Tide that season were Johnny Swann, Eddie Houston, Jerry Calvert, Buddy Lear, Charles Gray, Junior Howerton, Bobby Mercer, Buddy Fuller, and Stanley Ruby. Stan, according to Corky, was the only Jewish student at Central City High. And as for Buddy Fuller, well, he just may have pulled off the most disgusting prank in Central City High basketball history that Fall—one with Corky as its victim!

The Tide, like teams elsewhere then, used "Tough Foot," a pasty, gooey gunk applied to feet to prevent blisters—a common annoyance resulting from the old-style canvas basketball shoes. Following practice one day, Corky, clean and fresh from the showers, returned to his locker. Here, naked from head to toe, he bent forward to retrieve his slippers from the bottom shelf.

With this target fully exposed, Buddy Fuller, in a truly inspirational moment, grabbed a brush full of the sticky solution, and with a sweeping, swiping stroke up Corky's intergluteal cleft, glued his butt cheeks together! Now, amidst the howls and laughter of teammates, Corky found himself not only the "butt" of a joke, but left with a real sticky dilemma. "I couldn't get my cheeks apart," he laughingly complains, "but I sure wasn't about to ask any of them for help!"

Corky, although not above pulling similar capers himself, certainly could see no humor in this one, however. "I wanted to kill Buddy... I mean, I REALLY wanted to kill Buddy!" he stresses. "Some of my teammates laughed at first, but when they saw how mad I was, they all got quiet. Nobody said anything to me about it the next day at school... or at practice, either. They knew better."

After lumbering home best he could, Corky, desperate to remedy this dire and embarrassing situation, called on his mother for help. Flo Eva, handling the matter with a sense of resolve only mothers can muster, had her son drop his drawers, draping himself across his bed face down. Using lighter fluid and tweezers with surgical-like efficiency, the procedure proved successful, but not without pain. "I guess that whole experience qualified me as a genuine 'Tough-Ass,'" Corky concludes.

Just another day in the life of Corky Withrow!

With a roster full of talent, the pre-season respect for the Tide was noted statewide and first released in Dr. Frank Litkenhous's ratings that November of '53. To no one's surprise, the Tide was ranked as the top team in the 4th Region, but their statewide #15 ranking may have disappointed some expecting higher. Heading the ratings was Lexington Lafayette.

With their high ranking, and after a spirited afternoon pep rally, the Tide opened play by defeating Graham 55-45. Bobby Don Millard led the team with 13, while both Corky and Roy tallied 11 each. The Tide crushed Bremen 79-48 next. Despite sitting out most of the second half in foul trouble, Corky led the team with 24.

Corky followed this with 18 against Dunmor, 11 against Muhlenberg Central, 23 against Drakesboro, and 20 more against Hughes-Kirk. All were Tide victories, and Roy—"D.D." to his buddies—scored 19 in the 90-54 Hughes-Kirk blowout.

Although not in the starting lineup due to an infected arm, Corky produced 6 points in limited minutes in a victory over Calhoun. Hope stepped forward with an 18-point performance. With their 7-0 record, the Tide climbed to #7 in the Lit-ratings.

The Tide next faced Louisville Atherton at home. The Rebels, even with star player Charlie Tyra, a future Louisville Cardinals All-American and NBA performer, proved no match for Corky and the Tide. Although the Tide's crippled lineup forced Gish to use his reserves for much of the game, they still crushed the visitors 69-49. Billy Robinson, a reserve, scored 16; Corky, still ailing, 13.

With school dismissed for Christmas break, the team played their final pre-holiday game against Greenville on the 22nd. Although it was scheduled to be played in Greenville, the game was moved to Muhlenberg Central's much larger gym at Powderly in anticipation of a capacity crowd.

The game proved to be the Tide's first solid test of the season. Greenville, like the Tide, was undefeated and had its own sophomore sensation, Roger Newman, a 6'4" forward. This Blackhawks squad would prove the most competitive during Roger's years at Greenville, and a strong case could be made that these two teams were the region's finest that season.

The game lived up to the hype, and Legon McDonald, a local sportswriter, would later describe it as "one of the finest exhibitions of basketball ever witnessed in Muhlenberg County." It was close throughout, and with only thirty seconds remaining Greenville was clinging to a 68-66 lead. It appeared that Central City's streak might be about to end as the clock ticked down. But with only eight seconds remaining, Roy Withrow connected on what was his only field goal of the night. The horn sounded, sending the game into overtime.

With most of the Tide starters fouled-out, the overtime would find their reserves going against the Blackhawks' regulars. As overtime ticked down to the final few seconds, the Tide's Stan Ruby was fouled with the score knotted at 73. Ruby hit one of two, and the Tide held on for a 74-73 victory. For the victorious Tide, Corky and Larry Ray had 20 each. Greenville, led by Larry Sparks with 18, had suffered their first loss.

The game had done little in the way of proving which team was superior, but in only a few days, and in the Tide's Christmas tournament, the two rivals would square off again.

The CCIT, held on the 28th and 29th of December, featured four teams selected and invited by Coach Gish. The coach, with his talented bunch, wanted good competition, choosing to add a team from outside the county. This outsider would be the Hartford Mustangs from Ohio County.

Coached by Charles Combs, Hartford was sporting a 13-0 record and would be the favorite in their opening game against Greenville. But, to the surprise of most, Greenville upset the Mustangs 65-56 and awaited the winner of the Central City-Graham contest.

As expected, the Tide had no problems with Graham, winning 60-38. Corky, watching much of the game from the bench due to fouls, scored 12. Roy led the team with 19. Now, for the second time in a week, the Tide faced their biggest rival, Greenville.

Although Greenville would trail the entire game, it was the final quarter that would seal their fate. The Tide outscored them 24-9 during this time, pulling away for a 71-48 tournament title victory. Corky led his team with 20; Hope followed with 16. Roger Newman, despite fouling out, led the Blackhawks' effort, but with only 10.

The win upped Central City's record to 11-0, while Greenville notched only its second loss of the season, both to the Tide, and both in a one week span.

With the CCIT over, Drakesboro followed. Corky erupted for 27 in this one, a 64-51 Tide victory.

With a perfect 12-0 record, it was now time for Central City to face bitter rival Butler County. The yearly games between these two were always hard-fought and occasionally resulted in some ugly confrontations, sometimes involving fans.

The game played in Central City, the Tide just might have had an edge, but the Bears had the potential to give them all they wanted. Bobby Green, Bears guard and floor general, was, according to journalist Bobby Anderson, "an elusive all-court man," and when Green was teamed with their other starting guard, Wally Johnson, the Bears' style of tempo control had the potential to prevent the fastbreak offense preferred by the Tide.

As expected, Butler County opened with ball control in mind, but after quickly falling behind 12-4, was forced to play catch-up.

Failing at this, they fell to the Tide 71-54. Corky stole the spotlight, pouring in 25. Green led the visitors with 19.

Sedalia came to town next, but proved no match for the Tide. The home team notched a 74-58 win, with Millard scoring 22 and Corky 11.

Road victories at Bowling Green (75-60) and then Owensboro (67-39) followed. Corky hit for 21 and 22 in these two and followed this with 22 and 21 more in wins over Hughes-Kirk (81-58) and Daviess County (90-58).

Caverna came to Memorial Gym and gave the Tide a competitive game, but the Tide prevailed 74-67. Millard had 23; Hope, 19; and Corky, 15. The Colonels were led by Jim Godwin's 28 and Kenny Sidwell's 20.

Another home game followed, against Owensboro, and again the Tide won, this time 71-63. Millard was high man with 21. Corky added 15.

Two road games followed next. The first saw the Tide crush Murray 98-64, and then squeeze out a narrow 60-57 victory at Paducah Tilghman. Millard's 28, Hope's 23, and Corky's 19 paced the Tide in the easy victory at Murray, but in the contest against Tilghman, it was necessary for the Tide to resort to a "deep-freeze" in the final minutes. Corky scored 19 against the Blue Tornado, despite sitting out the entire third quarter with foul problems.

With the narrow escape in Paducah, the Tide headed home with their perfect record intact at 23-0. Their next game was against a 15-2 Madisonville squad, but the Maroons fell to the Tide 77-54. Corky's 25 led the way.

When the United Press Ratings were released that week, Kentucky's only undefeated team was ranked #4. The Tide trailed only Lexington Lafayette, Pikeville, and Inez. With only five regular season games remaining, Central City still had a chance to make history.

One team—and only one team—in Kentucky's high school history had gone through the regular season, district tournament, regional tournament, and state tournament without a loss. That team was the '48 Brewers Redmen from Marshall County, a team led by all-state performers Barney Thweat, Coy Creason, Van Mathis, and the soon-to-be 1949 "National Player of the Year" Mason Cope.

Now, with their unblemished record and only five very winnable games remaining, some thought the Tide could run the table as well. There were still tournaments to be played, of course, but no one in the district and region looked to be much of a challenger. With a favorable draw in the Sweet 16... why not? Would this be the year the Brewers' record was matched?

First, though, the Tide had those five regular season games. The first of these, at Bremen, was an easy win for the Tide, 87-47. Corky scored 29. Bremen's Joe Divine matched this total.

Greenville was the next to fall. Their record of 18-4 was impressive, but the idea that half their losses came at the hands of the Tide didn't sit well with these cross-county rivals. Feeling they had something to prove, the Blackhawks fought hard and for much of the game had a lead.

With only 2:37 remaining in the fourth, Hub Hope sank two free throws, igniting a Tide surge. Two more free throws by Corky iced the victory in the final minute for a 56-52 win. This marked the Tide's third win of the season over Greenville. Foul-proned, Corky had managed only 10, the same total that Roger Newman tallied for Greenville.

Heading to Louisville with a 26-0 mark, always tough St. X would, it was thought, be a big challenge. Played in the gymnasium at Male High, the game was never close, however, as the Tide spurted to an early 14-4 lead, moving on to a final 76-60 victory. Corky led the scoring with 26, one more than St. X's guard Jack Ramsey.

Now, with the path looking clear, only Muhlenberg Central and Calhoun remained. As expected, the game at Powderly was no contest, and the Tide rolled 90-46. Corky's 35 set a Central City individual scoring record. At 28-0, only Calhoun stood in the way of a perfect regular season.

The twenty-ninth victory came easily, as the Tide won 85-57. Let the celebration begin... but only for a moment. The district tournament was ahead, and a new season was beginning. The quest for perfection wasn't over.

Chapter 5

Eastward, Tourney-Bound, Loadin' Up, and Truckin'!

Coach Gish, for his undefeated regular season, was honored with a celebration after the victory over Calhoun. It was his twelfth go-round as Golden Tide coach, but this was his first time guiding a team through an undefeated season. With the team's 29 victories that season, his win total had grown to 304, a total placing him among the winningest in Kentucky's high school history.

After a mid-court ceremony that included a THIS IS YOUR LIFE look at his career at Central City High, Coach Gish was presented with a new, 1954 model Chevrolet—compliments of the fans and citizens of Central City. After a brief speech of thanks on the part of the coach, the ceremony concluded. It was now time to look ahead to tournament play.

The 1954 16th District Tournament Wednesday night opener at Muhlenberg Central featured Drakesboro against Graham, followed by Hughes-Kirk and Dunmor in the nightcap. Thursday evening games would match Central City against Greenville and Muhlenberg Central against Bremen. It would be the fourth meeting of the season between the Blackhawks and the Tide.

For good reason, most eyes focused on the Tide-Blackhawk game. These two were the highest ranked teams in the tourney, and many wondered if the Tide could defeat Greenville a fourth time. For most, the Blackhawks were considered the biggest obstacle between the Tide and an appearance in the Sweet 16. If so, this game was, in a sense, for the district and regional titles!

As expected, Greenville gave the Tide all they wanted and more. At the end of the first quarter the Blackhawks had a 13-12 lead. T.R. Newman's shooting and rebounding kept his 'Hawks in the thick of the fight, and a balanced attack from his teammates gave the Tide no breathing room.

On the Tide side, Bobby Millard proved a whiz at both scoring and on the boards, while Billy Robinson's inspired play helped put the Tide in the lead at half, 32-29. Millard continued his scoring in the third, connecting on four field goals, most from the deep right forward spot. Corky had scored several points, but had been hampered with personal fouls.

The Tide gained their biggest lead at 56-47 with six minutes remaining, but Greenville refused to quit. With two minutes left, the lead had been cut to two at 63-61, and many were starting to wonder if the Blackhawks were finally going to defeat their arch-nemesis and, worst of all, prevent the Tide from a return appearance in the regional tournament.

But it was not to be. When the horn sounded, Greenville was again on the low end, this time 69-64. The season was over for the Blackhawks, and their final record stood at 20-6. Of these half dozen defeats, four had come at the hands of Central City.

Leading the way for the Tide was Millard with 23; Corky with 18; Larry Ray, 11, and Roy Withrow, eight. T.R. Newman, Roger's older brother, was high man for Greenville with 19. Roger added 13.

The Tide could now turn their attention to a semi-final contest against Muhlenberg Central, a team defeating Bremen to advance. Few gave the Musketeers much of a chance against the Tide, and were right, as the Tide, led by Corky's 20 and Roy's 19, rolled to an easy 72-49 win.

In the other semi-final game Graham easily defeated Hughes-Kirk, and by so doing, earned a spot against Central City in the championship game. This final game would prove anti-climatic, however, as the Tide won 76-63. Corky tabbed 25; Larry Ray, 24.

The all-tourney squad included both Corky and Bobby Don Millard from Central City, but not Larry Ray. For many, including Coach Gish, this was a big disappointment. Bobby Anderson wrote: "If anyone ever deserved it, he did. He played sterling ball." Coach Gish certainly agreed.

With a perfect 32-0 record, and a district crown, the Tide could now look ahead to the 4th Region Tournament. Few questioned the Tide's role as the favorite, but not far behind lurked the dangerous—and despised—Bears of Butler County.

Excitement was at high tide in Central City that March. Basketball themed decorations dressed the store windows around town, all encouraging the Tide, as well as welcoming the visiting teams and fans.

In Jerry Adkin's Florist Shop window there was even a model basketball court displayed, one complete with players, cheerleaders, and an intense coach sitting on the sidelines chewing paper, a habit of Coach Gish. In the background were assorted colored streamers, each representing one of the eight schools in the regional tournament.

When the pairings were announced for the March 10-13 affair, Central City was slotted to play their first game at 8:30 on Thursday evening. Their competition, Hartford, sported a 28-6 record and was the same squad that had lost to Greenville in the Tide's CCIT back in December.

In the opening game on Wednesday night, Butler County ran their record to 29-5 by downing Leitchfield 61-43. In the next game Flaherty defeated Horse Branch 63-39. These two winners would face each other in the semis. In the first of two Thursday night games, Meade County defeated Graham 60-51 and awaited the winner of the Central City-Hartford contest.

In the second game on Thursday, the Tide rushed to an early 10-1 lead and soon stretched it to 18-4. Much of this early damage could be credited to Corky and Larry Ray. At half their lead stood at 31-19, and although Hartford rallied in the fourth, the Tide went on to win 69-56.

Corky led his team with 19, while Hub Hope, breaking out of a late season slump, added 18. With this victory, the Tide would face Meade County in the semis.

In the first semi-final contest on Friday evening, Butler County defeated Flaherty 68-57. The Bears now waited for the winner of the Central City-Meade County contest.

The Tide faced a Meade County team that started 6'7" Walter Coin, but his teammates had no way to match up with the balanced attack of Central City. As soon as the game started, a Tide barrage by Corky, Hub, and Bobby Don quickly buried any hope the Greenwaves had for an upset. When the squads left the court at half, the Tide led 43-17. Central City had hit on 19 field goals, the 'Waves on only three.

Meade County would lose to the Tide 70-39. Although the Tide reserves played much of the second half, Hub Hope continued the climb from his slump by scoring 18. Millard had 15; Corky, 13. Walter Coin managed to score 11 for Meade County, but had also earned a technical foul for letting out an "Indian-like war whoop" while protesting a call by referee Roy Winchester.

It was now down to two—Central City versus Butler County—and to the victors would go a trip to the Sweet 16. With the one point loss in the previous regional finals to Breckenridge County still haunting them, the Tide players were hungry. There was also the perfect 34-0 record, and this, plus the fact that the competition would be Butler County, certainly took the contest to another level of urgency as well.

But the game, despite the rivalry, wouldn't measure up to the hype that evening. The Tide started with a hot hand, and with 4:29 still remaining in the first, led 10-2. The lead continued to grow, and when the third quarter ended, stood at 63-38. With this lead, Gish went to his bench in the fourth, winning 79-63.

Corky led the winners with 28, and Hub Hope had another fine performance with 17. Bobby Don added 16; Roy Withrow, 11. Bobby Green had 19 for Butler County.

Corky, Bobby Don, and Hub were named to the all-tourney team along with Shields and Johnson from Butler County. Joining them were Hartford's Charles Newcom, Flaherty's Leslie Bickett, Graham's Jim Williams, Leitchfield's Bobby Lowery, Horse Branch's Adrian Cooksey, and Meade County's Neal Miller.

At the conclusion of the team's regional title victory, it was announced that the 35-0 Golden Tide would be facing the Inez Indians in their first Sweet 16 contest in Lexington. The game against the 15th Region champs would be played at 9:15 on Thursday night, March 18, and would be the final game of the tournament's first round.

Inez's record stood at 29-2, and they, like the Tide, were ranked in the state's top five. Inez and Central City had met in the state tournament on one previous occasion, that being in 1935. Inez won 20-15. The Indians of Coach Claude Mills were certainly not the favorable first round draw Tide fans had hoped for, but Central City was no favorable draw for Inez, either.

Central City was basketball crazy! Was there anyone not going to Lexington? But just in case they couldn't, there would be a live broadcast on WNES, and if, heaven forbid, anyone didn't care about the game, the 62" Drive-In would be opening the same night. Here, in the enclosed comfort of one's automobile, movie-goers could watch *Kentucky*, a horse-racing romance starring Loretta Young, and then the thriller, *Cat People*, a "flick" with Simone Simone in the lead role (Isn't one 'Simone' in a man's name enough?).

And if an outdoor movie wasn't on one's agenda, there was the State, where one could follow the antics of Red Skelton in *Half A Hero,* a hilarious comedy about life in the suburbs. Assuming the Tide would still be playing on Friday night, the theater's owner had even made plans to announce the Tide scores, by quarters, for their movie-goers.

For those planning to make the trip to Lexington, it was, indeed, a busy and exciting time. Central City's small, all-male pep band would make the journey, courtesy of the local Henry-Cisney Chevrolet dealership. This group would be traveling in a brand new Chevy station-wagon, compliments of the dealership's owner, Ed Henry, a man brave enough to risk his sanity by driving the loud and rowdy musicians himself.

The Generals of Lexington Lafayette were favored to win it all. Coached by Ralph Carlisle, and including all-state performers-Vernon Hatton and Doug Shively, the Generals had been at the top of the Litkenhous Ratings all season. They were also playing in their hometown.

Many, including the gambling crowd that hung out in the Phoenix Hotel lobby, felt Lafayette would likely be facing Central City in the finals on Saturday night. Still, though, that was days away, and neither the Tide, nor the Generals, had a clear path.

Few saw what was coming. In the second game of the first round on Thursday morning, tournament favorite and #1 ranked Lafayette fell to Newport Public, 50-45. Then, in another upset in the first game of the Thursday evening session, powerful Louisville Male lost to Dilce Combs, 66-62.

Now, with two tourney powerhouses eliminated, Tide fans were feeling even better about their chances. If they could just get by Inez in their opening game! Few questioned that Inez was good, but were they good enough to hang with 35-0 Central City? After all, no team had arrived here with a perfect record since Brewers High in '48, and that team won it all! Could this be an omen?

Central City opened on a good note against Inez, as Corky, Roy, Hub, and Larry combined to give the Tide an early 8-0 lead. But Tide shots soon failed to fall, Millard began picking up fouls, and behind the Indians' Billy Ray Cassady, Herbie Triplett, and Orville Blankenship, Inez pulled ahead 10-9 as the game clock hit five minutes remaining in the first quarter.

The boys from Muhlenberg did take one more lead, 11-10, but Inez responded with eight straight to stretch their lead to 23-14. During this time, almost nothing seemed to be going right for Corky, as time and again his shots bounced off the rim. By halftime, his team, to the shock of most everyone in Memorial Coliseum, trailed 40-25.

In the second half, the Indians stretched their lead to an imposing 47-26. While the Tide had to depend on steals to get back within range, the Indians relied on free throws from Tide fouls. Fourteen of Inez's final 16 came this way and would prove to be too much to overcome, although Millard's hot hand managed to cut the Tide deficit to eight on three different occasions.

When the final horn sounded, Tide dreams had been crushed 72-57. The perfect season had ended with a not-so-perfect performance. With the Tide's 35-1 record, Brewers' 1948 achievement was still theirs alone.

The scorebook told a frustrating story. The Tide had taken 96 shots, hitting on only 25 for a miserable .26 percentage. By contrast, Inez had taken barely more than half the total of Tide shots, but had connected on 23 of 51 attempts. Central City, as awful as their shooting had been, had two more field goals than Inez, but free throws had settled the matter.

Bobby Don Millard, in his final high school game, led his team with 19. Hub Hope, also in his final game, added 14. Corky, in his self-proclaimed "sorriest game ever," had 10. Roy Withrow finished his Tide days with seven, and Larry Ray his with four.

It was a dejected Tide gathering in the Memorial Coliseum dressing room after the game. For most, it would be the final game. For Corky there would be another day, and even more Sweet 16 games in the future, but for now he was devastated. Corky accepts much of the blame for his team's loss. "If I'd had even a normal game," he calculates, "we could have won."

The Inez dressing room was a happier place. They had knocked off a tournament favorite, and with the elimination of Male and Lafayette earlier, the odds of winning the tournament now appeared in their favor.

Inez's Cassady had been superb with 27 points. Herbie Triplett found the range for 17; Omar Fannin, 13; and Orville Blankenship, nine. Two nights later these same four mountain lads, with their teammates, would have even more to celebrate—this time as Kentucky State Champions!

Corky didn't remain in Lexington to watch other games, instead, choosing to fly home with Dr. Davis, a Tide supporter and volunteer team physician. The flight in the small, privately owned plane would be Corky's first.

Along with All-District and All-Region honors, there were other accolades coming Corky's way. One was local, as the *Times-Argus Messenger* named an All-County team. Seven seniors, a junior, and two sophomores received this honor. The sophomores were, of course, Roger Newman and Corky Withrow.

With seven of eight possible votes cast by local coaches, Corky trailed only Hughes-Kirk's Carl Carver for the top spot. A columnist at the paper wrote:

> Corky Withrow is probably the most talked about basketball player in Muhlenberg County today, and the compliments do not stop with county borders. He is high on the list of all regional choices and with sports writers over the state. The reason for this is his 6-4 frame, which carried him to the varsity as a freshman and as the leading scorer for the team this season. Playing on a well-balanced team like Central City's has both its advantages and disadvantages. Because the four remaining players score well, his scoring output is slowed, but his rebounding, especially on the offensive board is tops. He also shoots well from the floor.

The Tide's Bobby Don Millard was also named to this countywide team. He was thought by many to be the Tide's most outstanding player that season, primarily due to his willingness to find open teammates. This, no doubt, cut into his scoring average, but still he managed to toss in 12.8 per-game. Butler County's Wally Johnson remembers Millard, claiming, "If Bobby Don got loose in the corner, it was over... you might as well turn around and head the other way. He could really shoot.... I was glad when he graduated."

As good as Millard was at basketball, he, like Corky, was as good or even better at baseball. His pitching talents would eventually lead to a professional stint with the Chicago Cubs organization, but an injury to his throwing arm curtailed his baseball career.

There was a third Tide player named to the All-Muhlenberg squad, as Hub Hope was recognized for his 10.4 scoring average and steady play on both ends of the court. Despite the harassment and verbal abuse Central City endured due to his transfer from Drakesboro, Hub truly proved to be the Tide's "missing puzzle piece."

The Central City honorees didn't end with players, either, as Delmas Gish won "Coach of The Year" honors in Muhlenberg

County. To go with this honor, he racked up a number of other awards as well: Regional "Coach of The Year," "State Prep Coach of The Year" by the *Louisville Courier-Journal,* and "Coach of The Year" by the *Paducah Sun-Democrat.*

Along with the All-Muhlenberg County squad, the Central City newspaper also saw fit to name an All-Regional squad. Corky and Bobby Don made this one, and joining them were Roger Newman, Carl Carver, Bobby Broyles, Denny Wester, Jimmy Williams, Shirley Wilson, Charles Shultz,and Leslie Bickett.

For Corky, his teammates, and coach, it had been a wonderful ride, but to their frustration, had fallen four victories short of their goal.

Chapter 6

Much A-Do About Corky... and a Little A-Don't

When the 1954-55 school year arrived, the Golden Tide was minus five of the crew that had put together the 35-1 record. With the losses of Millard, Ray, Hope, Swann, and Roy Withrow, only Corky and Billy Robinson were returning with any significant experience.

Still, with the influx of several promising players, the squad looked to be pretty good, but no one could reasonably expect another perfect season for this inexperienced and youthful bunch. It was definitely wait-and-see.

Billy Robinson and Billy Mason would form the starting guard combination, while senior Jerry Calvert would fill a backup role. The front line would consist of Corky, Stan Ruby, and Eddie Houston, but newcomers Carl Jamison (6'1"), Jimmy "Duck" Swann (6'3"), Billy Ray "Dilly-ball" Duvall (6'2"), and Winfred Thompson (6'0") would see time as well. But even with all these fresh faces, Tide fans expected good things, and with Corky again in the mix, expectations were amplified.

Not only did locals expect good things, but there were those across the state that did as well. In fact, the first issuance of the Lit-Ratings that November placed the Tide as the state's fourth best, after only Coach McCoy Tarry's Sedalia Lions, Ralph Carlisle's Lexington Lafayette Generals, and Stan Arnzen's Newport Wildcats. It's safe to say most of the Tide's lofty ranking was due to the presence of Corky, especially considering the quality of the graduated players from the previous squad.

The Tide showed early signs of living up to these high expectations. In the opener, against Muhlenberg Central, they won by 50,

76-26. Corky logged only twenty minutes in this one, but poured in 36. This was not only a personal high, but would set the pace of scoring he would maintain throughout the season. He followed this with another 36 points in a 74-58 win over Graham.

The Tide's third game was closer, as Drakesboro stayed with the Tide until late in the fourth. The final score gave the Tide a 66-57 win, but it took a Billy Robinson steal and layup to give them the push needed to seal the deal. Corky led the team with 22; Robinson had 17.

Next to fall in the Tide's wake was Dunmor. Corky was unstoppable, scoring 40 in 29 minutes of action. His per-game average was now 33.5, and the Tide record stood at 4-0. When the second issue of the weekly ratings was released, the Golden Tide had climbed to the top spot in the state.

Central City picked up their fifth win at Bremen by crushing the Eagles 86-41. Corky scored 42 in this one, raising his average to 35.2—the highest ever attained in Muhlenberg schoolboy history! Billy Mason had 12.

Win #6 came at Beechmont, where The Tide defeated Hughes-Kirk 89-51. With 34, Corky again led the Tide. Robie Harper led the Tigers with 19.

The Tide now at 6-0, the St. Xavier Tigers paid a visit. Powered by Corky's 39, the Tide defeated the visitors 76-63. Billy Mason scored 13 and Stan Ruby, 12.

Central City played host to Greenville next. Still stinging from their four losses to the Tide the previous season, Greenville could do nothing to reverse the outcome this time. The final score was 70-52. Corky accounted for 34; Billy Mason, 18.

With Christmas vacation came the annual CCIT. The games, played on the 27th and 28th, featured Drakesboro against Graham, and Central City versus Hartford. Admission, since it was a tournament, was increased to 50 cents for students, 75 cents for adults. But still they came!

In the opening round Graham defeated Drakesboro 51-48, followed by the Tide's 78-58 win over Hartford. Corky scored 25; Mason, 18; Robinson, 12; and Eddie Houston, 10. Central City mauled Graham 76-48 for the tournament title in their next game. Corky scored 34; Billy Mason, 20.

With the new year, the Tide, at 10-0, were ranked fifth in the state. Corky had racked up 342 points for a 34.2 scoring average.

With school back in session, the Tide headed to Calhoun. Corky was still on his game, this time scoring 40. It was a big game for his team as well, as they became the first Central City squad to break the 100-point barrier, this at 102-69.

From their highest total to their lowest came next, when stalling, deliberate Hughes-Kirk came to town. Coach Ben Topmiller's plans slowed Corky a bit, but failed to produce a win. The Tigers fell to Central City 63-38. Corky spent most of the second half on the bench with foul problems, but still managed to score 28. Mason added 14.

With a 12-0 record now, the team traveled to Butler County to take on the upset-minded Bears. These Bears were grouchy ones when the state's third-ranked team walked into their Morgantown den that night, Jan. 10, 1955. Hankerin' to avenge their '54 regional final tourney loss to their rivals, Butler County was primed and loaded.

This 4th Region "headliner" matched the region's top two teams. Butler County, with its all-business-like coach, William C. "Bill" Warren, was sporting a solid 12-2 record and was, according to one local journalist, "a smooth-working, steady-grinding team." The Bears featured excellent guard play with Allan Shields and Wally Johnson, and tenacious board work from the Hammers brothers, Raydean and Lowell.

Although Central City entered the game as the favorite, the Bears saw it as an opportunity. Corky, describing a chance meeting between his brother and a Butler County player days prior to the game, tells, "Roy ran into Wally Johnson a few days before the game. Wally told Roy if they could hold me to 35 or less, they thought they could beat us. I don't know how they arrived at that number, but that's what Wally told Roy, and Roy told me. He was right. I only scored 28, and we lost the game."

The Bears stood claw to toe with the Tide that evening, and by the time the final seconds wound down, had pulled away on the scoreboard, earning a 65-54 win. With the loss, the Tide record dropped to 12-1, and their long regular season winning streak of forty-four games—one stretching back to the Male loss in 1953—was over.

With the bitter loss to their rivals behind them, Central City went home to face Owensboro Catholic. For three quarters the Aces stayed close, but a late third quarter surge pushed the Tide on to an eventual 69-59 win. It was their thirteenth victory, but the previous loss to Butler County dropped the Tide to tenth in the latest state rankings.

Wingo, the Tide's next opponent, was ranked #17 in Kentucky. After Wingo would come Sedalia, a team ranked #20. In the first of these games, played in Graves County on consecutive nights, the Tide faced Wingo. The Indians were undefeated and were led by their all-state performer, Ken Wray. To go with Wray was another solid performer, Frank Waggoner. Even with this duo, the Indians couldn't whip the Tide. Central City won 84-73. Corky scored 27. Wingo's Waggoner scored 24; Wray, 19.

The following night the Tide took on Sedalia, coached by McCoy Tarry, the former coach of the 1948 undefeated Brewers team. The Lions were led by Bob Wilson, their all-stater. If looking for a fitting description for Central City's performance in this game, try "bowed unceremoniously," as they were totally embarrassed in a 75-59 loss. The Tide never led, and early, frequent fouls by Corky, Mason, and Robinson had much to do with their demise. Corky had 20, his lowest output of the season. Billy Mason scored 17, and Winfred Thompson, 13. Bob Wilson led Sedalia with 23.

Corky, offering an oddly amusing excuse for his poor personal performance that night, explains: "We had a great game against Wingo on the first night and then went to our motel in Mayfield. For some reason, I ended up sharing a room with Jack Day, our assistant coach. The room only had one bed, and I didn't much like that... but that was okay... we had to share beds with teammates sometimes. I finally fell asleep, but after a while, I woke up and realized Jack had rolled over and thrown his leg and arm over me. He was asleep and didn't know that. I didn't know what to do, so I laid there awake all night. I sure wasn't going to wake him and embarrass us both. In the game that night I was dragging and was too tired to help my team."

After Corky's sleepless night, and the Tide's defeat at the hands of Sedalia, their record fell to 14-2. They had lost two of their last three contests and were now only a week away from an appearance in the Louisville Invitational Tournament. It would be the Tide's first appearance in the LIT since the 1950 team had participated five years earlier, and there was great excitement.

The Louisville Invitational was held on Friday and Saturday, Jan. 21-22. The Tide had been chosen as one of only four teams from outside the Louisville area. The remaining three state-at-large squads were the Adair County Indians, Newport Wildcats, and Inez Indians.

When the drawings were announced, the Tide had a first round bye, with their first game coming against the winner of the Atherton-Newport contest. The Tide would be playing at 3:30 on Friday afternoon.

But before Central City headed to Louisville, there was one more game to be played locally. This game was against Owensboro, at Central City. Red Devil strategy involved stopping Corky with double, and sometimes triple, teaming, but proved all-for-naught, as he poured in 37 in the Tide's 80-57 victory. The Tide could now focus on their trip to the LIT.

The team checked into the Kentucky Hotel in downtown Louisville. Here, with a first round bye, they waited to learn the outcome of the Atherton-Newport contest. Almost no one expected Atherton to win, even though they had Charlie Tyra. The nay-sayers proved right, as the Johnny Turner-led Wildcats easily disposed of the Rebels. John Turner and Charlie Tyra would later be teammates at the University of Louisville.

With Newport as the tourney favorite, the Tide-Wildcat contest had the potential to be a real dogfight. But when the game began, it seemed Central City was the bigger dog. Scoring at will, Corky racked up 16 of his team's 28 first quarter points, and when this period ended, the Tide held a 28-18 lead. The lead widened to 32-18 in the second, but Newport clawed back to cut the Tide's lead to 44-37 at half.

The third stanza saw the Newporters cut deeper into Central City's lead, and when it ended, the margin had been whittled down to 49-47. Much of the Wildcats' success came from increased efforts to shut down passing lanes to Corky. In response, the Tide had no answers, and Corky was continually denied the ball.

The fourth was more of the same and saw the Newporters grab their first lead at 55-53. A free throw extended that lead to 56-53, and by the time the clock had ticked down to 4:30, the 'Cats had forged farther ahead at 64-55, a lead that was never overcome. Newport had inflicted the Tide's third loss of the season, 69-62. Corky scored 31, a total slightly below his 32.6 average entering the game.

The Tide returned to their hotel rooms after the loss, and it wasn't long before Corky received a phone call from Harry Lancaster, the assistant coach at Kentucky. Lancaster asked Corky to meet him in the hotel lobby's coffee shop. The University of Kentucky had already been recruiting Corky for some time now, and even Coach Rupp had made a couple of trips to Central City to watch him perform.

After a few minutes of conversation, a Southeastern Conference letter of intent was placed on the table. This, if signed, would commit Corky to UK, but only if he chose to play at a Southeastern Conference school. "I was in no way pressured that day, but I signed, knowing I was going to do so sooner or later anyway," explains Corky. "I saw no reason to postpone.... I knew I wanted to go there."

Even with his signing, non-SEC colleges continued recruiting Corky, however. He could have gone most anywhere he wanted, but it was the local schools that most interested him. These included Louisville, Western, Kentucky Wesleyan, and Murray State, but others, including Furman in South Carolina, were visited. The Air Force Academy even came calling!

Corky recalls his visit to the Louisville campus, claiming, "It wasn't a good fit.... I didn't like the campus at all." Although the Louisville coach was Bernard "Peck" Hickman, a former Golden Tide star player and alumni, Corky never really considered signing with the Cardinals after that visit.

When asked about Western, Corky was kinder with his remarks, and of the colorful Western coach, Ed Diddle, Corky had this to say: "I really liked Coach Diddle. He asked me what other schools had offered, and I really didn't know what to say. The first thing I could think to say was 'clothes,' and when I said this, he pulled his coat open, pointed to a Bowling Green clothing store label, and told me he could get all the clothes I wanted."

With the LIT over for the Tide, and the papers signed with the University of Kentucky, Corky and his teammates headed home.

The first post-LIT tournament game for the Tide was against Drakesboro. The Tide won 68-55 with Corky's 26 leading the way.

Daviess County fell next. The game, played in Owensboro, saw the Tide put 103 points on the board and win 103-83. Corky was at his best, scoring 51, with 44 of these coming on his 22 field goals. Considering he spent seven minutes on the bench, the total is more impressive and also represented a new individual scoring record for a Muhlenberg high school cager.

Corky scored 33 and 35 in the next two victories against Muhlenberg Central (70-31) and Heath (79-72), but his 24 against Paducah Tilghman wasn't enough to prevent a 56-51 Tide loss, one dropping them to 18-4.

Central City followed their loss to Tilghman with a win over Calhoun 79-55. This gave the Tide their nineteenth victory. After twenty-three games, Corky had 759 points, and was averaging an even 33 per game. Second in the region was Roger Newman with 23.7, and third, Robie Harper with 20.6.

Next, against Madisonville at their place, Corky scored 24 in a 74-50 Tide victory and followed with 34 more in a 70-49 shelling of Bremen. His season total now exceeded 800—a first for a Muhlenberg cager!

Next up... Greenville! In this game, at Greenville, the 'Hawks hung tough, trailing only 49-42 at the end of the third. Then something happened... or rather didn't happen, as the Tide went without a field goal in the final stanza. Greenville, taking advantage, used free throws to knot the score at 49 with 3:30 remaining.

With Corky missing two shots in the final seconds of regulation, the game went into overtime. Then, after he missed a forty foot desperation shot at the buzzer, a second overtime was necessary. In this overtime, Roger Newman hit two free throws near the end, and the Blackhawks held on for a rare victory over their arch rivals. The final score was 51-49. The Tide record now stood at 21-5.

Corky's 16 points against Greenville was his lowest of the season. His six field goals were only two less than Greenville's team total of eight, but the victors had capitalized on 35 free throws. Central City could claim only 11. Roger Newman led all scorers with 25.

Following this loss another game of great interest, statewide, was slated to be played. Adair County, coached by John Burr, was coming to town. The Indians were ranked #4 and had lost only once during the season, that loss coming in the LIT. The Tide wanted back on the winning track, but against Adair County there would be nothing easy.

Adair County was very good and counted two first team all-staters on its roster. These two were 5'10" Terry Randall and 6'3" Ralph Shearer. Shearer recalls the contest at Memorial Gymnasium: "We lost that game by four, 73-69, but played it without one of our starters, Haskin Rowe. Corky and I had a shootout.... I think we both scored 39 each. Corky was a great player, but I remember Central City didn't play much defense at all. I pretty much could score at will since there was nobody guarding that close."

Shearer had been named an all-stater during his sophomore season in '54 and would be selected for this same honor in this, his junior season of '55. However, in what he acknowledges as a "big mistake," Ralph allowed "Bones" McKinney, the coach at Wake Forest University, to persuade him to attend a North Carolina prep school during his senior season in '56. Of course, Wake Forest provided the needed funds for this transfer. Shearer continues: "We had the best team in the state in '54 and should have won the championship. We lost to Inez 70-68 in the semi-finals, and they went on to win it all that year. The next year we made it to the finals, but lost to Hazard. I really believe we could have won it all in '56, too, if I'd stayed at Adair County for my senior season."

As it turned out, Ralph Shearer didn't play for the Demon Deacons of Wake Forest, either. Instead, Coach John Oldham convinced him to enroll at Tennessee Tech. But even this didn't last long, as Shearer played only two seasons before giving up college and taking a job at GE in Louisville.

The last of the Tide's regular season games came against Owensboro at the Sportscenter on Feb. 24. It was, in one writer's words, "an erratic, but hotly contested game, played more by football rules and football tactics than one usually witnessed in the normal run of a basketball season." It was also noted that several Tidemen finished the game "badly bruised and skinned." Corky's 21 led the Tide in this donnybrook, but he had struggled with a severe cold throughout. The Tide's 62-54 victory was their twenty-third of the season.

With the '54-'55 regular season in the books, the Tide's attention now turned to the 16th District Tournament to be held at Muhlenberg Central. Central City was scheduled to square off against Drakesboro in the first game, with the winner facing the survivor of the Graham-Muhlenberg Central contest. In the lower bracket Greenville was paired with Hughes-Kirk and Dunmor with Bremen.

In the opener the Tide started fast, and by half held a 34-25 lead. In the second half Drakesboro's Gale Buchanan got hot and brought his team to a 35-35 tie, but that would be it, as the Tide pulled away and won 77- 69. Corky scored 23, but was closely followed by Mason's 20.

Graham crushed Muhlenberg Central 51-34 in the nightcap, earning a shot at the Golden Tide. The Tide-Graham contest was fiercely fought, and Graham built a five point lead in the fourth quarter. Corky, after a back court steal, scored a few plays later, tying the score at 56. From here the Tide pulled away to a final 66-56 win. Corky's 25 paced Central City.

Central City was in the finals of the district once again, this time facing Greenville. The Blackhawks had earned their way to the finals by beating Hughes-Kirk, and then a good Dunmor team, 57-53.

The district final proved to be a "classic," at least to basketball fans in Muhlenberg County. Both teams were at their best, and the game was played at a high level. To some it was Corky vs. Roger, as the two played on even terms the entire game.

Central City raced to an early 24-16 lead, but Greenville fought back to trail by three at half, 38-35. The third quarter saw Greenville surge ahead and finish the period with a 51-48 lead. In the early stages of the fourth they extended this lead to 55-50, but the Tide fought back and edged ahead. With Greenville trailing 61-60, the usually dependable Newman was called for a lane violation, not once, but twice in a row! Corky, scoring both times, gave the Tide the final victory at 66-62.

Throughout the game Roger and Corky had battled evenly. Corky finished with 27, and so did Roger. Corky's points came on 13 field goals and a free throw, Roger's on 7 field goals and 13 free throws. Both had capitalized on what was given by the other team.

Central City had the district crown once again, but Greenville was heading to the regional tournament as runner-up. Of course, as only fate would have it, the two rivals would face each other in that as well.

When the 16th District All-Tournament team was announced, it included Corky, Billy Mason, and Billy Robinson from the Tide, Roger Newman and Larry Sparks from Greenville, Glen Thompson from Dunmor, Rondall Woodall from Graham, Robie Harper from Hughes-Kirk, Gale Buchanan from Drakesboro, and Gerald Divine from Bremen.

When the drawings for the 4th Region Tournament were held, by some hand of fate, perhaps, Central City was opening up against Butler County, with the winner facing the winner of the game between Breckinridge County and Greenville. These were considered to be the best four teams in the tourney by many, and Central City was a big rival with all three!

On Thursday night, March 10, the Golden Tide opened their regional play against Butler County at Powderly. The Bears (26-4) had defeated the Tide in early January, and the re-match promised to be filled with tension.

Early in the contest the Tide fell behind, but eventually took a lead at 13-12. From there, they would never trail. From a 19-17 first quarter lead, the Tide built a 46-36 halftime lead behind Corky's 22 points. Although he was in foul trouble during the second half, his replacement, Billy Duvall, had a hot hand from the field, pushing the Tide lead to 19.

When the game ended, the Tide's loss in Morgantown had been avenged 87-72. Corky's 26 points pushed his season total to 1,102, a new, one season high for a Muhlenberg cager. Billy Mason had 16; Carl Jamison, 15. For the losing Bears, Wally Johnson had 20; Ray Hammers, 13; and Allan Shields, 12.

Having won, the Tide would now face Greenville, the winner over Breckinridge County. For both Central City and Greenville, this routine was getting a bit old.

A shock to most, arch rival Greenville bowed out quietly this time. The Tide trailed by a point at half, but came out in the third with inspired play that pushed them to a 49-38 lead at the end of that stanza. From here, they were never threatened, and at game's end, had a 69-54 victory. Corky's 28 led the Tide. Newman totaled 23 for Greenville.

Next up for the Tide was the regional championship game and a matchup against Hartford. Hartford had made its way to the finals by defeating Irvington in the semis. A win over the Mustangs would put the Tide on the road to Lexington, but the game would prove the toughest hurdle on their tourney trail thus far.

Hartford had started regional tournament play with a 29-6 record. With Don Barass and Charles Newcom leading the way, they were not to be overlooked as a dark horse candidate in the race for the regional title. But with their narrow 55-54 overtime victory over Leitchfield in their opener, few gave the Mustangs much of a chance against the Tide.

The first half went as most expected, as the Tide took a 31-19 lead to the lockers. But when second half play began, the Tide quickly discovered the Mustangs weren't ready to fold just yet. By quarter's end, Hartford had cut the Tide's lead to 39-33.

After only scoring eight in the third, Tide shooting got even colder in the fourth. Out rebounded and in serious foul trouble, they struggled. Billy Mason, the Tide's #2 scorer, was already on the bench with his fifth personal, and Corky earned his fifth at the four minute mark with the score knotted at 45 each. Things didn't look good for Central City!

With only eleven seconds remaining, and with Hartford leading 52-51, the Tide, in desperation, fouled the Mustangs' Glenn Mills. Mills, if he could hit both free throws, would ice the game. At best, Tide hopes were slim now.

Miraculously for Central City, Mills—in what had to be Hartford's most frustrating basketball moment ever—missed both shots! Winfred Thompson, grabbing the rebound, threw an outlet pass to Carl Jamison who, in turn, threw ahead to Billy Duvall at mid-court. Billy, with desperate pleas from Jamison to shoot, launched a thirty footer that threaded the net for his only field goal of the game. The Tide had the victory, 53-52!

Emerging from the bottom of his team's celebratory pile-up, Duvall, with bloodied nose, was hoisted atop the shoulders of his teammates. At that moment no player in Golden Tide history had been a bigger hero than Billy, and it was he whom Coach Gish would later credit with "clutch work" in all six of their tournament games. And although only scoring 36 points in those six contests, Billy's final basket in this one was sending the Tide to the Sweet 16!

For the game, Corky had 18 before fouling out, Robinson had 12, and Mason, eight. Hartford's Newcom had 17; Barass, 11; and Glenn Mills, 10. Mills, it's safe to speculate, had several restless nights following this. Corky, seldom one to miss an opportunity for some good-natured ribbing, has since informed Glenn that he is the only non-Tide player ever inducted into Central City's Hall of Fame! So much for sensitivity.

When the All-Tournament team was announced, it included Carl Jamison, Billy Robinson, and Corky Withrow from the Tide, but, to the disappointment of Tide supporters, not Billy Ray Duvall. Others named to this squad were Donnie Barrass and Charles Newcom from Hartford, Larry Sparks and Roger Newman from Greenville, Ken Beard from Breckinridge County, Wally Johnson from Butler County, and Tony Carman from Irvington.

After the trophy presentations, Billy Duvall, although not part of the all-tourney squad, was again hoisted on the shoulders of his victorious teammates. Now, amidst the roar of elated Tide fans, he was carried to the locker room—a Golden Tide hero for all times to come!

With the Sweet 16 only days away, the sixth ranked Golden Tide now learned they would open state tourney play against the Pikeville Panthers of Coach John Bill Trivette. The Panthers' record stood at 24-5, and the game would tip-off at 9:15 on Wednesday night. The winner would face the winner of the game between the Glasgow Scotties and the Johnny Cox-led Hazard Bulldogs.

As in the previous year, Central City was pitted against a formidable team from the mountains. Once again, there would be no easy route.

The state tourney game against Pikeville proved close throughout. The Panthers' outstanding 1-2-1-1 full court press, applied with relentless pressure, forced turnovers and slowed the Tide's running game. The largest margin came when Pikeville built a 38-27 lead in the second stanza, but Central City fought back to trail by only five at half, 46-41. Ralph Gilliam, Pikeville's 5-9, bespectacled all-state guard, scored 12 in this second quarter.

Behind Corky and Billy Mason the Tide fought back in the third, taking a 61-59 lead as it ended. This would be the last Tide lead, however, and the last tie came at 67-67 in the fourth. The final score was 78-74, as the Panthers managed to outplay the Tide down the stretch.

Corky led the Tide with 28, but had fouled out in the late stages. Billy Mason, before fouling out, had 15. Winfred Thompson also hit double digits with 11. Pikeville's Ralph Gilliam had 33 to lead all scorers.

With their second straight first round elimination, the Tide headed home. For Corky and his soon-to-be senior classmates, there would be only one more chance to earn a state title.

Again, Corky gained statewide honors, being named to the Sweet 16 All-Tournament squad, and the *Paducah Sun-Democrat*

All-State team. With this last award, he finished second to Male's Kenny Kuhn in total votes and would join a list of outstanding players that included Johnny Cox of Hazard, Don Mills of Berea, Donnis Butcher of Meade Memorial, Ralph Shearer of Adair County, and Herbie Triplett of Inez.

Another honor was awarded Corky by the *Louisville Courier-Journal.* They gave him a spot on their All-State team, again finishing second to Kuhn in total votes. Dean Eagle, a Louisville sportswriter, placed Corky on his All-State squad, too.

During his junior season Corky had scored 1,086 points in 36 games, placing his average at 30.2 per game. His high game had been 51 against Daviess County, three times he had scored in the forties, and 13 times he hit the thirties. His rebounding was equally impressive, but the lack of official records leaves this total a question mark.

He had been named to every all-county, all-tournament, all-district, all-region, and all-state team he was eligible for, and had signed to play college basketball with Adolph Rupp and the University of Kentucky.

There would be many more awards and honors to come during his senior season, but the big prize—a Kentucky State Championship—was still out there.

After every Central City basketball season, there was a spring baseball season for Corky, too. The 1955 season would be Corky's most memorable.

Tide baseball, like most high school baseball of that day, took a very distant second (or third) to basketball. The Tide program was, according to Corky, "a stepchild or novelty." Very little money went into the program, and certainly even less was produced. Records, what few exist, are sketchy.

Still, though, they had a team, and it was coached by Jack Day. Without question, the team's finest performer was Corky Withrow, and he was already attracting the attention of several big league scouts.

Prior to this season, there had been other outstanding Tide players and good teams. Bobby Don Millard, a '54 graduate, held great promise and had a legitimate shot at a professional career as a pitcher. There had been some others with above average talent as well, but the program was largely just something to do between basketball season and summer vacation for most.

There had been no little league programs in Central City when Corky was younger, so for the most part, it had been sandlot and pickup games where he developed his skills. There was also his father, and surely the time Otis spent with his sons in their front yard on Resevoir Avenue deserves some mention. "D.D," Corky's brother, was a solid baseball player, too, and would go on to play college baseball for Kentucky Wesleyan, this on a team roster that included "King" Kelly Coleman.

But there was some organized baseball in the area, and that was with the American Legion sponsored teams. Corky spent a few summers on the diamond with their teams, and his 1952 Post 61 American Legion team even earned its way to the final game of the Legion's State Tournament in Louisville. Central City lost in the title game to Latonia's Legion team, but still a runner-up trophy was a big deal to those fifteen year old Muhlenberg County youngsters.

The '55 Tide team, led by Corky's big bat, had an outstanding season. Good enough to win the regional tournament at Madisonville, in fact, and then participate in the Kentucky High School State Baseball Tournament at Parkway Field in Louisville. This tournament, held on June 10-11, involved teams from the KHSAA's eight high school baseball regions.

In the tourney's third game (the first for the Tide), Central City faced the Tomcats from Ashland High. The Ashland pitcher that day was the hard throwing Jim Host. Host would go on to pitch at Kentucky and then play minor league ball in the White Sox organization. His career ended with an arm injury while pitching for the Lincoln White Sox, but Host would become a highly successful businessman and entrepreneur. Among his business related achievements would be his involvement with the building of the YUM! Center in Louisville and as CEO of Host Communications.

As good as Host was, he wasn't good enough to stop Corky Withrow and the Golden Tide on that June day in '55, however. Twice Corky blasted Jim's pitches off the high left field wall of Parkway,

305 feet away. For the game Corky went three for four, leading his team to a narrow 3-2 victory. "I had a single, a double, and a triple off Jim," Corky boasts, "and I reminded him of that when I saw him a few years ago."

Winfred Thompson was the winning pitcher against Ashland. Corky played shortstop that day.

With the win over the Tomcats, the Tide advanced to play the winner of a game between Louisville Manual and Greensburg. In this one, Manual's Crimsons easily defeated the Dragons, 8-1.

The following day Central City faced Manual in the semis. For Manual, it was almost the same as a home game, as Parkway Field was located only a very short distance from their campus.

In the other semi-final, Hall High School, from Gray Knobs, Kentucky, defeated Salem High 4-3. Hall would then advance to the final game to face the winner of the Manual-Central City contest.

Corky had another fine game against Manual, going two for three at the plate and blasting another shot off the left field wall of Parkway. But it wasn't enough, and the Tide fell to Manual. Although research revealed this final score as being 10-4, Corky insists his Tide team didn't score that many runs that day. Either way, four runs or less, it was a loss.

During his two games in the tournament, Corky had gone five for seven at the plate. His .714 batting average was the tourney's best, and for his performance here, and throughout the regular season, he earned All-State Baseball honors.

If anyone is interested, Manual defeated Hall in the championship game.

Chapter 7

The King and I

In the fall of '55 Corky began his senior year at Central City. Soon to be eighteen, and having gained the attention of most all the state's sportswriters and college coaches, he could pretty much write his own ticket.

Corky had his own automobile now, a 1937 four door Chevy sedan purchased from Ootsie Smith for $75 cash. The money came from some he had saved from earnings as a part-time employee at Villines, a local furniture store. Although his savings weren't quite enough to seal the deal, his parents helped with the difference.

His popularity was at an all-time high that fall, and he rode this crest of popularity right into the office of senior class president. The girls liked Corky, too, but he had a steady girl named Lavon Goff. Lavon and Corky were engaged, but the marriage date was set for some vague, undetermined time after graduation. Lavon, like Corky, was elected to high office as the class secretary that fall, and clearly this seemed to have the makings of a future family political dynasty.

Topping the music charts that August was Fats Domino with his hit single "Ain't That A Shame." Little Richard was soon to release "Tuitti Frutti," and at Sun Studios in Memphis, Sam Phillips was experimenting with a new genre called "rock-a-billy." Earlier that year Elvis Presley lamented the loss of his "baby" in his first #1 hit, "Heartbreak Hotel," and Johnny Cash was recording "Folsom Prison Blues."

"Teen angst" was in the air that fall of '55 also, at least in part due to the tragic car crash death of Hollywood teen idol James Dean. The accident, with Dean driving his '55 Porsche Spyder, happened on Sept. 30, just prior to the release of his latest and last picture, *Rebel Without A Cause*, a movie Corky recalls watching at Central City's State Theater a few weeks later.

No doubt, many parents were wondering what was going wrong with this generation of teens, especially with movies like Dean's and 1953's *The Wild Ones* starring Marlon Brandon.

Music was also becoming increasingly rebellious, at least in the minds of many parents who, for the most part, had come of age during the Big Band and Swing music era of the thirties and forties. It was, at least to them, hard to see any moral or social good that could result from songs with titles such as "Black Denim Trousers and Motorcycle Boots." Tragedy and teen music just seemed to have been made for each other!

There was, to be fair, teen music of a much less threatening nature. Two brothers, Phil and Don, sons of Ike and Margaret Everly, were able to explode on the music scene in February of '57. Their first hit single, "Bye Bye Love," certainly represented no challenge to adult authority, but even they would soon push the limit of adult patience when they followed with "Wake Up, Little Susie" in September of that same year. Shocking to many, the words were considered scandalous enough to be "Banned in Boston."

Regardless of what was happening on the movie and music scene, all that mattered to Corky Withrow was the current scene and happenings at Central City High. That was his world, and much of it revolved around him.

Although being the senior class president was a great responsibility, Corky had absolutely no intention of letting the burdens of office take any priority over basketball. That was first and foremost, and if his Tide fell short of a state tourney championship in his last high school campaign, the season would be a failure of massive proportions, at least to him.

This latest version of Golden Tide basketball was loaded with talent and experience. Expectations, although always high in Central City, would be at the highest level ever, as the team could claim a soon-to-be All-American and an excellent surrounding class and deep bench.

While reminiscing along the banks of Charlie Thurman's lake in Sonora, Hardin County, on a hot summer day in 2014, Corky talked about a few of his senior teammates from that season:

> Billy Mason was always smiling. He was a good ball -handler and shooter with lots of basketball savvy. He scored lots of points for us that season. His mother was a big booster of the team and was always bringing us cakes, cookies, and other things she baked. She was a single mother... bless her heart, and I don't remember her ever having a job... maybe she did. Looking back, I'm not sure how they made it. It had to be hard. We loved Billy's mother to death, but she did think Billy should be shooting more. Lots of parents think that. There was one time when Billy let her attitude affect his, and he convinced Carl Jamison to go along with him... but nothing serious. Before one of our games, they sat in the upper corner of the gym instead of sitting with the rest of us like usual. Coach Gish didn't much care for this and told me to get the team together and solve the problem. That's the way Mr. Gish was. We had a team meeting, including Billy and Carl, and worked it out. That's really the only time I can recall anything remotely close to a team problem that year.
>
> Carl Jamison was one of our guards. He was a gamer... and I mean this in a good way... the oddball of all oddballs. He averaged about 12 a game and was an absolute wild man on the court. But he was very physical and didn't know any other way to play. He was as hardworking as anyone on the team. We don't know what happened to Carl, though, and none of us have heard from him for years. Carl also played trumpet in the band, and that was his great passion.
>
> Both Carl and Billy Mason played trumpet, and they were in a small orchestra... maybe a dozen or so... called Men of Note. They were pretty good and played at dances and other school functions. Billy Duvall was an outstanding shooter... one of the purest I've ever seen. I saw Kelly

> Coleman, Jerry West, Oscar Robertson, and several other great ones, but Billy could shoot with any of them. Billy was really friendly and good-natured, too. He loved the girls... I mean, really loved the girls! But now school was a different matter. Billy didn't care much for school at all, but Mr. Gish kept us in line when it came to that. Coach was a silent disciplinarian and didn't have to say anything to keep us straight.

Another of Corky's teammates that season was Winfred Thompson, a junior. Winfred graduated from Central City in '57, signing to play for Coach Robert "Bullet" Wilson at Kentucky Wesleyan. Winfred would play his freshman season for Wilson, and then the next three years for T.L. Plain, Wilson's successor at the Owensboro college. After graduation Winfred returned to Muhlenberg County where he was a businessman until his death in September of 2002.

About Winfred, Corky had this to say: "Winfred was quiet and unassuming. He came from a good, hardworking family like the rest of us, and he worked at his father's service station in town. He was a good leaper and rebounder and could drive the lane really well. He scored several points for us, but wasn't selfish at all. Not one of us was selfish. As the season went on, Winfred came into his own. He got better and better every game, and with this, scored more points for us."

There was one more teammate Corky mentioned, but not related to any particular Tide basketball memories. "Buddy Lear was a reserve and was dating a Central City High girl, Ellie Durall," he explains. "But she didn't marry Buddy. Ellie married John Y. Brown later." Elleanor Durall Brown, it should be noted, would later own the ABA's Kentucky Colonels.

When the Tide took the court for the first game of Corky's senior season, the competition was Bremen. The Tide had no problems and quickly built a 21- 3 lead, rolling to a 66-47 victory. Corky led the way with 29.

Next up was Calhoun. Again it was easy, and the final score of 89-55 included Corky's 38 points. Dunmor followed, the Tide won 81-54, and Corky added 35 more to make a three game total of 102. Billy Mason had 22.

The Tide's fourth game found Corky tying his county scoring record with 51 against Hughes-Kirk. Central City won 107-69. Mason totaled 14. Hughes-Kirk's outstanding brother combination of Robie and Jimmy Harper scored 19 and 18, respectively, for their coach, Roy Withrow—Corky's brother! Roy, although only in his second year of college, still lived in Central City with his family and was in his first year as a high school head coach.

For the first showdown between the two Withrow brothers that season, their mother attended. Corky was on fire that night and couldn't miss. With his final game total of 51, he was sure his parents would be excited and proud, but upon arriving home after the game found just the opposite. His mother was upset, and the reason for her ill temper was Corky's unnecessary, excessive shooting and scoring at the expense of his brother. Corky, it seems, had forgotten his mother's other son. Roy hadn't been on the winning side that night!

"She was as mad as I'd ever seen her," Corky laughs, "and I remember Mom getting right in my face and telling me it wouldn't happen again!" With Flo Eva's warning came a choice. "Mom told me... either she was going to school to tell Mr. Gish she didn't approve of what I did against my brother's team, or I could tell Mr. Gish, myself."

What teenage boy wants his mother to come to his school in such a state of mind? Certainly not Corky, and with no viable options, he was forced to explain to his coach everything that had transpired in the Withrow home after the game. "Mr. Gish," Corky recalls, "said nothing until I finished, and when I did, all he said was 'I understand.'"

Even with his outstanding offensive display, Corky had absorbed a verbal beating from his mother. "Mom could be pretty mean when she wanted to be," he chuckles. A valuable lesson had been learned, though, and it was one that could have come, with some minor revision, straight from the Bible. This lesson was, as passed down from Flo Eva to Corky, "Brothers do not do these things to brothers."

The story of Roy versus Corky doesn't end with this game, however, as there would be another game played in the gym at Hughes-Kirk a few weeks later. Flo Eva was there to watch her sons again, this time seated behind a low wall separating the fans from the floor. "I knew not to do that again," Corky acknowledges. "I could barely see my mother's head peeking over the wall, but when I got the ball I looked for her. If she nodded yes, that meant I could shoot. If she nodded no, I passed to a teammate."

Even with the pre-arranged restraints of motherly advice, Corky still scored 30 that night, but it was a far cry from the drubbing he had inflicted on Roy and his Tigers in their first contest. And with that, Mom was okay.

About the same time as Corky's 51 point outburst against Hughes-Kirk, Central City announced the teams playing in the upcoming CCIT on Dec. 23-24. The visiting participates would be Graham, Todd County, and, to the delight of most, the Wayland Wasps from the mountains of Floyd County. Wayland's roster included eastern Kentucky's most noted player, "King" Kelly Coleman, and he was what all the excitement was about.

There was also another tournament ahead, as the Louisville Invitational committee had, for a second straight year, invited the Golden Tide. This tourney was scheduled for the 27th and 28th, three days after the CCIT.

But there were still regular season games to be played prior to these tourneys. The first of these found Drakesboro coming to town. The Tide had no problems, easily winning 74-49. In only three quarters of play, Corky scored 35. The following night he scored 30 more in an 84-44 beat down of Muhlenberg Central at Powderly. Thompson added 19.

Graham came to town next and, like the Tide, had an undefeated record. But here their streak ended, as the Tide handed the visitors their first defeat in twelve games by whipping them 88-69. Corky totaled 24; Carl Jamison, 21.

Following was a trip to Greenville. Wasting no time, the Tide blasted out to a 17-0 lead in the first quarter. Greenville didn't give up, however, and behind Newman's 20 straight points, cut the Tide lead to 33-32 at half.

The third period saw the Tide stretch their lead to 39-32, and then pull away for a 69-51 victory. Before departing the contest with foul problems, Roger Newman had scored 30. Corky, with the same problems, had 22.

With school dismissed for Christmas break, it was tournament time. With their high rankings, and with both Todd County and the Wayland Wasps coming to town for the CCIT, anticipation was high.

In the opener Wayland faced Graham. With Kelly Coleman leading the way, Coach "Copper John" Campbell's Wasps got off to an early 17-6 lead. At half, their lead stood at 32-19, and by the end of the third, it was 47-33. When it had ended, Wayland had the victory at 65-53. Coleman had lived up to his billing with 40 points. Now, if Central City could win their game, tourney organizers would get their wish—"King" Kelly versus Corky!

The Tide played well that night, too, and at the end of the first quarter had a 24-16 lead over the Elks. The second period went much the same, and by half, the lead had grown to 53-35. At the end of the third, Central City led 68-49, so the fourth saw plenty of action for the Tide reserves. Corky led his team with 26, and when the game ended, it was 85-63 in favor of the Tide. The much anticipated game between Wayland and Central City lay ahead.

Wayland High School, located in the mountainous coal mining community of Wayland in Floyd County, had been invited to make the long, winding, arduous trip in hopes of matching Kelly Coleman against Corky Withrow. With these two on the court, the game would be one for the ages and draw statewide attention.

According to Coleman, he had been called to Lawrence Price's office at Wayland High early that season. Price was the school's principal, and with him in the office that day was Wayland's coach, Copper John Campbell.

The two informed Kelly of the team's invitation to play in the CCIT. It was a long day's drive from Wayland, and the team would be playing a game on Christmas Eve, they explained. Hoping for a favorable response from their unpredictable star, the two then asked Kelly for his opinion. But a positive response is not what they received.

Instead, Kelly claims he told Price and Campbell he didn't want to go for a "sure loss in a set-up game." With this negative reaction, the two men told Coleman the school would receive $800 for participating, and assured him the money would be used for much-needed new uniforms for the team. With such a guilt-trip placed at his feet, Kelly backed off his initial refusal, agreeing to go with the team. "I couldn't let my teammates down," he says. "We really needed those new uniforms." Corky, not one to cut Kelly much slack these days, agrees: "Wayland had the most pitiful looking uniforms I ever saw... ugly blue and gold... faded and worn!"

Kelly remembers little about the team's travel to Central City, but can recall riding in the car with his coach and principal, and then being given a single room next to theirs at the motel. "They weren't about to let me out of their sight that weekend," Kelly laughs. "I guess they figured I'd sneak out and get some beer!"

The motel where the Wasps stayed that weekend was on the outskirts of town and was most likely the Rambler Rose. Here, according to Kelly, he and his teammates were stumped when trying to break open a coconut. "We'd stopped somewhere on the way to Central City and had bought a coconut," he laughs. "We hadn't seen one that was still in the shell and didn't know how to bust it open. One of our players, Curtis Ray Slone, I think, smashed it open by slamming it down on the motel's concrete floor."

Although the Waylanders did travel the long distance to Central City, played the games, and received the $800 paycheck for their efforts, the uniforms never materialized. Kelly claims the team never saw any new uniforms that season, and still doesn't know what the money was used for. "It sure wasn't used for us," he complains. "We even had to borrow warm-ups from McDowell High when we played in the state tournament later."

When asked if he had heard anything about Corky and Central City before traveling there, Kelly explained he had. "Yeah... I'd heard a little about him my junior season," he recalls. "We knew he was a good scorer and knew they had a good team, but I also knew we were going to lose that game. It was a made-for-television game... without the television, and they set it up to be me against him."

Although the two had never met, there was almost a meeting on the Saturday morning prior to the game when Corky and a few teammates went to the Central, a downtown pool room. Here, they noticed some Wayland boys in their letter jackets. "They stared at us, and we stared back. That's all that happened," Corky explains. Kelly remembers being at the pool room with his buddies that morning, but denies having noticed any Tide players there.

Although the game didn't start until 7 that evening, it is told the ticket line began forming around 2 that afternoon. Corky recalls "people with their chicken baskets lined all the way down the street," and Kelly confirms the same.

There is no question the game was a big deal in western Kentucky, but it would also garner a substantial amount of attention elsewhere, at least as much as could be garnered statewide in 1955-56. It was, as Gary West labeled in his insightful biography, *King Kelly Coleman: Kentucky's Greatest Basketball Legend*, "East against West, and Kelly versus Corky."

Although most came to see Corky and Kelly square off, the two were not guarding each other that night. Instead, Corky's responsibility was guarding Wasps center Melvin Robinson, and with this, he registered a shutout. Robinson was held scoreless, as was his backup, the coconut-smashing Curtis Ray Slone.

The referees that night were Don "Quack" Butler and "Doc" Farrell. Many stories have been told about their refereeing that night, and Kelly still, tongue-in-cheek, perhaps, complains about several traveling calls made against him. "I was hardly ever called for traveling my entire career," he insists, "but Doc and Quack called me for five that night!" Corky, after listening to Kelly's complaint, countered: "Three or four steps before shooting might have been allowed in eastern Kentucky, but in western Kentucky, a player was required to dribble."

Starting that night for Wayland were Billy Ray Fultz, Billy Ray Combs, Melvin Robinson, Elmond Hall, and Kelly Coleman. Facing them were Winfred Thompson, Billy Ray Duvall, Billy Mason, Carl Jamison, and Corky Withrow.

At the beginning Corky was hot... Kelly was not. Corky scored 14 in this period, and the Tide held a 22-15 lead when the quarter ended. Kelly, after a slow start, heated up and finished this quarter with nine.

In the second stanza the Tide stretched the lead to nine, taking a 36-27 lead to the dressing room at half. In this quarter Kelly had scored 10, while Corky, after cooling off, added six to his total. At halftime it was Kelly with 19 and Corky with 20. But the "King" had three fouls!

The second half opened with Wayland trailing by nine. Kelly was playing well, but with three fouls, and still irritated by the traveling calls, he had to play smart.

As the intensity of the game picked up, it became more of the Kelly vs. Corky contest that many expected. When Kelly scored, the hometown crowd expected Corky to answer with the same. Corky was usually successful at this, but had picked up some fouls as well. With these came time on the bench, while his replacement, Jimmy "Duck" Swann, filled in.

When the third ended, the Tide lead was at 10, 63-53. Kelly had added 10 to his game total during this stanza, and Corky 14 to his. Corky, with 34, led Kelly, who could claim 28. Although Tide fans were happy with the 10-point lead, they couldn't rest yet. Wayland had the "King", and with him on the court, no lead was safe.

By now it was obvious to many that Central City's bench was deeper than that of Wayland, and with this, plus the fact Kelly had foul problems, Tide chances looked good. The fourth quarter saw Kelly bring Wayland back to within four, but by this point he had picked up a fourth foul. However, Corky had four fouls, too!

The Tide dug down deep now, regrouped, and pushed their lead back out to eight, and that was that. The game ended 83-75 in favor of Central City. The scorebook showed Corky with 40 points on 15 field goals and 10 free throws. Kelly also had 40, his coming on 14 field goals and 12 free throws. Both had finished with four fouls.

"Kelly versus Corky" was a stalemate, but Central City versus Wayland ended with a Tide victory. But, as Kelly often points out, it was on Central City's court, in their tournament, on Christmas Eve, a day's hard drive from Wayland and, in his words, "with Central City's referees."

As for the game being a "set-up," one can only look at the scorebook for answers. There were 21 fouls called against Central City, 15 called against Wayland. Still, though, Kelly insists it was. "A few years later I ran into Quack Butler," he explains. "Quack told me there was no way they were gonna let a bunch of mountain boys come down there and beat Central City."

In some ways this Christmas Eve game was a true "classic,"largely because two All-Americans met on the court that night. But, after all, it was just a regular season game—albeit a tournament atmosphere—played between two non-rivals a few hundred miles apart. It would be the only time these teams would battle each other that season, but Kelly insists his Wayland teammates desperately wanted a rematch with Central City during the Sweet 16 that March. "When we played Central City in December, I was the only one on my team with any experience," he states, "but by tournament time, we were much more experienced and were a much better team. We really wanted to play Central City again, and I have no doubts we would have beaten them in a re-match. We should have won the state championship that year."

Chapter 8

The Bloody Butler County Kerfuffle of '56

With the win over highly regarded Wayland, the Tide had a brief Christmas break before the Louisville Invitational on the 27th and 28th. Ranked #3, the Tide would be taking on the state's top ranked team, Newport Public.

Everything went right for the Tide when they took the floor against Stan Arnzen's northern Kentuckians on this day. A hot start propelled them to a 23-6 first quarter lead, and by halftime, this became a 44-15 lead. Of these 44 Tide points, Corky had totaled 22, with 11 coming in each period.

The second half was more evenly played, despite the loss of Newport's Ron Bridewell to fouls in the third. John Turner, a future U of L and NBA star, finished as high man for Newport with 21 points, but it wasn't enough, as Central City crushed Newport 90-60.

Earl Cox, sportswriter for the *Courier-Journal*, wrote: "You can't take a thing away from this Withrow, a strapping 6-4 center. In addition to his 38 points, he controlled rebounds on both ends of the floor, was a terror on defense before he tired badly in the late stages, and had at least 10 assists."

Corky's 38 points set an LIT tournament record. To go with these were Winfred Thompson's 18, Billy Duvall's 14, and Billy Mason's 10.

With their easy win over Newport, the Tide now faced the Berea Pirates, a team ranked #4 by Dr. Litkenhous. Berea, behind Don Mills' 38 record-tying points, had also crushed their first-round opponent, Louisville Southern, 98-40.

Berea was big. In addition to the 6'7" Mills, a future Kentucky Wildcat, was 6'4" Darrell Bicknell, a future Western Hilltopper.

To go with their size, the Pirates also had quickness, mostly on the part of a diminutive guard named Jimmy Williamson. Williamson could score, too, as evidenced by his 23 points in Berea's romp over Southern.

In their game against Central City, the Pirates used both Williamson and Mills to slow Corky down. Williamson camped in front; Mills camped behind. This combination of size and speed more than neutralized the Tide on the backboard, at the same time limiting Corky's time with the ball.

Central City had its final lead of the game at 22-21 and trailed Berea 37-30 at intermission. The third quarter was played evenly, ending with a 57-50 Pirate lead.

The fourth saw the Tide make a run to cut the lead to 62-60, but with four minutes remaining Bicknell scored what proved to be the back-breaker. Leading by six, and with two minutes to go, Berea resorted to ball control. When the buzzer sounded, the Tide was on the losing end, 76-64.

Game totals found Corky with 22, a disappointment for him. Jamison had 14; Mason, 12; and Duvall, 10. The All-Tournament team included Corky and Winfred Thompson from Central City, Calvin Bird from Corbin, John Turner from Newport, Jimmy Jeans from Valley, Terry Litchfield and Jimmy Self from Manual, Ed Shackelford from Eastern, and Darrell Bicknell and Don Mills from Berea.

With New Year's Day, 1956, around the corner, the Golden Tide's record stood at 12-1. Tournament season was over for now, and it was back to district play. The first of these would find them on the road against Hughes-Kirk. Again, Corky would be facing his brother's Tigers.

This time, again under the critical eyes of his mother, Corky and the Tide won 85-66. With a nod of her head, yes or no, Corky scored 30. This total was acceptable to Flo Eva, and no scoldings followed.

Now, with a 13-1 record, the Tide prepared for the hated Bears of Butler County. The game would be played in Central City and, like all Tide-Bears showdowns, was expected to be a tension-filled, hard-fought contest.

The Bears rolled into town with revenge in mind, having lost their last Tide meeting in the '55 regional tournament. Coach Bill Warren's squad was solid and was determined to knock off the Tide. The two teams were bitter rivals at a heightened level and would tangle, both on and off the court. The results would have consequences beyond the game, and for the Tide, throughout the remainder of the season.

Tempers flared early, and it was obvious that the 700 Butler County fans in the gym had no inclination to sit cordially and politely in their rival's house. In fact, they proved to be the guests from Hell.

The Bears' fans seemed to take as much pleasure in verbally harassing Corky as they would get from any victory their team might achieve. Razzed and provoked throughout the game, it was all Corky could do to keep his competitive temper in check.

According to some, one particular incident was the spark that ignited the powder keg. The Butler County pep band, during the pre-game warm up drills, began to unnerve Corky, the bass drummer in particular. According to Corky, there had already been some tense moments during the "B" team's game, and when his squad took the court for the varsity contest, they found Butler County warming up on the goal normally used by the Tide. "They had our basket!" Corky explains. "We always took the goal on the right for the first half, and they knew that. They beat us to it that night, and I'm sure it was done to upset us."

Corky was right. Just ask Butler County's Wally Johnson. "Everything we did was pre-scripted," Johnson admits. "Coach Warren always had things prescripted, and he covered every detail he thought would give us an edge. He wanted to disrupt anything that was part of their normal routine." And the Bears coach, according to Johnson, "was determined to beat Central City that night."

Having taken over a largely unsuccessful Morgantown High basketball program only four years prior, the all-business coach had built a basketball powerhouse at what had become Butler County High shortly after his arrival. "I respected Coach Warren," Johnson says, "but I didn't like him then. If I passed him in the hall during the day, I wouldn't even look at him. But if he was talking to you, you'd better look him eye to eye." Wally, later a head coach at

Flaherty High, North Hardin High, and Bardstown High, came to admire and appreciate his former coach, but only after his graduation. "I eventually came to understand why he had handled us like he did. Looking back, I can see he was one of the biggest influences in my life."

Taken out of their normal routine that night, the Tide had no choice but to take the goal opposite their usual one. This goal was in front of the Bears cheering section and, worst of all, in front of their pep band. "Their bass drummer sat on the floor in the front row and was beating the drum like a red-haired stepchild," Corky complains. "It was making me mad!"

Understand, it wasn't that Corky didn't appreciate music, but he certainly didn't enjoy the Bears drummer pounding away on his end of the court. Finding this extremely irritating, he resolved to take it on himself to stop the music for his own sanity as well as that of his teammates. He had, it should be noted, reached his drummer-toleration limit. With this limit reached, Corky took action.

"I took a basketball, walked over and... accidentally, of course... threw it through their bass drum," he laughs. Corky's action certainly solved what he viewed as one problem, but didn't do much for any reasonable hopes for a peaceful and cordial night of basketball played with sportsmanship and good will.

After a few moments of discussions between assorted school officials, order was temporarily restored, but the tone had been set. The game had now become as much Butler County versus Corky as it would be Bears versus Tide. It would be ugly.

Central City began the game on a good note and built an early nine point lead. It was not maintained, however, and by the third quarter the Bears had forged ahead. With the lead, and with the ball in the hands of their designated dribbler, Wally Johnson, Butler County went to their stall game. This included shooting, but only when available.

Johnson, a savvy competitor, kept the ball from Tide reach for most of the game's final twelve minutes. During this time the Bears stretched the lead to ten. Tempers were on edge throughout, players had to be separated, and more than once these scuffles involved Corky.

Fans were not above the fray, either, and when Corky went to the floor for a loose ball, a Bears supporter jumped from the stands to taunt him. Some even claimed this fan pinched Corky, but he has no recollection of this happening.

Amidst the scuffles and general turmoil, the game-clock wound down. The Tide, with only twenty seconds remaining and trailing by five, was forced to foul Johnson, a solid free throw shooter. Wally, an early practitioner of "trash-talking," recalls a snide and snarky comment he made to a Tide guard while stepping to the line. Remarked Wally, "Looks bad for the home team, don't it?"

With Johnson at the line, Tide hopes were now zero. Ray Hammers, Butler County's best rebounder, stepped in the block on the left side of the goal; Corky took the right block. "All night we had used a strategy where I'd hit the first foul shot, but miss the second," Johnson notes. "I was a good free throw shooter and could make the rebound come off on Hammers' side of the goal when I missed. Hammers would rebound and stick it back in. It worked several times that night."

Corky had noticed this when Johnson was at the line, and knowing the game was lost, was determined it wasn't going to happen again. "I decided," he confesses, "if the ball came off to Hammers, I'm choppin' his ears off!" That's exactly what happened, and Corky, executing his plans flawlessly, came down with his hands on both sides of Ray's head, in the process clipping both ears. Hammers, reacting viciously, came out swinging! "Ray hit me in the nose, drawing blood," Corky cites. "I grabbed him and we both went to the floor."

Carl Jamison, meaning well, but hampering Corky's ability to defend himself, grabbed Corky and pulled him back—an action that allowed other Bears to get to him. "I pulled loose from Carl and got a few more good licks in," Corky assures, but by this time many fans were pouring onto the court in anticipation of entering the fray.

Wally Johnson describes the post-game activities from the Butler County vantage point: "We were still on the court and completely surrounded by fans from both schools. There were so many people on the court, you couldn't see the floor. We had to fight our way to the dressing room, and then had to stay for at least two hours after the game ended. I never got settled down during that whole time. I was really glad to get out of there."

There were police in the gym that night, but things were way beyond anything they could control or stop. Reports of a knife being drawn on one of the referees were sketchy, but Johnson claims it happened. "I know it's true... I saw the knife!"

When some measure of order had been restored inside, it spilled outside. When ketchup and mustard were found smeared on the seats of a Butler County bus, Central City Superintendent George Taylor took it on himself to clean them. But when the Bears team bus left the school parking lot and headed through town, it was pelted with rocks and assorted projectiles by a dozen or more irate Tide fans lining the city's sidewalks.

Officially, the game ended with a 54-47 Butler County victory. For Corky, it officially ended with his ejection. But due to the rioting that followed his ear-cropping of Raydean Hammers, the refs wisely decided not to bring players back to the court to finish the final seconds. Butler County had the victory anyway, and it was deemed best to get them dressed and on their way back to Morgantown as quickly as possible.

The referees, Norman and Eugene O'Nan, had ruled Corky's actions as a "flagrant action of unsportsmanlike conduct," and Corky admits it had been intentional. "I was mean and competitive back then and wasn't above playing dirty if I thought it was warranted. I'm not proud of that now, but that's the way it was then."

For the record, Corky had 23 points in this losing effort. However, the suspension and penalties that came their way soon after cost him and his team more than just a loss on their record sheet. But, in partial defense of Corky, the penalties were as much for the actions of Tide fans as they were for his fight with Ray Hammers. "I don't remember Mr. Gish or anyone saying anything about it being my fault, but I sure lost some sleep over it," he admits.

With the fight, the ejection, the threatening of referees by Tide fans, and the damages to Butler County buses, strict and swift retribution in the form of penalties were sure to come their way.

On the 19th of January, thirteen days after the fight-marred game, the penalties were released to Delmas Gish in the form of a letter from Ted Sanford and the KHSAA office in Lexington. It read:

> Gentlemen: You are hereby notified that Central City High School has been suspended from the KHSAA for a period of three weeks beginning Jan. 19 and both Central City and Butler County High School are placed on probation for a period of one year from the date. It is my opinion that both violated provisions of KHSAA by-law 17 on the evening of Jan. 6 when certain representatives of the schools conducted themselves in unsportsmanship manners.

After additional references and explanations, Sanford concluded:

> I do wish, however, to enumerate briefly incidents which have caused your schools to receive penalties mentioned. The Central City High School is being suspended because near the end of the Butler County-Central City game, played in Central City on the evening of Jan. 6, a Central City player, Corky Withrow committed an apparent flagrant act of unsportsman like conduct against a Butler County player, Raydean Hammers, for which he was ejected from the game by officials Norman and Eugene O'Nan, and for disgraceful conduct of some 10-15 Central City supporters, who threw rocks at the Morgantown buses as they were going through Central City following the game.

When all was said and done, Central City was barred from any games and organized practices for a period of three weeks. There was also one year of probation. The penalties, especially the suspension from games in the current season, was a crushing blow to the players and fans.

Even with the penalties, the team was allowed to practice on their own and were not barred from the gym. No coaches could be present, however. But since Gish had a set routine of drills for his practice sessions anyway, Corky and his teammates carried on.

Following the loss to Butler County, and the rioting that followed, the Tide resumed play. The letter and suspension that would come from the KHSAA office had not yet arrived, so games were still to be played.

First, the Tide traveled to Owensboro to take on the Aces of Catholic High at the Sportscenter. The Tide earned their fourteenth win, 64-56. Corky, despite fouling out, led the team with 22.

A double-header in Memorial Gymnasium followed. In the first game Greenville played Wingo, and in the second it was Central City against Sedalia. Greenville and Central City switched opponents the following night. Corky was back in form with 36 against Sedalia, but it wasn't enough. The Tide lost their third game in the last four, this time 87-83. The following night Central City crushed Wingo, 116-77. Corky tallied 32; Mason, 21; and Jamison, 19. The Tide's record after these two contests stood at 15-3.

The Tide traveled back to Owensboro next, and in their final game before learning the results of the KHSAA investigation, thumped the Red Devils 85-58. The reserves played much of the second half, but Corky still managed to score 39.

After learning of the suspension and probation, Central City was forced to cancel three weeks of games. However, they could, if opposing schools agreed, reschedule those cancelled games for post-suspension play.

The time away from competition proved to be tough for the Tide players, coaches, and fans. "We knew all of Coach Gish's drills and his practice routine, so we just did the same," Corky notes. "But I still think the three weeks with no actual, competitive games really hurt us."

During their exile, the school rescheduled their cancelled games in preparation for a return to action. When completed, the Tide's post-suspension schedule listed eight remaining games.

With the lifting of the suspension, the Tide players were chompin' at the bit, especially Corky! First, against Bremen, he set a Muhlenberg County individual scoring record with 53 points in a 104-63 victory. The following night found Corky scoring 42 more in an 81-47 win over Madisonville. It was obvious he hadn't lost his scoring touch during the layover.

Greenville was next. Resorting to a stall, the Blackhawks still fell by a lopsided 63-27 score. Corky had 29; Roger Newman 10, and the Tide record climbed to 19-3. Calhoun, in another slow-down effort that failed miserably, fell 68-28. Corky had 35; Winfred Thompson, 12. It was win number twenty, and in the last four contests Corky had tallied 157 points!

A game against Daviess County followed. Central City won this one 93-79, despite losing Corky to fouls with 4:40 left in the game. He pumped in 38 in this one—18 more than the 20 tallied by Bobby Rascoe, Daviess County's talented sophomore star. Rascoe would go on to lead his team—one coached by the colorful Buck Sydnor—to impressive Sweet 16 runs in both '57 and '58. Along with this, he would earn All-State honors both years, and then follow with All-American honors while playing for Ed Diddle and the Western Kentucky Hilltoppers. Pro basketball would come next, first with the Phillips 66ers, and then with the ABA's Kentucky Colonels.

Bobby recalls his trip to Central City to face the Golden Tide in '56, but can't remember many specifics. "It was the first time Coach Sydnor put me in the starting lineup for a game, and I was so excited I guess I just didn't pay attention to all the details and things going on around me," he says. "I know Corky scored a ton of points, but getting 20 in my first time as a starter was pretty exciting to me. I got to play more and more every game after that."

Drakesboro was next to try the stall against the Tide, but again to no avail. Although Corky was held to 18, the Tide won 47-27.

Win number twenty-three came at the expense of the Owensboro Red Devils. Corky scored 38 in the 77-65 win. The Tide closed out their regular season schedule with an 84-55 victory over Muhlenberg Central at Memorial Gymnasium. It was Corky's final regular season game in a Tide uniform, and he didn't disappoint, scoring 34. With the season in the record books, the Tide record stood at 24-3. Not bad in a suspension-interrupted season.

With tournament time only days away, Central City was ranked as the state's second best, behind only Berea. Now, and for Corky's final time as a high school cager, it was district, regional, and the state tournament ahead.

In the 1956 16th District Tournament at Muhlenberg Central, Central City opened their play against Hughes-Kirk. Once again, much to his family's dismay, Corky would be facing his brother, the Tigers coach. But this time the stakes were higher.

"The district drawings were held in the newspaper office on a Sunday, and I can still see Roy getting out of his car and walking in the house after the draw," Corky recalls. "His head was hanging like a whipped puppy. I knew he had drawn us in his first game, and I can assure you, it wasn't a happy house that night."

For the first three quarters of this third brother vs. brother showdown, the Tigers relied on ball control to prevent the Tide from running up a big score. The problem was Hughes-Kirk failed to score much, themselves. When the first quarter ended, the Tide led 12-5, and when the second ended, it was 14-6. Central City had taken only two shots in that quarter.

The Tide was more aggressive in the third and quickly moved out to a 24-8 lead. Coach Withrow was forced to step up his team's offensive effort in the fourth, but to no avail. Central City won 48-22. Corky's 22 points matched the Tigers' 22.

Roy Withrow wouldn't be at Hughes-Kirk the following year, as he would accept the coaching position at Temple Hill High in Barren County. Although his coaching career would be short, he stayed in education after earning college degrees and eventually would become superintendent of the Barren County schools. Roy passed away, a victim of cancer, in Glasgow in 2011. Corky describes his brother as having been respected and loved by all who knew him, and as one who, throughout his life, had been "straight as an arrow and honest in everything he did."

With the win over Hughes-Kirk, the Tide next faced Greenville and their "Demon of Destruction," Roger Newman. It was their third showdown of the season, with the Tide winning both previous affairs.

Once again, the Tide faced a stall. This time it almost worked as Greenville never trailed by more than four and, at times, led by three. With one minute left in the contest, the Blackhawks led 29-28 and had possession of the ball. It was a golden chance to upset the Golden Tide!

But with things looking bleak for the Tide, Billy Mason alertly stole the ball, driving the length of the court to score. The Tide took a 30-29 lead.

The ball was now in the hands of Newman, but after missing a field goal, Roger fouled Corky in a struggle for the rebound. Corky proceeded to sink both charity tosses to up the Tide lead to 32-29. With only seconds on the clock, a Greenville basket at the horn made the final score 32-31, but it wasn't enough. Central City had dodged a bullet.

The Blackhawks were led by Newman's 22. Corky led the Tide, but his 10 were the lowest of the season. Much of this could be credited to Roger's outstanding defensive work, once again proving the Greenville phenom could play both ends of the court.

In their parallel careers at the neighboring schools seven miles apart, Corky's Tide and Roger's Blackhawks had faced each other fourtenn times. Roger played in eleven of these, Corky in all fourteen. Greenville won only once during the Newman-Withrow Era, and in the eleven head-to-head contests, Corky tallied 204 points; Roger, 197.

During Roger's career at Greenville, his team won 66 and lost 50. Twenty of these 66 victories came during the '54 season, but four of the Blackhawks' six defeats that same season came at the hands of the Tide.

It is also worth noting that Roger's teams were defeated by the Tide in the district tournament four times. Only once, in '55, did the Blackhawks appear in a regional tournament, this as district runner-up, and again the Tide ended their season.

Roger, when asked about the Central City-Greenville rivalry, had this to say:

> As far as any rivalry... yeah, we were rivals, but I never disliked Corky and Central City. I know there was never any bitterness about the losses and rivalry on my part, and I think that was true of Corky, too... maybe more for the fans than us. I enjoyed playing those games against Corky, and I really enjoyed good competition and teams. I always hoped the games would be competitive, and I know Corky felt the same way. We were both highly competitive, but not in a nasty way at all. Our fans may have felt that way, but I don't ever remember having those feelings.

Roger's first coach at Greenville had been Robert "Bobby" Todd. Todd was there in this capacity from Roger's 7th grade season through his junior year. "Coach Todd was a fundamentalist in every aspect of the game," Roger notes, "and was really outstanding when it came to that. He was a great coach even though we didn't have that many outstanding players."

Todd left before Newman's senior season, taking a coaching position in West Texas where he, according to Roger, "achieved great success." With Todd's resignation, Greenville hired Ben Topmiller away from Hughes-Kirk. This, in turn, opened the door for the hiring of Roy Withrow by Hughes-Kirk.

Roger Newman would go on to play basketball at Kentucky, but only during his freshman and senior seasons for various, mostly personal reasons. A few years after his graduation from Kentucky, he accepted a position as a commodities broker in Chicago. Today he resides in Florida, but still owns his parents' farm—his childhood home—in Muhlenberg County. He also owns a home north of Chicago. This home, as well as his Muhlenberg farm, are currently for sale.

With the semi-final victory over Greenville in the '56 district tourney, the Tide advanced to play Dunmor for the championship.

The game would prove anti-climatic, however, as Central City demolished Dunmor 94-49. Trying to run with the Golden Tide was a foolish thing to do.

When the all-tourney team was announced, Greenville's Roger Newman was called. So was Central City's Corky Withrow, Winfred Thompson, and Carl Jamison. Robie Harper represented Hughes-Kirk, and Jim Williams represented Graham. Others included R.C. McElwain from Dunmor, and Gale Buchanan from Drakesboro.

Now, for the fourth time in his high school career, Corky and his Tide teammates were headed to the 4th Region Tournament.

One of the most memorable games of Corky's basketball career came in a semi-final game during the 4th Region Tournament in Morgantown in 1956. The opposing team was Clarkson High from Grayson County. The Redhawks were coached by Bowman "Bo" Davenport and had advanced to this game by defeating Irvington 79-75.

From the beginning it was clear Coach Davenport had no intention of playing racehorse basketball. After watching the Tide's narrow 32-31 victory over Greenville, and then the 96-49 rout of Dunmor, he wisely chose to play the slower pace. No rocket science needed here!

Clarkson, from their first possession of the night and throughout, was in slow motion. When the first quarter ended, they trailed 9-7, but things were about to get even slower... really slow.

The second quarter passed with neither team scoring. So did the third! Then, in the final quarter, and with only two minutes remaining on the clock, Allen Herron, the Redhawks' clever, ballhawking guard, fired up a twenty footer. He connected, tying the score at 9-9.

For Clarkson, it was all Herron all the time. In fact, all seven of the Redhawks' first quarter points had been his, and now he had put his team in position for a major high school upset by scoring all nine of his team's points.

Concludes Corky, "We should have pressed. Although we had faced stalls before, we hadn't seen it taken to this extreme. It was a novelty to us, and we got caught up in it. We stood back instead of forcing their hand."

At one point in the game Corky claims he took a break. "I got tired of standing out there. It was obvious they weren't going to shoot and didn't want us to have the ball, so I just stepped off the court, sat down on the edge of the stage, and watched Herron dribble. I just figured nothing was going to happen anyway... why not take a rest?"

As the clock wound down in the fourth, the fans, especially those from Clarkson, were hysterical. Central City was on the ropes! Even the Butler County fans in the gym smelled blood in the water.

After Herron's game-tying shot, the Tide, not wanting to put the ball back in his hands, decided to go into a freeze of their own. Holding the ball for a final shot, Corky, with six seconds left, turned to the basket and connected with a jumper. Game over. Tide wins 11-9!

In one of the most bizarre games in Central City memories the scorebook showed Allen Herron with all 9 Redhawk points, and Corky with 8 of the 11 Tide points. The other three came from Winfred Thompson. Eight points was a season low for Corky, but still he was the hero.

Looking back at that game fifty-eight years ago, Corky realizes Clarkson's team had to be devastated with the loss. "I know how that feels, and I'm sure those guys still feel they could have won. They came real close... believe me."

Years later, in 1976, Bo Davenport coached Edmonson County to an upset win over Christian County to win the Kentucky State Championship. This upset, many believe, saved Kentucky's Sweet 16 basketball format.

Now, as if ordained by fate, the Tide had struggled their way to the regional final to play—you guessed it—Butler County. In a disrupted season they would be facing the team that had been the major cause of it. For the Bears the rematch could validate their claim as the region's best, but for Central City it could be the sweetest kind of revenge.

Neither team expected the game to be easy. It was going to be all-out war from tip-off 'til the last second, and nothing else should be expected. Coach Warren's Bears weren't going to put the ball in the deep freezer as Clarkson had tried, but they wouldn't go to the racehorse style, either. Their strategy would be a deliberate style, one limiting the Tide's ability to control the game's tempo.

This strategy proved to be an effective one for the Bears, as Wally Johnson's ball-handling skills kept the Tide from mounting any runs. At half, the score was knotted at 27. Tempers, for the most part, were still under control—perhaps suppressed would be a better choice of words. There was still probation hanging over both programs.

The third quarter was more of the same, but near the end, Butler County pulled out to a four point lead. The game had gotten slower as the defense had gotten better. It was as if things were now in slow motion in Morgantown. "Tense," is the way Corky describes that final quarter.

With a 41-41 score, it was now the Tide resorting to a stall game. With twenty seconds remaining, Corky turned near the foul line and popped in a two-pointer to put his team up by two. But there was still time on the clock.

"I got the ball, came across the line, shot, and scored. Coach Gish was about half-mad at me for shooting that soon," Corky explains, "but what could he say? I scored!" Butler County, with the ball and time on the clock, came down the court. Allan Shields got off a good shot, but the ball rolled around the rim and fell off. Corky grabbed the rebound, clinging to it tightly. "That's the happiest I ever felt after a basketball game," he claims, "and... if I'm completely honest... the fact that we were going to the Sweet 16 at the expense of Butler County made it even better."

Corky thinks the only thing preventing a riot after that game was the fact that Ed Diddle was in the crowd and had come on the court to congratulate the All-Tournament team. "Nobody wanted to act ugly in front of Coach Diddle," he figures.

Corky scored 22 of the Tide's 43 that night, while his counterpart, Ray Hammers, led Butler County with 14. Wally Johnson added 11. Among those on the all-tourney squad were Johnson, Hammers, Billy Mason, and Corky. Allen Herron, the Clarkson guard who engineered the near-upset of the Tide, was also honored.

It would be the final time Corky faced the despised Bears on a basketball court. It was sweet revenge for their previous, fight-filled game, and the suspension and probation that followed. Due to the fight-marred earlier contest, the two schools would discontinue their season series, however, and wouldn't play for several years after.

Today, Wally Johnson, the Hammers, and Corky Withrow replay those games with lots of laughter and good-natured teasing. After all, it was just a game. Right? Maybe not! Wally, a resident of Florida now, recently told Corky, "If folks back in Butler County ever find out I'm a friend of Corky Withrow, I'll never be able to go back there again." In response, Corky asked Wally, "Why would anybody in their right mind ever want to go back to Butler County, anyway?"

Old rivalries never die... they just seem to fade away.

Chapter 9

Ebb Tide

Corky has always felt the drawings for the 1956 State Tournament were "rigged." The fact that three of the state's highest ranked teams—Central City, Carr Creek, and Wayland—were slotted in the same bracket, and away from hometown favorite, Lexington Lafayette, seems odd to him. Carr Creek's legendary coach, Morton Combs, sometimes hinted the same, and Kelly Coleman, not one to mince words, is even more emphatic in his belief that the KHSAA was interested in protecting Lafayette and the big crowds they would draw.

Although we'll never know if this was truly the case, Corky's conclusion is based on some seemingly plausible notions. "The drawings were not open to the public then, so no one really knows what went on," he explains. "Ted Sanford ran the KHSAA office from Lexington, and they wanted to protect Lafayette since they would draw large crowds to their games. The longer they stayed in the tournament, the more money KHSAA would bring in." To both Corky and Kelly, it appeared Central City, Wayland, and Carr Creek had been bracketed together for the purpose of elimination prior to any match-up against Lafayette in the final game. In the case of Central City, there was also that ugly incident, suspension and probation, a few weeks earlier. Would Sanford have held this against them?

Regardless of how the teams were bracketed, fairly or unfairly, a game against Carr Creek High in the first round was a tough way to start tournament play. But then it was like that in '54 with Inez and in '55 with Pikeville.

On the day prior to their opening game, Central City was alive with excitement. Their beloved Golden Tide was headed to Lexington with a legitimate chance to win it all. Store front windows in town displayed their loyalty and excitement with gold and black crepe paper streamers, pom-poms, and posters, while Tide washing powder boxes hung from every imaginable place.

The school's afternoon activities that Tuesday didn't include much in the way of education, as the students were eagerly anticipating a big pep rally to send the team on its way. A caravan of decorated cars followed the team through town, and with horns blowing, the caravan made its way to the "Y" on the outskirts of town. Here, the cars carrying the players turned east on 62 toward Lexington. Most of the caravan dispersed here, waiting to make the journey the following morning.

Corky remembers riding in the car of Mac Houston, the team's scorekeeper. With them were Billy Mason, Billy Duvall, and Winfred Thompson. Winfred was to be Corky's roommate once the team checked into their rooms at the Phoenix Hotel. The team always enjoyed their stays at the Phoenix, and to Corky it was especially exciting being with the other teams when eating together in the hotel's dining room. "I don't remember ever seeing Kelly during our time in Lexington," Corky claims. "But I do remember how much we wanted to play him and Wayland again, especially after the leaflets about him and Wayland were dropped all over the city. Those leaflets made us mad, and I'm sure some of the other teams felt the same way... but you can't blame Kelly for those. He didn't like that happening, either. It really wasn't fair to him."

At 10:45 on Thursday morning, Carr Creek's Bobby Shepherd walked to the center jump circle at Memorial Coliseum. Facing him was Corky Withrow. Standing over the large "K" painted on the floor, the two shook hands, then stepped back to await the opening toss.

It was a matchup of two teams regarded as Kentucky's finest. The Indians, representing the 14th Region, were ranked as the state's #1 team in the Litkenhous poll, but their 78.5 rating was only slightly better than the poll's #2 team, Central City, one with a rating of 78.3. The game was a toss-up in most people's opinion, and, according to *Courier-Journal* columnist Johnny Carrico, "was a game that would have been more fitting as a championship struggle than a first-round game."

With Shepherd on the court at tip-off were Indian teammates E.A. Couch, Warren G. Amburgey, Ed Richardson, and Freddie Maggard. All five were seniors, seasoned and experienced enough to respect, but not fear, the oncoming Tide. Coach Morton Combs and assistant Willard "Sprout" Johnson had prepared them well, instructing them to "just do what you always do." This was man-to-man defense and fast break offense. It was their defensive skills their coaches felt would be their biggest advantage over the Tide.

As for matching up with Carr Creek, Coach Gish and assistant Jack Day had no reason to concede any weaknesses, either. Central City was big, with no starter shorter than 6'1", and they could shoot, rebound, and run better than most. They, like the Indians, used man-to-man defense—never a zone—but their roster, unlike Carr Creek, included a soon-to-be named first-team All-American in Corky Withrow.

"We really had it all that year," Corky boasts. "Shooters, rebounders, speed, ball handlers... we had it all. I still feel... and know for a fact… we were the best team in the tournament. No question about it."

All this may have been true, but the Tide lineup that morning was not quite the same one as had started throughout the season. Missing was Billy Duvall. Duvall was with the team, but rather than a Tide uniform, was now dressed in street clothes. In his place on the court was Jimmy Swann.

Billy's absence was a big blow to the team, to Coach Gish, to the Tide fans, and more importantly, to Billy, himself. "It was hard to see him on the bench, but not able to play," Corky recalls. "I know he must have felt he was letting us down, and we definitely missed him. He averaged about 14 a game I guess, and I've always felt we would have won the tournament had he been able to play. He would have made a big difference for sure."

The reason for Billy's inability to play was an injury to his ankle, one suffered during the fourth quarter in the district semis. The ankle was broken when Duvall's foot came down on the foot of Roger Newman. Without Duvall, the Tide had defeated Dunmor in a high scoring affair, and then Clarkson and Butler County in slow downs, but Carr Creek, with balanced scoring and rebounding, would be a bigger challenge.

The game between the Indians and the Tide didn't start well for the black-clad boys from Muhlenberg County. During one span in the first, the Tide went more than five minutes without a field goal. And, to make matters worse, Corky picked up three fouls in a four minute span. During this time Carr Creek spurted to leads of 8-3 and then 12-7. However, three quick baskets by Thompson, Mason, and Jamison brought the Tide back for a 14-14 deadlock when the quarter ended.

Corky was still on the bench to begin the second period. Coach Gish was not gambling on a fourth foul against his star, especially in the first half. Carr Creek was determined to take advantage of his absence, and Bobby Shepherd, with help from sophomore reserve Jim Calhoun, catapulted the Indians to a 31-19 lead during this time.

"I felt totally useless sitting on the bench and watching my teammates fall behind like that," Corky groans. The Tide was struggling mightily, enough so, one journalist later wrote, "Probably no Central City team ever made so many mistakes in one period as the Golden Tide did in the second period against Carr Creek."

Corky, recounting those moments on the bench, claims he took it upon himself to make a move. "When we got that far behind, I told Mr. Gish I wanted back in the game. There wasn't much use of me just sitting there watching the game get away from us," he says. "I don't recall Mr. Gish saying a word when I told him I was going back in. I just told him I was, ran to the scorer's table, and checked myself in."

With Corky's return there was renewed hope for the Tide and their fans. The Tide surged, and with nine straight points cut the lead to 33-28 as the half ended. For his foul-plagued half, Corky had managed to score 10, despite sitting six minutes on the bench.

To begin the second half, it was all Corky. He went through, over, and around the Indian defense at will. He connected on 10 of the Tide's 11 field goals, rebounded superbly, and held in check Bobby Shepherd. His third period scoring total of 20 was a tournament record for one quarter, and during this time he had missed only one shot!

His explosive performance in the third still ranks as one of the tournament's finest, and with it the Tide had built a 63-56 lead by the end of the period. There was now a collective feeling the "ship had been righted."

Things were going well for the Golden Tide now. Their offense was on track, and solid defense continued to deny the ball to the Indians' center, Bobby Shepherd.

Midway through the fourth quarter, things began unraveling, however. Errant passes, missed shots, and what Corky describes as "dumb decisions," came to the forefront. "We just threw it away. It still hurts," he acknowledges.

In agreement with this assessment is Greenville's former star and Tide rival, Roger Newman. "There wasn't any way Central City should have lost that game," Newman tells. "When I was a freshman at UK, I was on the team with Bobby Shepherd and E.A. Couch. They were both good players, but they shouldn't have beat Corky and that Central City team... no way!"

As a result of the Tide's ragged play in the final quarter, the lead shrank. Carl Jamison, with a chance to put the game away, missed the second of two free throws with 13 seconds to go and the Tide leading 68-66. "But Carl didn't lose it with that foul shot," Corky says in defense of his teammate. "We all played poorly that quarter and still had chances to win after that. We can't blame Carl."

The Indians grabbed the rebound and threw the ball to E.A. Couch. Carl Jamison, playing his usual aggressive game, fouled Couch while attempting to steal the ball. Trailing by two, Couch stepped to the foul line. He hit both, tying the score. The Tide failed to answer, and regulation ended with the score knotted at 68. The Central City crowd was stunned.

Corky won the overtime tip, but after controlling the ball for several seconds, a Carr Creeker stole it from a Tide player. The Indians, with guard Freddie Maggard taking charge, went to their stall. Then, with only nine seconds on the clock, Maggard shot a jumper from behind the foul stripe. It was perfect, and Carr Creek had grabbed a 70-68 lead.

The Tide did get off a desperation shot, but for the third time in three years had lost a first round Sweet 16 game. Heads hanging and tears flowing, they headed to the locker room.

The scorebook showed Corky with 34 points on 15 field goals and four free throws. Winfred Thompson had 18 points; Carl Jamison, eight; and Billy Mason, four. Jimmy Swann and Donnie Moore had two each. One might wonder how many Billy Duvall would have added had he been on the court that morning.

Bobby Shepherd led Carr Creek with 27, Maggard had 17, E.A. Couch and Jim Calhoun tallied eight each. Warren Amburgey added seven and Ed Richardson, four.

Corky's record-breaking third quarter performance was, no doubt, a determining factor in his selection to the All-Tournament team two days later. His 10 field goals in this period, plus two more in the fourth, would earn him a spot in the record books as well. Today, in 2015, his one half performance with 12 field goals ranks fifth all time, tied with Richie Farmer and Terry Davis. These 12 are only two shy of the record 14 field goals set in that same tournament by Kelly Coleman.

Although the team remained in Lexington for the duration of the tourney, Corky chose not to attend any more of the games with the exception of the finals on Saturday night. "I felt sure we were the best team there and couldn't stand watching teams that I considered to be lesser ones advance," he unapologetically admits. "I don't remember much about what I did on Friday and Saturday. I guess I just roamed around Lexington. I do know I wasn't having a good time."

By not attending the semi-final consolation game between Wayland and Bell County, Corky didn't see Coleman's 68-point, record-setting performance. The tournament had truly been "one for the ages," but for both Corky and Wayland's Kelly Coleman, it had been spoiled by Carr Creek—both on shots from Freddie Maggard in the closing seconds. Coleman, like Corky, believes his team was the best in the tournament that year. "I was the only one with any experience when we played Central City earlier that year, but by tournament time, after my teammates got some experience, we had the best team in the state. We really wanted to play Central City again and should have beaten Carr Creek in the semi-finals," Kelly claims.

When the All-Tournament squad was named, Corky, in coat and tie, came to the floor. It was his second time honored with this award, having been named to this same squad after the '55 tournament.

"King" Kelly was also named to the team, of course, but was nowhere to be found when his named was announced. Linda Carol Coleman, Kelly's fifteen year old sister, accepted on his behalf. In a photo of this group, Linda Carol can be seen on the back row standing next to Corky. The whereabouts of Kelly that night, regardless of numerous reported sightings, still remains somewhat of a mystery.

Missing from the All-Tournament team was Carr Creek's Freddie Maggard, the tournament's hero. He had hit game-winning shots against both Central City and Wayland, but had been left out when the voting was tabulated. Kentucky's General Assembly, righting the perceived wrong, passed a resolution unofficially naming him to the squad a few days later.

Now, with his high school career concluded, Corky could look forward to a bevy of statewide honors, and a post-season crammed with basketball all-star games. His name would soon appear on several All-American rosters as well, among these *Scholastic Magazine* and *Dell Sports*.

Chapter 10

To Be an Actor, or More Likely, Not to Be

From the fall of 1952 through the spring of '56, Corky had been a student at Central City High, and these years were special to him. His friends say he was "smart as he wanted to be," but for the most part, and by his own admission, he did what was required.

"At my best I was a 'B' student," he confesses, "but Roy was more brainy than I ever was. I couldn't match him. Every time grades were issued, he was always going to have good ones, but with me it was more of a question. It wasn't because I couldn't make good grades; it just wasn't a priority."

To Corky, school was "fun" and "a place to be with friends," but his mother, Flo Eva, had a different perspective. With this, Corky claims, "The general overall happiness in our household depended on grades I brought home. Sometimes it wasn't quite as happy as others."

Corky didn't just hang with basketball and baseball teammates. He was considered an "all-around good guy," and that meant being friends with all, or at least most, of his classmates. Close buddies he mentioned included Billy Mason, Buddy Lear, and Kenny Lamustus, and there was an older pal named Charles Gray. "Charlie was a senior when I was only a freshman," he explains, "but he had a car."

Another buddy, Joe Pruitt, was a student at Muhlenberg Central, but with Corky, attended Sunday School and church services at First Baptist in Central City. "Joe's mother was absolutely the best cook around, and every Sunday after church I rushed to their house so I wouldn't miss her Sunday dinner. Usually I beat them back to their own house," Corky adds.

Like most of us, Corky also has memories of special teachers. "I had a big-time crush on Miss Jenny Foster," he laughs. "She was one pretty lady, and whatever class it was that she taught was my favorite subject. I think it was English." Corky told Jenny about this crush at his fiftieth class reunion in 2006. "She laughed, but seemed flattered," he reports.

There were other favorites for Corky, and these included Bob Forsyth, his gym teacher; Lyle Baugh, his math teacher, and Alex Cather, his history teacher. "The first day of Mr. Cather's history class, I got in trouble for eating a candy bar while he was talking, but I really came to enjoy his class that year. I visited him in his home shortly before his death a few years ago, and we talked about those days at Central City," Corky notes.

Corky wasn't above mischief by a long shot, and during his senior year pulled a prank during a practice session for the annual senior class play. But to understand the origins of the prank, one must go back days before when Corky and Byron Pinson, a Henderson basketball star, journeyed to New York City to watch the NCAA's East-West College All-Star game in Madison Square Garden. Corky and Byron were there courtesy of Furman College of Greenville, South Carolina, a school recruiting both for their basketball skills.

Furman had paid for them to fly (via Ozark Airlines) to Greenville, tour the campus, and then board the plane to attend the game. While in New York the two found time to visit Times Square. Here, in some obscure novelty shop, Corky noticed a brown plastic item for sale, one swirled and shaped to appear as a fresh pile of doggie-doings. Corky, enamored with the unlimited possibilities this item would lend itself once back in Muhlenberg County, bought it! Such a novelty would, without a doubt, be the talk of Central City students for weeks to come. It was truly a must-have item!

The play was to be held on the stage in the school's auditorium. Corky, clever and talented thespian he was, saw an opportunity to use his plastic pile-'o-poop during one of the rehearsals. It would, in his opinion, add some extra dramatics and much needed excitement to the otherwise routine rehearsal.

Sue Vincent, his unsuspecting and targeted classmate, was about to recite her lines when Corky's plan was put in motion. "I was standing behind Sue and had placed it on the floor behind her," he explains. "I'd put it under the water faucet to make it look wet and shiny," he added. But even Corky was shocked at Sue's reaction when she turned and noticed the disgusting object at her feet. Explains Corky, "She started screamin' and carryin' on like I'd brought a bomb in there!"

When Sue was calmed down and order was restored, the teacher/director was not amused. With all fingers pointing to Corky as the culprit behind this diabolical and barbaric act of depravity, he was ordered to leave the premises. It seemed, sad to say, his acting career had come to a screeching halt. This was certainly not the first time he had been ejected from a school activity—the Butler County ballgame, for example—but it was, as far as he knows, the only time a Central City student had been kicked out of his senior play.

Fortunately, for both Corky and the acting world in general, the following day brought a reconsideration on the part of the play's director, but only if Corky would give a most heartfelt apology to Sue. To this he agreed. Relying more than ever on his God-given ability as an actor, the apology was made, and Corky's theatrical career was back on track.

Being the senior class president at any high school in America brings with it tremendous burdens and responsibilities as we all well know. With Corky's resounding victory in the fall of '55 elections, he understood the enormous amount of time required, as well as the pressure, prestige, and power that came with such an exalted position. Still, he had no intentions of letting these responsibilities get in the way of his main priorities, basketball and baseball.

Nearing the end of his tenure in the spring of '56, one of Corky's final acts of office was to give a speech to the senior class at their graduation. Corky, with his years of acquired knowledge and wisdom, was certainly one qualified to be passing on advice to classmates, and understanding this, he, it could logically be assumed, spent hours in preparation. After all, his legacy as senior class president depended on it!

Corky, hopeful of finding just the right words to convey this advice to his classmates, put much thought into this all-important speech. He owed this to them. And just how did he accomplish his goal? "I got the school librarian, Mrs. Lamb, to write it for me," he confesses. Then, with a laugh and shrug of his shoulders, he added, "I don't remember a thing I said that night, if you want to know the truth about it."

If all the truth be told, his classmates probably can't remember, either!

Growing up in Central City had been pretty much like growing up anywhere else in the state in the '40s and '50s. The teenage boys spent a great deal of time playing "check pool" for dimes in the local pool rooms of which there were several. One could choose Baxter's, or Beasley's, if desired, but Corky's place of choice was Willard Vincent's Central. Here, among some of the county's most proficient "sharks," Corky became highly skilled with a pool cue, and it would be a passion he would maintain over the years.

Many good times were experienced in the pool rooms, but there were also those occasional fights and arguments. Corky, at age fourteen or thereabout, witnessed Bernie Ray Harper's brutal beating of "some old fellow" here, and as a result, was called before a Muhlenberg Grand Jury as a witness when Bernie Ray was hauled into court, the result of a lawsuit filed by the beaten victim.

Corky can't remember all the facts of the case, but does recall the argument began during a poker game at the so-called Chigger Club on a bluff overlooking the Green River, not far from town. Bernie Ray lost all his money in this game, and claiming to have been cheated, went home, got a shotgun, returned, and proceeded to take the others' cash at gun point. The dispute, one way or the other, found its way to Baxter's pool hall a few days later, and Corky was there to see the one-sided beating unfold.

Bernie Ray Harper was eventually killed with a shot to the back of his head in an unrelated incident. Bernie's killer was his brother, "Fatty" Harper, a former National Marble Champion as a youngster. Oddly enough, Bernie Ray had called his brother a "son-of-a-bitch," an insult Fatty, for some reason, found highly unflattering. As if all of this wasn't enough, Fatty, as Karma might have ordained, was shot dead in another unrelated incident in an Owensboro bar. The Harpers were, in Corky's opinion, "something else."

Corky's first encounter with our legal system is just one example of acquired learning traced back to time spent in Central City's pool rooms. However, it was not the kind of learning his mother might have found necessary for her sons' education. "Mom would get mad if she knew we were in there after 9:00 at night," Corky notes. "She set a curfew for us through the week, and if we missed it, she'd send Dad to pick us up. Dad would be laughing about it when he brought us home, so Mom would get mad, knowing he didn't take our curfew as seriously as she did."

Along with the pool halls and the real-life education that came from time spent there, movies were big in Central City, too. Corky and his friends spent many hours in the bubble-gummed seats and concession areas of the theater, but the air conditioned comfort made hot summer days and nights tolerable and well worth dealing with the sticky messes. Corky recalls a special night at the State in November of '56 when he and Lavon, his steady date and fiancé, viewed Elvis Presley's first movie, *Love Me Tender*. "Other than going to the movies, there wasn't much to do in Central City," he explains. "Most times we'd just watch television at Lavon's parents' house, or drive around town... but occasionally we'd go to Owensboro."

Viewers could also be entertained with matinees, complete with cartoons, serials, "B" westerns, and unbelievably bad and cheaply made horror films. Corky and pals spent many Saturdays with just such a line-up of cinematic delights. On one particular Saturday a local paper ran an ad explaining that—for only a few cents and a handful of soda bottle caps—movies could be viewed from 10:00 a.m. until midnight. Among the features to be shown: Alan "Rocky" Lane "blasting outlaws in a big land grab" in *Marshall of Cedar Rock*, followed by a cosmic Frankenstein intent on terrorizing earth in *The Magnetic Monster* starring Richard Carlson. With such classy entertainment available at such a reasonable cost, who could possibly argue that the young folks in Central City were being culturally deprived?

If serious shopping was necessary, and one had the time and transportation, there was always Owensboro, some thirty miles up the road. This was necessary sometimes, as Owensboro had a variety of stores that Central City didn't.

To be certain, the necessities for every day living were available in Central City. Ben Franklin, Western Auto, Firestone, and a "Five and Dime" were popular places to shop, and for a really good chocolate malt, one could grab a counter seat at the soda fountain at Miller's Drugs. Corky loved their chocolate malts.

A local teen hangout was a little restaurant that sat directly across the street from the school. The name of this concrete block diner was the Chile Bowl, a place Corky claims had "really good hamburgers and fries and a jukebox always filled with several of the latest rock-n-roll songs." Like the school building, nothing of the Chile Bowl remains now. But the memories of time spent "hanging out," flirting with the girls, and dancing to the latest tunes are cherished ones.

If Coca-Cola, Pepsi Cola, Grape Nehis, malts, or shakes were not on the menu plans for the evening, there were stronger brews to be found as well, but not legally. To acquire these stronger beverages, a trip outside town to the Hilltop could take care of that. Corky claims the proprietor of this establishment was "a man ahead of his time," as his illegal bootleg whiskey business included a drive-thru window.

Perhaps even more revolutionary was a mobile moonshine business under the management and ownership of a man Corky, for some reason, refuses to reveal, even sixty years later. This unnamed entrepreneur delivered his home-brewed product in an old school bus, and on any given day might be seen rolling through the streets of town. Alerting his regulars by blowing the bus horn, he would then park the vehicle to allow customers to come aboard. To avoid any legalities, such as city taxes, licensing, etc., the actual transactions would be completed while driving along the city streets. If requested, this enterprising fellow even made home deliveries.

Although Corky would never claim to have been angelic during his high school days, he wasn't much of a drinker. "I drank beer some," he admits, "mostly because my buddies did, but I never cared much for the taste."

Chapter 11

With a Fist Full of Dollars

After Corky graduated in the spring of '56, he was invited to play in a slew of high school all-star contests in Kentucky and neighboring states. With him in these games would be his former rival, Roger Newman. Playing together, these two represented western Kentucky against eastern Kentucky, and then represented Kentucky against the best from Indiana, Ohio, and West Virginia.

The two also represented the South All-Stars against those from the North in a nationally prominent game held on the campus of Murray State. This contest, the North-South Chuck Taylor Classic, featured players from across the nation and was, for all practical purposes, the forerunner of the modern McDonald's Classic. First held in 1949, this '56 game would mark the final clash of this series.

The East-West series, held each summer, had been originally organized by Pikeville High's legendary coach, John Bill Trivette. Among the players named to the West squad were Byron Pinson and Pascal Benson from Henderson, Barry Gager from Henderson Holy Name, David Denton from Bowling Green, Rex Story from Mayfield, and, of course, Corky Withrow and Roger Newman. This squad was coached by T.L. Plain. Among those playing for the East were Don Mills from Berea; Freddie Maggard, E.A. Couch, and Bobby Shepherd from Carr Creek; Lowell Hughes from Prestonburg; and "King" Kelly Coleman from Wayland. John Bill Trivette coached the East.

Kelly Coleman, suffering from an ankle injury suffered during an independent league tournament held in Williamson, West Virginia, a few weeks prior, didn't participate in all these East-West contests, however. "I was injured with a pick-up team from Floyd County when a teammate landed on my foot during a game," he explains. "I was in a cast for several weeks after that, and the only East-West game I played in was the one in Pikeville. By the time of all the All-Star games, I was tired of basketball anyway, so I really didn't care."

Corky recalls the Pikeville game against Kelly and the East, not just for the actual game, but also for the trip he, Roger Newman, and David Denton had taken in Kelly's car. "I don't recall why," Corky says, "but Kelly had a car there and drove Roger, David, and myself around town. It was an older car, I think, and I remember Kelly pulling a pistol out of his glove compartment to show us." Kelly, when reminded of this, laughed, then added, "It was a .38, but what I didn't show them was the dynamite I had in the trunk. That's what I used when I went fishing and always carried it with me. It was easy to get dynamite in Wayland. All I had to do was ask somebody for it."

In this three-game East-West series held in Paintsville, Pikeville, and Whitesburg, Corky averaged 24 points per game and earned Star of Stars honors. Newman was impressive also, especially with a 24-point performance in a game won by his West squad.

After both performed well in these games, Corky and Roger were selected to represent Kentucky in a two-game series against Indiana, a game against West Virginia, and two more against Ohio's best. The Kentucky All-Stars, coached by Ed Diddle and Ted Hornback from Western, presented Corky and Roger an opportunity to play against Jerry West and Oscar Robertson, both first team All-Americans along with Corky.

The first contest against Indiana was played at Butler Fieldhouse in Indianapolis on June 23, and the second at the Armory in Louisville two nights later. Kentucky lost both games to the Oscar Robertson-led Hoosiers, but it should be noted that Kelly Coleman was still suffering from the earlier ankle injury and resulting out-of-shape condition that followed. He did play some in both contests, but only after Coach Diddle convinced him that he owed it to the fans who were paying to see his performance. Corky was also at less than full strength, at least for one of the two games, as he fell victim to a food poisoning episode on the day prior to the game in Louisville. Both played, but with less than usual efficiency. Robertson was unstoppable and clinched the MVP honors.

Kelly, it should be added, was Kentucky's "Mr. Basketball" that season, and as such, wore jersey #1. Corky, having finished as runner-up in the balloting to Kelly, wore jersey #2 during these games.

Roger Newman recalls playing with both Corky and Kelly in these games, and of each, notes:

> I didn't know much about Kelly before that summer. We [Greenville] didn't play many games outside Muhlenberg County, let alone games in eastern Kentucky. Central City played everywhere, including Louisville, but not us. As far as playing on the team with Kelly, I will say this: Of the three of us—Corky, Kelly and myself—Kelly did more shooting! Corky could do most everything well. He was a good shooter at up to about fifteen feet and was especially good at running the floor. His weak point may have been defense, but that wasn't uncommon for a shooter then. You really couldn't ask more from a scorer. When we played Central City, he wasn't guarding me. Winfred Thompson did that.

In one of two games against the Ohio All-Stars, this one played in Bowling Green, Corky was awarded the Star of Stars trophy. He earned this by scoring 28 points, but is quick to point out Roger had 28 rebounds in this same game. Coleman was a no-show for both of these, as well as the contest against West Virginia.

The North-South Classic, held on the campus of Murray State, was a single game affair played on June 16. The participants, chosen from across the country, reported on the 10th of June and had been selected by a committee headed by a man named M.O. Wrather.

Playing with Corky and Roger on the South roster was a 6'7" high scoring "lefty" from Minden, Louisiana. His name was Jackie Moreland, and he, like Corky and Roger, had signed a conference letter to play with Coach Rupp at Kentucky. He had scored 5,030 points as a high school cager in Minden, but Kelly Coleman is quick to point out that Louisiana high school teams played several more games each season than those in Kentucky.

Rupp, after watching Moreland play twice while a high school junior, is reported to have said: "Give me Jackie Moreland and four other players, and I'll beat anybody in America." It is also noted that Rupp claimed he would win three NCAA titles with Moreland aboard. With Corky and Roger on the same UK roster, who would have bet against Rupp?

Corky, Roger, and Jackie, thinking they would soon be Wildcats, bonded. "We hung together quite a bit that week," Roger recalls. "We figured we'd be playing together at Kentucky, but it didn't work out that way."

No, it didn't. Moreland, in one of the most bizarre college recruitment adventures of that day, had also signed with North Carolina State, Texas A & M, Centenary, and who knows where else. He actually enrolled at North Carolina State and was attending classes. But after the school was placed on probation for recruiting violations involving him, Jackie spent a year as the absolute best college intramural basketball player in America—maybe of all time! Eventually, Moreland landed at Louisiana Tech, where he played three years of varsity ball. After graduation, he turned down a $30,000 baseball signing bonus with the Pittsburgh Pirates, opting to accept a basketball contract with the NBA's Detroit Pistons, instead. Eight years of NBA and ABA play followed, but in December of 1971, at age 33, Moreland died, the result of cancer.

Corky and Roger enjoyed their week on Murray's campus, especially with the extra benefits that came their way via an unnamed Murray booster intent on acquiring their basketball services. "We were provided a convertible, a fishing boat and tackle, and a wad of money to spend," Corky admits, "but as far as I know, none of the others had these things available." Roger, when asked about this, laughed, said "yeah," but remained non-forthcoming with any additional information.

For the record, if all-star game results mean anything, the South was victorious over the North, scoring over 100 points in the contest. Neither Corky nor Roger reached double figures that night, but with minimal playing time available, the same could be said of most others on the roster. Kelly Coleman, though selected for the South squad, was, once again, a no-show.

Today, enclosed in a glass case in the Central City Gymnasium and Convention Center, the all-star uniforms worn by Corky that summer of '56 are on display.

After four stellar years of Golden Tide basketball, followed by the nine summer all-star games, it was decision time for Corky. The decision was not about his college choice—that had been made in early '55—but instead, involved baseball. This was not one to take lightly, and would, in ways he could never have imagined, affect the remainder of his athletic career and beyond.

On the one hand was the grant-in-aid he had already signed with UK. On the other was a contract offer from the Milwaukee Braves. Basketball or baseball? Most any boy in Kentucky would be thrilled with just one of these opportunities, but Corky had both.

There was also the money... big money in the eyes of a teen-aged boy. "If I'm completely honest, it all came down to the money," Corky acknowledges. "It was $4,000 in cash signing bonus, and that was a fortune to me. My family wasn't poor, but that sure seemed like an awful lot back then."

Corky, looking back, is sure it would have been better had he played basketball at Kentucky, but for one reason that may surprise. "I have some regrets about not going to Kentucky," he confesses, "mainly because the minimum baseball signing bonus was raised from $4,000 to $10,000 the next year. I would have made $6,000 more if I'd waited."

Still, he defends his decision to sign the baseball contract, claiming he wouldn't take anything for the time spent in baseball, especially that with the St. Louis Cardinals. "That month," he says, "was the fulfillment of my boyhood dream, and few who ever had that dream saw it come true. I did."

Corky had pondered these choices for several months, but as decision time neared, it was clear where his heart was leading. He was tired of basketball, at least for now, and the disillusionment and heartbreak that followed the Carr Creek loss had dampened his enthusiasm.

Withrow and Newman Sign With UK

For the first time in history a Muhlenberg County basketball player has signed a basketball grant-in-aid to the University of Kentucky. And while one is considered a good average, Muhlenberg had two accepting the offer issued by Kentucky.

Corky Withrow of Central City and Roger Newman of Greenville, given up by far as being the two most outstanding basketball players to ever perform in Muhlenberg, signed on Saturday with Coach Adolph Rupp of UK. Both signed in Nashville where the Wildcats were playing, and losing, to Vanderbilt.

Thus ended speculations as to the choice of both boys, who were known to have had offers from many colleges, wanting their basketball services.

At present both boys are idle in the basketball picture, thus robbing Muhlenberg of its two greatest drawing cards. Withrow, who leads the county in scoring with a 31.7 average, is sitting out a three-week suspension with the Golden Tide, while Newman is out with a broken bone in his left foot.

And it was also known that Coach Rupp had wanted both boys badly, as had Western and other schools in this area. Withrow had tabbed UK as his first choice early, but had made no decision until Saturday, while Newman was reportedly interested in Murray and Vanderbilt before signing with UK.

Both boys will probably enroll at UK this fall, and will be eligible, and probably starters on the freshman team.

Corky Withrow

Roger Newman

Corky Withrow Signs Kentucky Grant-In-Aid

LEXINGTON, Ky. (AP) — Corky Withrow, who gained all-state basketball honors last year as a junior at Central City High, signed a grant-in-aid with the University of Kentucky Saturday, he announced.

In a radio interview at Nashville, where Kentucky met Vanderbilt Saturday night, Withrow said he planned to enroll at Kentucky next fall.

With his decision to sign the Braves contract, many Wildcat fans would be upset and dismayed, but it was his life and his decision. His fans would just have to deal with it. So would Adolph Rupp.

The signing of a major league baseball contract was a big deal in Muhlenberg County, and Corky Withrow was a major celebrity, at least to the folks in Central City. In fact, it was big enough for WNES radio station owner Ronnie Bean to air the signing live on his radio show. "It wasn't the way kids have television signings and press conferences today with all the drama," Corky explains, "but it was a real big deal to me. Dick Keely, the Braves scout who followed me at Central City, was at the station that day."

Corky didn't receive the $4,000 check on signing day. That would come in the mail from Milwaukee a few days later. "It was pretty exciting to get a check that big, and one of the first things I did was trade my '37 Chevy for a black, 1950-model Mercury. It looked like one James Dean would drive," he chuckles. "The rest I put in the bank."

Prior to the signing day at the radio station, Keely had informed Corky of his assignment to the Evansville Braves, one of several Class B clubs connected with the Milwaukee organization. This suited Corky fine, since family and friends would be close and could attend games with little effort. But it would be late in July before he could report, and chances for much playing time would be slim.

Evansville, with a minor league history dating back to 1915, played at Bosse Field, a stadium dating back to that same year. Their first team, the River Rats, had a player named Frank "Kid" Withrow, but no family connection has yet been found.

Bosse Field holds a significant place in baseball history. The ballpark lays claim to being the third oldest still in use in the United States, with only Boston's Fenway and Chicago's Wrigley claiming to be older. Due to its age, it has been called the "The Fenway of the Minor Leagues," and with its early 1900s ambiance and appearance, even found its way to the big screen as the homefield of the Racine Belles in *A League of Their Own*.

When Corky reported to Evansville that July, there were still several road games remaining, as well as those to be played at Bosse. Traveling on a bus to ballparks in such non-exotic cities as Terre

Haute, Waterloo, Keokuk, Peoria, Quincy, Burlington, and Cedar Rapids may not sound exciting to most, but was certainly a dream come true for an eighteen year old baseball player fresh out of high school!

Evansville was well on their way to winning the TRIPLE I League title that summer, but with their set line-up, skilled players, and deep roster, Corky would see very little playing time. He played a few innings, however, but in his only two at bats had no hits. Still, it had been a rewarding experience, one allowing him to "just sit back and learn all I could," he explains.

When asked about his manager at Evansville, Corky looked puzzled. After being reminded that manager had been Bob Coleman, he responded with a smile as memories returned. Coleman, Corky recalls, "was an old man by that time and always sat in a 'cubby-hole' in the corner of the dugout." With Coleman was his constant companion, an old dog.

Bob Coleman, born in Huntingburg, Indiana, in 1890, had been in baseball since 1910. By 1916 his playing days were over, but a long managing career would follow. His career peaked between '43-'45 when he followed Casey Stengel as the manager of the Boston Braves.

As a young man playing with a Springfield, Illinois, TRIPLE I team, Bob was on a roster with Ray Chapman, a native of Beaver Dam, Kentucky. As most any good baseball historian knows, Chapman would be killed by a "bean ball" thrown by Yankees pitcher Carl Mays in a 1920 game against Cleveland. Mays, a reputed "head-hunter," was later exonerated by a New York Grand Jury, however. Chapman died during surgery and remains the only major leaguer to have died from such an injury. He was 29 at the time of his death and, at least according to contemporary newspaper reports, had planned to retire at the end of that season.

Robert Coleman—a.k.a "Uncle Bob," "Marse Bob," and "Old Carpet Slippers"—died of pancreatic cancer in a Boston hospital in 1958, only two years after Corky had played for him at Evansville.

Although Corky's first professional baseball season had been a short one of little note, he has fond memories of his time at Evansville. But when it ended, and with strong encouragement from his mother, Corky agreed to give college and basketball another try.

Chapter 12

Corky Goes to College

Although Corky chose to pursue baseball over basketball at UK, there would be college basketball for him elsewhere. But not without controversy.

Rex Alexander, coach at Murray State, had long been recruiting him to play with the Racers in the Ohio Valley Conference. Most of Murray's recruiting efforts involved a Central City and Murray State booster named Dan Carroll. "Dan was kind of a go-between for Murray and me," Corky explains. "He told me if I signed with them, there would be a bank account opened in a Murray bank, one in my name, and with $7,000 in it. Since I was already ruled ineligible at Kentucky, I was ready to sign."

Didn't happen, though. Carroll, bearer of sobering news, informed him the Racers were withdrawing their scholarship offer since receiving word "professional athletes" had been ruled ineligible on OVC rosters. "That rule came out of the blue," Corky grumbles, "and I've always felt Rupp was behind it. He was upset when I signed the baseball contract, and with the kind of power and influence he had in this state, I feel he was trying to prevent other Division I colleges in Kentucky from signing me."

Regardless of the reason for the sudden OVC rule change, Murray State, like Kentucky, was out of the picture now. Corky again looked elsewhere, but admits his interest in going to college had been greatly reduced.

Arad McCutcheon, coach at Evansville, wanted him on the Aces' roster, even offering free room and board in the McCutcheon home while Corky played baseball for the Evansville Braves that summer. Corky accepted the room and board, of course, but confesses to having had no real interest in playing basketball at the Evansville school.

There were others vying for Corky's talents as well, but when decision time arrived, he chose Kentucky Wesleyan. Robert "Bullet" Wilson's Panthers played a big-time schedule, and the program seemed to be on the rise. With no conference ties to raise eligibility issues, the school seemed to be a perfect fit.

But there were other incentives to sign with Wilson and the Panthers, and they were big ones! Along with Corky's scholarship would be one for Lavon Goff, his fiancé, and still another for Roy, his brother. For Roy, the scholarship also came with a role as a student manager for the Wesleyan basketball squad. Roy was already a student at the Owensboro school, having enrolled a year prior to this. And although not playing basketball for Wesleyan, he had already earned a spot on the Panthers' baseball roster, one that included "King" Kelly Coleman.

Practice with Wesleyan went well that fall, and Corky enjoyed the time with Wilson and his teammates. He had always enjoyed playing in the Owensboro Sportscenter with his Central City teams, and the thought of playing an entire season in this venue was especially appealing.

Ironically, the first game on Wesleyan's schedule was against Murray State. Corky was slated to be a starter that night, and he eagerly awaited the opportunity to compete against the school that had previously withdrawn his scholarship offer. But his plans were about to be dashed.

Prior to game time, Corky was told to report to Coach Wilson's office. Here, to his dismay, he was informed that Murray State was refusing to play the game if Corky was uniformed and on the court. The reason offered was the OVC rule barring "professional" athletes from team rosters, but in this case the rule was being applied to an opponent of an OVC team. Since the OVC classified Corky as a professional athlete, their teams would no longer be allowed to play against a team listing him on their roster.

But there was more bad news. Kentucky Wesleyan, due to another NCAA ruling, had declared him ineligible, too! Corky was devastated. So was Bullet Wilson. "Coach Wilson was on the phone quite a bit that day," he recalls, "but there wasn't really anything he could do."

Corky stayed in school to finish his classwork that semester, but only half-heartily. In his Western Civilization class—one he was attempting to drop—his professor convinced him to remain for the duration of the semester. "He assured me he would help, and things would work out fine," Corky explains. But when final grades were posted, he found this not to be the case. Laughs Corky, "That son-of-a-bitch gave me an F!"

Corky even attended a few of the Panthers' home games that season, but soon found these too painful to watch. "I was a lost ball in high weeds," he moans.

Although several doors were slammed closed to Corky during the '56-'57 basketball season, another was opened thanks to Bob Davis, head coach at Georgetown College. Davis, after hearing of Corky's most recent problems, traveled to Owensboro with hopes of enrolling him at Georgetown. Here, since the Tigers played in the KIAA of the NAIA, he wouldn't be subject to NCAA rules.

Coach Davis had known Corky since the all-star games earlier that summer, and word of Corky's ineligibility at Wesleyan was all that was needed for him to take action. Coach Davis recalls:

> I had followed Corky and Roger Newman around the state during the all-star games. Roger's brother, T.R., was playing for me at Georgetown, and I had gotten to know them pretty well by this time. I jumped in my car and drove to Owensboro when I heard what had happened to Corky at Wesleyan. Corky was in his dorm room when I got there and walked in. I picked up a suitcase that was in his room and began throwing his clothes in it. He wasn't sure what was going on when I told him, 'Get up Corky; I'm taking you back to Georgetown with me.' He was surprised, of course, and said "hold on coach!" So I backed off a little, and we sat and talked.

Coach Davis explained that Georgetown's president, Dr. Judd, was an ex-baseball player and fan and had just recently accepted the top job at Georgetown. Davis assured Corky that Dr. Judd understood his situation, and that they could work out an arrangement allowing him to play both basketball and professional baseball. This arrangement would include doubling-up on schoolwork during the fall and winter, and then being allowed to leave school early for spring training. Coach Davis also assured there would be no eligibility issues with the NCAA since the school was an NAIA school. With this understanding, Corky agreed to visit the campus.

Corky liked Coach Davis, the Tiger players, and the Georgetown campus. The fact that the school was small, Baptist-supported, and highly acclaimed for its academic standards certainly were strong selling points with his mother.

The Kentucky Intercollegiate Athletic Conference (KIAC) was an eight team league consisting of the Georgetown Tigers, Bellarmine Knights, Berea Mountaineers, Centre Colonels, Pikeville Bulldogs, Transylvania Pioneers, and Union Bulldogs. All eight were Kentucky colleges, and the KIAC was one of several members belonging to the National Athletic Intercollegiate Association (NAIA).

Corky, soon to turn twenty, would play his first season of college basketball during the '57-'58 season. His teammates on the Georgetown roster were Larry Phillips, Charlie Grote, Don Duvall, Pusey Carter, Gerry Gering, Bill Otis, Gordon "Goose" Montgomery, Jack Williams, Harold Pike, and T.R. Newman. There was considerable talent here, and the season would prove one of the Tigers' finest.

Corky, recalling his first practice at Georgetown, tells:

> I walked in the gym and was watching the others who were already on the floor. They were doing a drill that involved fighting over a single basketball thrown on the court. Coach Davis was also the football coach, and to me this looked more like a football drill. The players were knockin' each other's brains out to get that one ball, but I didn't see the point and told Coach Davis I wasn't doing that. I pointed to the ball rack and told him there were plenty of balls in that rack, and I wasn't going to hurt myself fighting teammates over just that one.

According to Corky, Davis said nothing. But the drill was never used at practice again, at least as far as he knows. This is not to say rules were bent to suit Corky. Far from it, in fact, and another story proves this.

After most practices, the team was required to run laps around the court, and then up and down the gym bleachers. On one occasion, the team had been running an unusually long time with Coach Davis nowhere to be found. Corky, deciding he had run long enough, sat down under the basket, removing his shoes and socks. With teammates still running laps, Corky headed to the locker room to shower.

While Corky was showering, Tom Chaney, the team's student manager, darted in, explaining—"sheepishly," according to Corky—that Davis was mad, and that the team would continue running until he returned to the court to complete his laps. Now, realizing his teammates were suffering due to his decision to quit early, Corky hurriedly grabbed his shoes and shorts, hustling back to continue running. Coach Davis admits to having been "pretty mad" at his players that day, but also feels he "probably made them run too long."

Charlie Grote, a Georgetown player, remembers this incident, too, claiming, "We were awfully mad at Corky that day, and for the next couple of weeks shunned him. We wouldn't even talk to him!"

Although Corky's anger would occasionally get the best of him, his admiration, respect, and love for Coach Davis is immense. "He was a football coach first," Corky explains, "but his great success in basketball was due to his tremendous ability to motivate young men. He could have coached anything and been successful."

Davis's coaching success at Georgetown would ultimately result in his hiring by Auburn University a few years later. Along with this, there would be induction into both the NAIA Hall of Fame and the Georgetown College Hall of Fame. There was also a term as Vice-Chairman of the U.S. Olympic Committee.

While at Georgetown Corky was active on the social scene as well as in the gymnasium and classroom. As a member of Kappa

Alpha fraternity, he even appeared in a talent show on stage at the college's auditorium. Coach Davis was in the audience that night and describes the affair as having been a contest between fraternities, each one performing an act of "some type."

"The auditorium was packed that night," Davis recalls. "Corky, Larry Phillips, and 'Hoot' Gibson, one of my football players, were dressed like Alvin and the Chipmunks and mimicked one of the Chipmunks' songs. They were awful; they looked awful, sounded awful... it was outrageous, but was so funny they won the contest. I laughed 'til I cried. I'm not sure Corky would remember that, but I do."

On campus Corky was popular. He was well liked by everyone—teachers, students, and teammates. "He was a wonderful kid," Davis beams, "and everyone would go out of their way to do things for him."

Charlie Grote is equally complimentary of Corky as both a person and as an athlete. "He was quite remarkable... a better person than he wanted people to know. He had the best hands I ever saw and was very fast. He would have been an absolutely great football player and had amazing confidence at everything he did."

To illustrate Corky's confidence, Charlie described a game in which the Tigers were struggling against an opponent's zone defense. A timeout was called, and the team huddled in hopes of finding a solution. "Corky," Grote recalls, "told us to throw him the ball in the middle, and then get out of his way." This new strategy worked and was used against zones the remainder of the season.

Grote was no slouch, either, having been All-City at South High in Knoxville, Tennessee, before his family's move to Pikeville, Kentucky. At Pikeville he played for John Bill Trivette, and was on the Panthers' squad that suffered a double overtime loss to Inez in the '54 tournament. Grote, after another family move from Pikeville to Georgetown, played his senior season at Georgetown High in Scott County. Charlie was recruited by several universities and colleges, including Tennessee and South Carolina, but his affection for the city of Georgetown was a major factor in his decision to play for Davis and the Tigers. His decision, like Corky's, proved to be a good one for Georgetown College, as both would later be named NAIA All-Americans.

Although the season was a great one for Corky and his teammates, one game still haunts him. Not because of his play, but rather, his lack of play—the result of being held out of a game for the same reason he had dealt with previously. This time it was the University of Louisville causing his misery.

Days prior to the Tigers' yearly match against Louisville, Peck Hickman, Cardinals coach and Central City graduate, informed Coach Davis there would be no game played if Corky was with the team when they stepped on the court at Freedom Hall. Hickman, citing the NCAA ruling and claiming Corky was a professional athlete, also threatened to end the long-running series.

Corky, having experienced this twice before, was mad, finding it especially appalling that a fellow Central City alumni would make such a threat. Even harder to understand was why Coach Davis had given in to Hickman's demands. After all, Davis had assured him there would be no more eligibility issues! Corky may have had a point, but perhaps his rejection of Hickman's scholarship offer a year earlier had voided any Hickman-Withrow mutual admiration. As for Davis's decision to sit Corky out and play the game, one should consider the then-hefty paycheck Georgetown would have forfeited had the game not been played.

Corky, although not able to suit-up and play in the game, did make the trip to Freedom Hall with the team. Here, unable to help his teammates, he sullenly watched his Tigers fall to Louisville by over 20 points. Revenge, if the opportunity ever came his way, was on his mind as they headed home.

Despite missing the big game against the Cardinals, things went fine otherwise. Corky's scoring average hovered around 25, and his rebounding average was nearly 14.

Georgetown won the regular season KIAC championship, followed by a title in the KIAC Tournament. With this tourney title came a spot in the league's playoff game, with the winner representing the KIAC in the NAIA National Tournament in Kansas City, Missouri.

Georgetown proved successful in the KIAC playoff, and with the win, headed to Kansas City. The 1958 squad was the first to make this trip from Georgetown, and Coach Davis, in simple but heartfelt words, describes this team as one "very special" to him.

The team traveled to Kansas City by automobile, unlike the other larger schools traveling by plane. Corky rode in the car with Coach Davis, as was the usual arrangement for the Tigers. All thirty-two teams in the single elimination tourney were lodged in the same hotel, including the all-black Tennessee A&I squad from Nashville, as well as the all-black team from Texas Southern.

The Tigers performed superbly in Kansas City's Municipal Auditorium, despite some disadvantages. "We weren't as big as the other teams there, but we made up for it with heart," Coach Davis emphasizes.

The Tigers opened play against Rider College of New Jersey. Georgetown won 93-76. The following contest went to the wire before the Tigers pulled out a 92-91 win over Pacific Lutheran. The winning shot in this one came on a field goal by Corky after the team fought back from a 17-point deficit.

In their third game, against West Virginia Wesleyan, Georgetown came out on top 83-74. What began as a thirty-two team tournament was now down to the NAIA's "Final Four."

The two remaining games would pit Georgetown against Western Illinois and Tennessee A&I against Texas Southern. The two winners would play for the national title, but the two losing squads would also play again, this one in a consolation game for third place.

The Fighting Leathernecks of Western Illinois were coached by Leroy "Stix" Morley and led by their star-performer, Bob McAfoos. Morley's team came into this contest with a perfect 26-0 record, but only as an "at-large" team selected to fill a vacated spot belonging to the Louisiana regional representative. It may have been to Georgetown's advantage had the original representative been able to participate, however, as the Tigers fell to the Leathernecks 86-81. Groans Corky, "They were absolute beasts on the boards."

With this loss, dreams of a national title were gone, but there was still a consolation game facing the Tigers before departing Kansas City. The opponent would be Texas Southern, loser to Tennessee A&I in the other semi-final. It is worth noting that Texas Southern was the first all-black basketball team Corky faced during his athletic career. The KIAC had no such rosters, and Corky can recall only one black player during his two seasons of play in the KIAC. That player performed for Pikeville.

TSU was coached by Ed Adams and had the NAIA's leading scorer, Bennie Swainn. Swainn, a 6'8" All-American forward/center, was averaging over 27 points per game and would be selected by the Boston Celtics as the eighth pick in the '58 NBA draft a few weeks later.

The game proved to be a high scoring affair at 121-109, but it was Swainn and his Texas Southern Bobcats (now Texas State) claiming the victory. "They were big and tough, and I got my eye split open early in the game," Corky grimaces. "They put a bandage on it, but I stayed in the game. It was a consolation game, and we... if I'm totally honest... didn't take it all that seriously. There wasn't much defense played, and it was more of... like... you shoot it this time, and I'll shoot it next time."

With their second loss in a row, Georgetown had finished fourth in the national tournament, but had gained experience against the best the nation had to offer—at least on the NAIA level. Hopefully, this experience would pay dividends in the following season.

In the championship game that followed, Tennessee A&I defeated Western Illinois. This win earned A&I their second of three straight NAIA national titles, and they weren't through yet! Interestingly, Georgetown would play A&I in Nashville the following season, and the fact that the Georgetown players were able to watch the Tigers in the '58 championship game against Western Illinois proved invaluable.

Charlie Grote, Georgetown's All-American guard, was named to the NAIA All-Tournament squad, but Corky wasn't. "It was the only time during my high school and college days that I failed to make all-tournament, and I was hurt," he admits. "Charlie told me later I was the tournament's leading rebounder and fourth leading scorer, so I never understood why I wasn't on the NAIA's All-Tournament team with him. Maybe that seems petty and insignificant now, but that would have been special to me."

One humorous memory Corky has from the trip to Kansas City involved Coach Davis. This story has been told by Corky and others numerous times, but since stories such as this tend to be embellished over the years, one wonders just where the line between truth and exaggeration falls. Corky explains:

> Coach Davis decided he needed a haircut while we were in Kansas City, but he didn't know any barbers there. I don't know why he waited to get out there to get a haircut, but he did. After looking around, he finally found some barbershop, walked in, got his haircut, and returned to the hotel. The haircut didn't look good... kind of like someone had turned a bowl over his head and cut everything bare from the top down to his ears. He didn't like this, so went looking for someone who could do whatever to make it look a little better. He found someplace... maybe a 'beauty shop'... and they used black dye to cover the bare spot where his hair had been cut too close. From a distance it didn't look too bad, but up close... not so good. At the game that night the gym was hot, and Coach Davis took his coat off. He had a white shirt and tie on, and the dye, because of the heat, got to running down his forehead and ears, and then on his white shirt. His shirt was starting to look striped, and all of us on the team were getting tickled looking at him. Everybody thought it was funny but him.

With the conclusion of the NAIA tournament and the return to Georgetown, Corky packed his clothes and left school. His classes were still in session, but with the pre-arranged deal with Coach Davis and President Judd, Corky was headed for a brief visit home, and then on to spring training in Waycross, Georgia.

There were a few "loose-ends" to tie up, of course, and one of these fell to his coach. Who better, Corky figured, to find excuses for his thirty-eight "chapel cuts" that school year than his trusted coach, Bob Davis.

There would be one more season of basketball at Georgetown College for Corky, and it would come after the conclusion of his second full season of minor league ball in Wellsville, New York. However, when he left Wellsville that fall, Corky's plans didn't include a second season of basketball. "I wasn't going back to Georgetown, or any other college, for that matter," he explains. True to his word, when enrollment time rolled around, Corky was a no-show.

Flo Eva wasn't particularly happy with his decision to pass on college that fall and frequently reminded him that baseball might not work out. But Corky was sure his baseball future was bright and felt he truly deserved some rest and relaxation time. With this in mind, and some money to burn, one of the first things on his agenda was to travel to Madisonville to purchase a new Honda 125 motorcycle.

"Mom and Dad let me keep my motorcycle in the basement," Corky says, "and I was sitting on the seat when I heard some people coming down the steps. I looked up, and there came Larry Phillips, Charlie Grote, and Bill Otis, my teammates from Georgetown."

The trio, on orders from Coach Davis, had come to Central City to persuade Corky to return to Georgetown and the team. These instructions from the coach had been followed with a "don't bother returning unless he's with you" suggestion, one the boys took seriously. At first Corky held out, refusing his former teammates' pleas. But Larry, Charlie, and Bill, recalling Coach Davis's instructions, had no choice but to continue their efforts.

"I felt hogtied," Corky claims, so, to the relief of the trio of Georgetown go-betweens, he agreed to return to the team.

Georgetown's team played extremely well that season, entering tournament play with a 21-5 record. Impressive wins over two nationally prominent powerhouses deserve special note and would still have to rank among the school's finest all-time regular season victories. Corky explains:

> We played the University of Louisville at Freedom Hall. They had a real good team, one that would beat Kentucky in the NCAA tournament that year. John Turner, Bud Olsen, and Al Goldstein were on that team. Peck Hickman kept me from playing in this game the year before. We always played Louisville early in the season, and he tried to keep me from playing in this one, too. It got me riled up pretty good, but Coach Davis refused to back down from Hickman this time. I guess Louisville didn't want to lose the income from the game if it was cancelled, so he (Hickman) finally gave in and agreed to play us, even with me in the lineup. I'm sure he probably regretted it later.

Corky claims he played the game with a "big chip" on his shoulder and describes it as having been "a fun game against big-time players." He was at his absolute best, as was his teammate, Charlie Grote. Charlie led the team with 28, but Corky was right behind with 26. Combined, they led the Tigers to an 84-78 upset victory over the Cardinals. Tiny Georgetown College stood mighty tall as they walked off the Freedom Hall court that night.

Peck Hickman and Louisville, embarrassed by the loss, ended the thirty year series with Georgetown.

As impressive as the win over Louisville had been, another Georgetown victory that season may rank even higher on the "top wins" scale. Like the Louisville victory, it also came on the home court of their opponent.

Tennessee A & I (now Tennessee State) was an all-black college located in Nashville. Although the school played NAIA ball, there were those who felt the Tigers could play with the best the NCAA had to offer. Their coach, John McLendon, was a Kansas graduate and understudy of Dr. James Naismith, and on the roster were several outstanding players. Among these were Dick Barnett and John Barnhill.

Coach McLendon had built a basketball powerhouse at tiny A & I, and much of that success was owed to the fact the school was in Nashville, the site of the yearly national basketball tournament for black high schools. Coach McLendon took full advantage of the recruiting opportunities this afforded, and with this came top-notch recruits and resulting national championships. His achievements ultimately led to a short stint as an NBA coach and eventual induction into the College Basketball Hall of Fame.

The A & I gymnasium was at capacity that night, and of the 5,000 or so in the stands, Corky estimates, "only about forty were white." These fans had made the trip from Georgetown to root on the team, but few of these, if truth be told, gave the Tigers even a slight chance of beating the undefeated A & I team. Corky recalls:

> It was the only time in my athletic career that I went into a game thinking there was not even the slightest possibility we could win. I mean, I actually felt we had zero percent chance, and I know Coach Davis and the others felt the same way. We may not have said it, but we felt that way. I was completely intimidated... the thought of going into their gym against a great team like that. If I'm completely honest with you... going into an all-black gymnasium was unknown territory for us. We didn't know what to expect, but knew they were awfully good. They were undefeated, and we had watched them win the national championship the year before. I remember being awed by the things they could do. That whole team was nothing like we had ever seen before. They were absolutely amazing.

The A & I team was led by 6'4" Dick "The Skull" Barnett. Barnett, originally from Gary, Indiana, had been recruited by Coach McLendon at the national tournament in Nashville. During his college career at A & I he earned All-American honors three times and led his Tigers to three straight NAIA national titles. In the 1959 professional draft, he was selected by the NBA's Syracuse Nationals as the fourth pick, and after fourteen seasons (nine as a

Knick), he had amassed 15,358 points. During this time he earned a Ph.D from Fordham University and was also inducted into the College Hall of Fame.

But Barnett wasn't the only outstanding player at A & I that season. There was John "The Rabbitt" Barnhill, a quick, savvy guard from Evansville, Indiana, and Porter Meriwether, a three-time All-American and team captain. Other notable Tigers were Hillery Brown, Rossie Johnson, Eugene Werts, Ben Warley, Jim Satterwhite, and Melvin Davis.

When Georgetown took the floor, the A & I gymnasium was rockin' with noise. The crowd was unlike any Corky and his teammates had seen before, as the A & I cheerleaders, with their enthusiastic and colorful yells, had the place roaring and shaking. "It was fun, but it was intimidating at the same time," Corky admits. "They had some real chants."

Coach Davis recalls the same and credits Corky with relieving some of the tension and anxiety his players felt as they left their dressing room for the court. Davis explains:

> When we left the dressing room, everyone was nervous and tense. Right next to our locker room was the room where the A & I cheerleaders dressed. Their door was wide open, and some of them were only half-dressed when we walked by. Nobody said anything, but I could see my boys staring at the girls. One of their cheerleaders looked out and saw Corky staring at her. She looked at him and said, "What's the matter white boy, haven't you seen any of these before?" Corky said, "Yeah, but not any that color!" When my boys heard him say this... well... it was so funny to them, you could just feel all the tension melt away. We went out and played great after that.

It wasn't only the A & I cheerleaders and fans that caught the attention of the Georgetown players, but also A & I players who were putting on quite a show during the warm ups. "Everyone of them was dunking, some with both hands behind their heads," according to Corky, "and some of us, including myself, sat down on the court just to watch them go through their drills. They were just so much fun to watch."

What followed surely must rate as Georgetown's finest basketball game. Some might even call it "a miracle." Corky does, describing it this way:

> I was psyched out that night. I was intimidated going in, but with all the excitement and things going on, I played the best I had ever played. I'm not sure how many points I scored—maybe 26 or close to that—but it felt like I was jumping higher and farther than I had ever jumped, and it just seemed like the perfect game. I know it was my greatest game ever, and the whole team played the perfect game that night. That's the only way we could have beaten them, and I still consider that game as the pinnacle of Georgetown basketball.

When the final horn sounded, Georgetown had beaten A & I 88-83. Corky attributes part of this to some things that he, Charlie Grote, and, of course, Coach Davis had noticed while watching A & I in the NAIA championship game the previous season. "We noticed when they came down the court, they started their offense with a pass to the side. This allowed them to go over and around the defense," Corky explains. "We remembered this, and that night we concentrated on cutting off that first pass to the side. It worked pretty good."

Corky also remembers the silence when the game ended. The A & I crowd was stunned with the loss, of course, and the Georgetown players weren't quite sure what to make of this silence. Corky, recalling the moment, continues:

> Everyone in the gym, including us and our fans, were shocked that we had beaten them. It was so quiet at first I was kind of worried, but their players had been great to us, never an unkind or negative remark all night as far

> as I know. They were true gentlemen and came over and shook hands with us after it ended. As we were walking across the court to the locker room, it completely caught us by surprise when their crowd gave us a standing ovation. That was really special and was one of my greatest sports-related memories. I'll never forget the moment A & I's fans gave us that ovation.

A few years ago, ESPN filmed a documentary on that A & I team and season. It was broadcast on television several times, and in the documentary it was told, more than once, that their team lost only one game that season. However, much to Corky's chagrin, not once was it mentioned that Georgetown College was the team that beat A & I.

With wins over U of L, Tennessee A & I, and another KIAC regular season championship title under their belts, the Tigers headed to the KIAC tourney in Pikeville. In their opening game they defeated Centre College 97-83 and followed this with a 73-54 victory over Berea. The tournament final, a high scoring shootout, resulted in Georgetown defeating Pikeville 102-94.

One team stood in the way of a return to Kansas City now, and that team was, once again, Pikeville College. The winner of this playoff game would represent the league in the NAIA National Tournament. Georgetown, a squad having already defeated defending NAIA champ Tennessee A & I, seemed like a good bet to return to Kansas City, but Pikeville had other ideas.

"We always had problems with Pikeville," Corky grumbles. "Even when we beat them, they always played well against us." That was true on this night, too, as Pikeville kept it nip-and-tuck until the final few seconds. The game ended on a controversial call on a tip-in, and with this, Georgetown's season was ended. Corky credits Pikeville's George Carroll for most of their opponent's success. "He was a shootin' son-of-a-gun... from Ashland High, I think. He must have scored 40 that night. We just couldn't stop him."

This loss ended Georgetown's dreams of another run in the NAIA National Tournament, but Corky's performance throughout the season earned him some individual national recognition. He was named All-KIAC for a second time, as well as being named to the third team NAIA All-American squad. Charlie Grote, his teammate, was selected first team All-American. Coach Bob Davis earned national honors as well, as he was named "Coach of the Year" by the National Association of Intercollegiate Athletics.

The Pikeville loss would prove to be Corky's final college game. It wasn't because of any decision he made, but because KIAC college officials declared him ineligible for any future play. "I couldn't believe it was happening again," Corky claims. "Why after two years? But by now I was at the point where I really didn't want to be in college anyway."

Dr. Bob Davis, summing up his thoughts on Corky's bittersweet college basketball career, adds, "I wish I could have been his coach two more years, but it didn't work out. I'm so sorry I didn't have him for his junior and senior years. He would have been great had he stayed with basketball, anywhere he went. He got better every time he was on the court, but I think his baseball hurt his basketball."

With a farewell to his teammates, friends, and Coach Davis, Corky again left Georgetown before the semester ended. His name is still prominent in Georgetown record books, and despite never graduating from the school, was inducted into Georgetown's Hall of Fame in 2010.

Flo Eva Allison Withrow, Corky's mother

Otis Earl Withrow, Corky's father

Roy Duane "D.D." (left) and Raymond Wallace "Corky" Withrow. Photo taken ca. 1939 in Beckley, West Virginia.

Cartoon "Corky", a favorite of Otis Withrow.

Otis Withrow in the road near their home in High Coal.

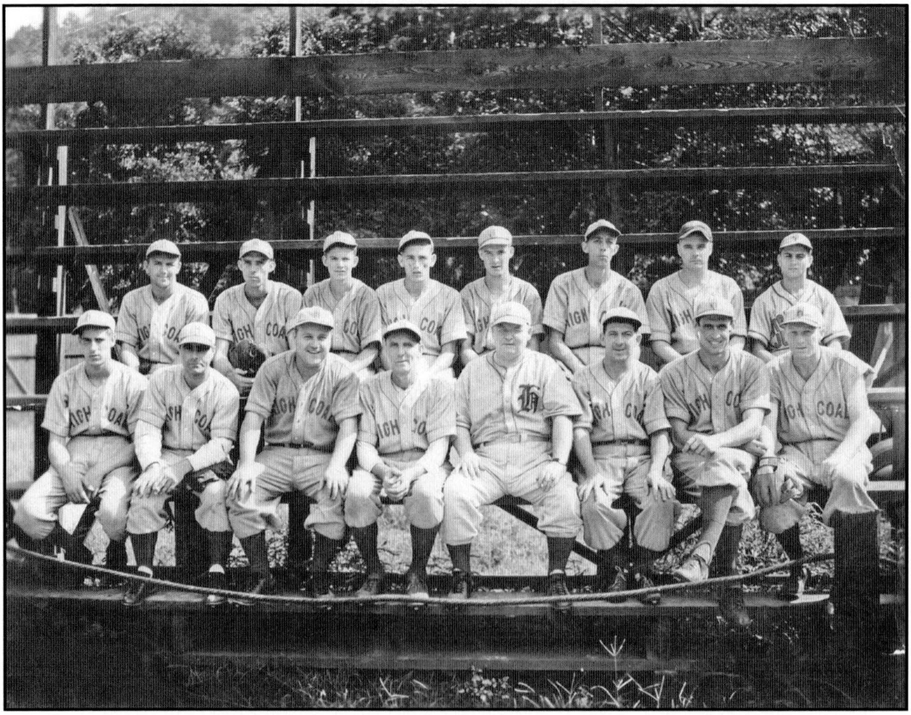

High Coal's (West Virginia) baseball team. Front row, second from right: Otis Earl Withrow. Front row, fourth from right: Manager Stitts, the team's owner.

Cleopatra Brown Withrow (1891-1938), wife of Etsel Lee Withrow, mother of Otis Earl Withrow, and paternal Grandmother of Corky.

Roy Duane, Peggy Sue, and Raymond Wallace "Corky" Withrow, children of Otis and Flo Eva. Photo taken ca. 1943 in Beckley, West Virginia.

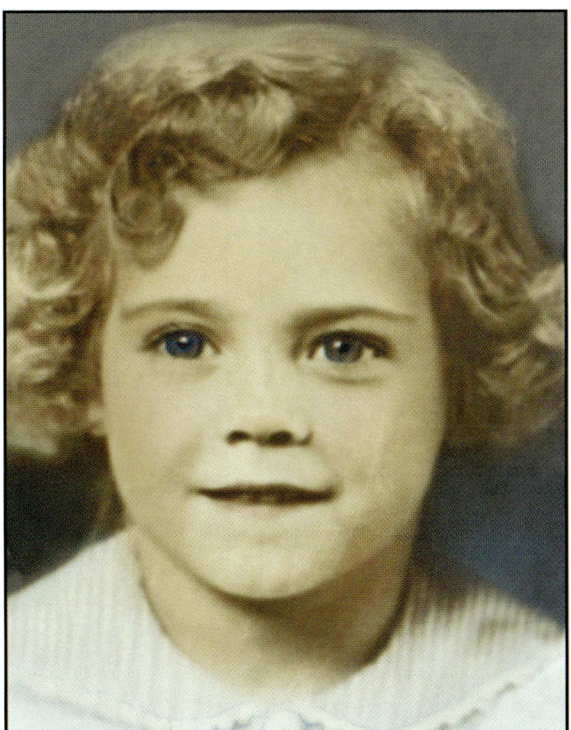

Peggy Sue Withrow, sister of Corky

Above four photos show Otis Withrow with sons, Roy and Corky, at their home in Central City. Photos ca. late '40s/early '50s.

Otis Earl and Flo Eva Allison Withrow

Corky in front of his boyhood home on Resevoir Avenue in Central City, KY.

Otis Earl and Flo Eva Withrow with their sons (Roy and Corky), their daughter-in-laws (Barbara and Betty), and grandchildren (Keith, Kelly Lynn, Duane and Chad)

"Hail to the Black and Gold,
Hail to you,
Hail, Alma Mater
Ever so true.
We love no other,
So let our motto be
Victory, Central High Varsity."

CENTRAL CITY HIGH SCHOOL
Central City, Kentucky

Central City grade school and high school. A victim of consolidation, the school was closed in 1990, and since has been demolished.

Memorial Gymnasium, home of the Golden Tide from 1952 through 1990.

The 1952-53 Central City Golden Tide. Standing left- right: E. P. Doom (Manager), Bobby Mercer, Bobby Don Millard, Stanley Ruby, Dick Wolfe, Corky Withrow, Charles Owen Gray, Coach Delmas Gish. Kneeling left-right: Billy Lee Robinson, Larry Ray, Eddie Houston, Roy Withrow, Junior Howerton. The squad finished with a 25-9 record, losing to Breckenridge County in the Regional Semis.

The 1953-54 Greenville Blackhawks represented the Tide's biggest rival. This squad finished the season with only six losses, but four of these came at the hands of the Golden Tide. Roger Newman, the Blackhawks' talented sophomore, is pictured in the back row (#10). Roger's brother, T. R., is #14.

The 1954 Golden Tide celebrated the season with a team banquet in the "Old Gymnasium". Roy Withrow is third from right, back row, while Corky stands to his right.

Roy Withrow's 1954 Central City High senior class portrait.

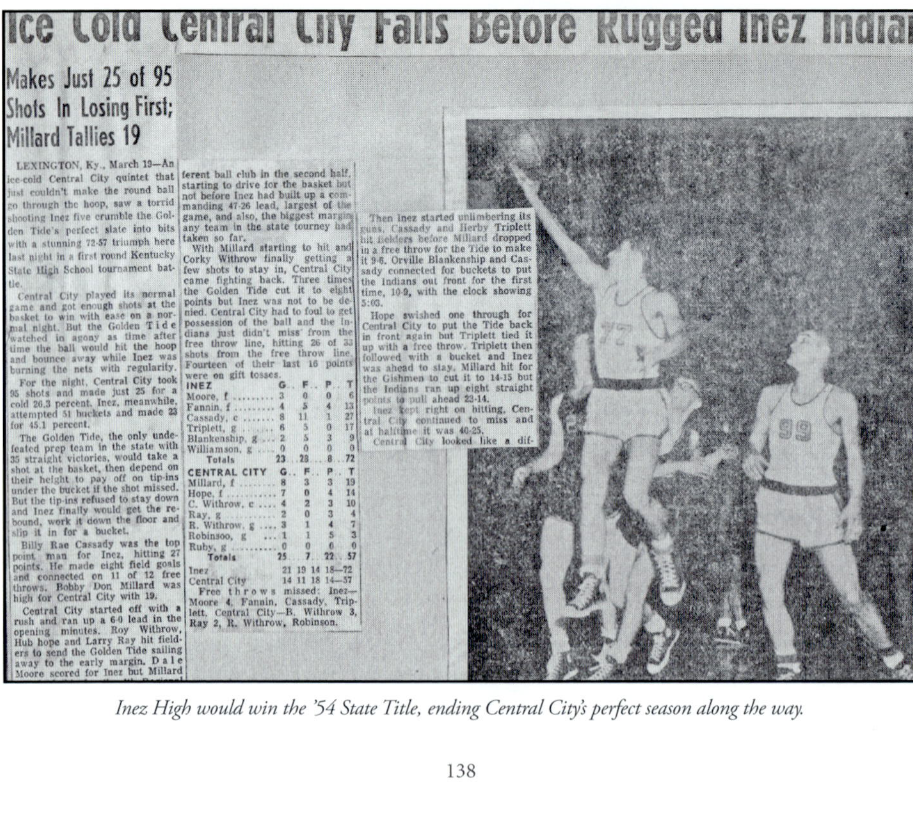

Ice Cold Central City Falls Before Rugged Inez Indians

Makes Just 25 of 95 Shots In Losing First; Millard Tallies 19

LEXINGTON, Ky., March 19—An ice-cold Central City quintet that just couldn't make the round ball go through the hoop, saw a torrid shooting Inez five crumble the Golden Tide's perfect slate into bits with a stunning 72-57 triumph here last night in a first round Kentucky State High School tournament battle.

Central City played its normal game and got enough shots at the basket to win with ease on a normal night. But the Golden Tide watched in agony as time after time the ball would hit the hoop and bounce away while Inez was burning the nets with regularity.

For the night, Central City took 95 shots and made just 25 for a cold 26.3 percent. Inez, meanwhile, attempted 51 buckets and made 23 for 45.1 percent.

The Golden Tide, the only undefeated prep team in the state with 35 straight victories, would take a shot at the basket, then depend on their height to pay off on tip-ins under the bucket if the shot missed. But the tip-ins refused to stay down and Inez finally would get the rebound, work it down the floor and slip it in for a bucket.

Billy Rae Cassady was the top point man for Inez, hitting 27 points. He made eight field goals and connected on 11 of 12 free throws. Bobby Don Millard was high for Central City with 19.

Central City started off with a rush and ran up a 6-0 lead in the opening minutes. Roy Withrow, Hub hope and Larry Ray hit fielders to send the Golden Tide sailing away to the early margin. Dale Moore scored for Inez but Millard

Then Inez started unlimbering its guns. Cassady and Herby Triplett hit fielders before Millard dropped in a free throw for the Tide to make it 9-6. Orville Blankenship and Cassady connected for buckets to put the Indians out front for the first time, 10-9, with the clock showing 5:03.

Hope swished one through for Central City to put the Tide back in front again but Triplett tied it up with a free throw. Triplett then followed with a bucket and Inez was ahead to stay. Millard hit for the Gishmen to cut it to 14-15 but the Indians ran up eight straight points to pull ahead 23-14.

Inez kept right on hitting. Central City continued to miss and at halftime it was 40-25.

Central City looked like a different ball club in the second half, starting to drive for the basket but not before Inez had built up a commanding 47-26 lead, largest of the game, and also, the biggest margin any team in the state tourney had taken so far.

With Millard starting to hit and Corky Withrow finally getting a few shots to stay in, Central City came fighting back. Three times the Golden Tide cut it to eight points but Inez was not to be denied. Central City had to foul to get possession of the ball and the Indians just didn't miss from the free throw line, hitting 26 of 33 shots from the free throw line. Fourteen of their last 16 points were on gift tosses.

INEZ	G	F	P	T
Moore, f	3	0	0	6
Fannin, f	4	5	4	13
Cassady, c	8	11	1	27
Triplett, g	6	5	0	17
Blankenship, g	2	5	3	9
Williamson, g	0	0	0	0
Totals	23	28	8	72

CENTRAL CITY	G	F	P	T
Millard, f	8	3	3	19
Hope, f	7	0	4	14
C. Withrow, c	4	2	3	10
Ray, g	2	0	3	4
R. Withrow, g	3	1	4	7
Robinsoo, g	1	1	5	3
Ruby, g	0	0	6	0
Totals	25	7	22	57

Inez	21	19	14	18—72
Central City	14	11	18	14—57

Free throws missed: Inez—Moore 4, Fannin, Cassady, Triplett. Central City—B. Withrow 3, Ray 2, R. Withrow, Robinson.

Inez High would win the '54 State Title, ending Central City's perfect season along the way.

The 1954-'55 Central City Golden Tide finished the Season with a record of 28-6. The sixth loss was to Pikeville High in the opening round of the State Tournament. Pictured here: Back row left-right: Lawrence Simpson, Billy Duvall, Jimmy Swann, Stan Ruby, Eddie Houston, Donnie Moore. Front row left-right: Buddy Fuller, Mgr., Billy Mason, Carl Jamison, Corky Withrow, Winfred Thompson, Billy Robinson, Delmas Gish, Coach and Principal.

The Adair County Indians, Coach John Burr and led by first team all-staters Terry Randall and Ralph Shearer, lost to the Tide 73-69 in a showdown at Central City. Left to right: Coach John Burr, Louis Pendleton, Terry Randall, Haskin Rowe, George Cheatham, Ralph Shearer, Tony Baker, Ray Daugherty, Ralph McQuary, Bill Conover and Roger Pickett. Photo courtesy of Ben Burr, Bardstown.

Corky Breaks Scoring Records With 51 Points, 22 Field Goals

Thar she blows, boys!

And thar goes all the records in Bobby Anderson's little book. All because Corky Withrow snowed the Daviess County Panthers in with a barrage of buckets that helped break four Muhlenberg County records and at least five Central City records, as the Golden Tide rolled to a 103-83 verdict over the Panthers Friday night at Owensboro.

Withrow, Central City's sensational junior center, played only 25 minutes Friday, but bucketed 51 points to smash by seven the scoring record of an individual in Muhlenberg County, heretofore held by Carl Carver of Hughes-Kirk, set against Utica on Feb. 23, 1954, with 44 points. In addition to the 51 points, Withrow broke his own field goal record, one he held jointly with Don Raymer of Muhlenberg Central. Both he and Don had scored 20 field goals in a single game. Withrow hit for 22 against Daviess County.

As a matter of team records in the county, the total of 186 points broke by 18 the record held by Hughes-Kirk and Irvington and the 83 points scored by a loser broke the 79 held by Hughes-Kirk.

For Central City records, both Withrow's total and field goals set a school record as well as the 103 points for the team, which broke the old record of 102 set against Calhoun recently, and the 83 points by an opposition team, and the total by two teams. As for the game itself, Central City went out in front 28-17 in the first quarter with Withrow scoring 11. Corky sat out the most of the second period, in which the Panthers outscored the Tide 22-18, but Central City still held a 46-39 halftime lead.

Withrow, hitting from all sides, scored 16 in the third period, and the Tide outscored the Panthers 25-20, and in the third and fourth in one stretch scored 16 straight points for the Tide. Withrow hit his 51st point with 1:45 to go and send Central City out ahead 99-77. Billy Mason then hit two free throws to send the count to 101.

Withrow's 51 points was the most spectacular feat of the game, but the Tide was not without other stars, as Soph Winfred Thompson hit for 15 from his forward position, and the guards, Billy Mason and Billy Robinson hit for 16 and 12 respectively.

Central City (103)	fg	ft	pf	tp
Thompson, f	5	5	5	15
Jamison, f	2	1	5	5
Duvall, f	0	2	1	2
Ruby, f	0	0	1	0
Withrow, c	22	7	4	51
Swann, c	0	0	1	0
Robinson, g	4	4	5	12
Mason, g	6	4	2	16
Houston, g	0	2	5	2
Moore, g	0	0	0	0
Totals	35	25	29	103

Daviess Co. (83)	fg	ft	pf	tp
Mayfield, f	2	3	3	7
Burns, f-c	6	8	4	20
Peercy, f	0	2	1	2
Claypool, c	6	6	5	18
Pagan, g	9	3	2	21
Cline, g	3	3	5	9
Roberts, g	3	0	4	6
Curry, g	0	0	0	0
Totals	29	25	24	83

Tide ... 28 18 25 32—103
Panthers .. 17 22 20 24— 83

Free throws missed: Tide—Thompson 2, Jamison 2, Withrow 3, Robinson 2, Duvall, Houston, Moore 2. Daviess County—Mayfield 11, Burns 4, Claypool 3, Pagan 5, Cline, Peercy 2.

Officials: Omar and Teague of Madisonville.

JAN. 28, 1955 51 PTS.

In late January, 1955, Corky scored 51 points against Daviess County. This mark established a new individual scoring record for a Muhlenberg County Cager.

Delmas Gish (1908-1998) graduated from Central City High in 1925. With a degree from the University of Kentucky in '29, he began a teaching and coaching career at McHenry High, but returned to the Alma Mater as a Math teacher and Basketball Coach. In 16 seasons as Head-Coach from '42-'58, his Tide teams won 407 games while losing 120. He was later inducted into the Kentucky Athletic Hall of Fame, the Kentucky Hall of Fame for Officials, and the Dawahares/KHSAA Hall of Fame.

The American Legion Post 61 Team (Central City) finished as runner-up in the 1952 State Legion Baseball Tournament in Louisville. The team lost in the title game to Latonia. Shown, front row, left-right: Bobby Don Millard, Connie Lile, Lynn Wilkins, Coach Chris Lemastus, Lowell Ward, Jimmie Lemastus, Glen Mohon, and Ronnie Higgs. Back row, left-right: Claude Alexander, Bobby Young, Simon Sanders, Larry Sparks, Murriel Cobb, Corky Withrow, Jimmy Sheffield, Mgr. Bobby Anderson, and Larry Stone.

The 1955-56 Golden Tide Team–Corky's Senior season–would finish with a 30-4 record after losing in the State Tournament's opening round to Carr Creek in overtime. Back row, left-right: Coach Delmas Gish, Eddie Brand, Donnie Moore, Jimmy Swann, Earl Goode, Johnny Lile, Bob White (Manager). Front row left-right: Carl Ray Jamison, Billy Ray Duvall, Corky Withrow, Winfred Thompson, Billy Mason.

On May 13, 2011, Kelly Coleman (right) returned to Memorial Gymnasium in Central City where he and Corky both scored 40 points in the Christmas Eve '55 Showdown. It was Kelly's first visit to Central City since that game. With Corky and Kelly is Jack Day, the former assistant coach of the Tide.

Memorial Gymnasium's Court. Corky played here from 1952- '56. Photo taken by Glenn Braden in September, 2015.

The Rambler Rose Motel on the outskirts of Central City was the motel where the Wayland Wasps stayed during the Central City Invitational Tournament on December 23-24, 1955. This postcard aerial view features the motel.

"King" Kelly and Corky on the floor of Rupp Arena prior to a game at the 2010 Kentucky State High School Basketball Tournament. Corky played in three State Tournaments '54, '55, '56–while Kelly rewrote the record books in the '56 State Tournament; enough so for it to be labeled "King Kelly's Tournament"

For Three Weeks; Both Are On Probation One Year

A telehone call at press time from Kentucky High School Athletic Commissioner Ted Sanford informed The Messenger, The Times-Argus and Radio Station WMTA that Central City High School has been suspended from the Kentucky High School Atheletic Association for a period of three weeks beginning today (Jan. 19), and that both Central City and Butler County High School had been placed on probation for a period of one year from date. The complete report in the form of a letter to Principal-Coach Delmas Gish of Central City and Foyest West of Morgantown is as follows:

"Gentlemen: You are hereby notified that Central City High School has been suspended from the KHSAA for a period of three weeks beginning Jan. 19, and both Central City and Butler County High School are placed on probation for a period of one year from the date. It is my opinion that both violated provisions of KHSAA by law 17 on the evening of Jan. 6, when certain reresentatives of the schools conducted themselves in unsportsmanship manners. It is not necessary for me to review all evidence presented at the hearing in my office yesterday, attended by you gentlemen, (names those present) in explaining reasons for my decision. All of you are familiar with evidences which has been presented. I do wish, however, to enumerate briefly incidents which have caused your schools to receive penalties mentioned. The Central City High School is being suspended because near the end of the Butler County-Central City game, played in Central City on the vening of Jan. 6, a Central City player Corky Withrow committed an apparent flagrant act of unsportsmanship-like conduct against a Butler County player, Radean Hammers, for which he was ejected from the game by officials Norman and Eugene O'Nan. And for disgraceful conduct of some 10 to 15 Central City supporters, who threw rocks at the Morgantown busses as they were going through Central City following the game.

"The two schools are placed on probation because of numerous acts of unsportsman-like conduct, on part of the supporters of each team during the game. Norman O'Nan stated in his report to this office that one Central City man drew a knife on him immediately after the game and he and his brother were threatened with knife as the officials left the floor.

"Supts. Taylor and West have made every effort to determine the identity of the men in order that a warrant may be sworn out for their arrest. To this date they have been unsuccessful. All of the other evidence presented to me indicated that is is probable that nobody had an open knife while near an official. Officials of the law were present at the game and these officers ejected promptly one or more trouble makers when asked to do so by the officials and Principal Gish.

"Concerning the vandalism which took place in one of the Morgantown busses while parked on the lot adjacent to the gym, the identity of those responsible for these acts have not been determined, and consequently my decision is in no way influenced by this incident.

"Other acts of unsportsmanship-like conditions mentioned at the hearing were as follows: (1) A Butler County man picking or pinching at Corky Withrow as he lay on floor after diing for a loose ball. (2) A booing of referees and of Central City players on numerous occasions. (3) Failure of supporters of both teams to exhibit the courtesy commonly given players attempting to pitch free throws. (4) Several supporters of both teams rushed to the playing floor immediately following the Withrow-Hammers incident as a result the officials thinking it necessary to announce over the PA system that the game would be forfeited if the floor was not cleared immediately. When an incident such as this one mentioned Occurs it appears certain individuals in your community have failed to learn the purpose of high school athletics. If a basketball game cannot be conducted as a friendly contest between teams representing two neighboring schools then the entire program of our interscholastic competition breaks down instead of sports helping in education they become a detriment. May I say I appreciate very much the fine attitude of all you men who attended the hearing yesterday.

"Nobody could have been fairer than you were in the matter of bringing to my attention the factual evidence, which you could get. We are all school men and we are all working for the same objective. We cannot solve problems of poor sportsmanship, however, by ourselves. In your past cases, you are going to need the co-operation of the school patrons of your community who believe as we do concerning the proper place for sports and physical education in the school program, to solve some of the problems which exist.

"Regardless of what happened on the evening of Jan. 6, I am sure that the good sportsmen in each of your communities are in the great majority. (Signed) Sincerely yours, Theo. A. Sanford, Commissioner."

A result of the '56 Butler County-Central City fight and riot was a three-game suspension and one year probation.

Roger Newman would go on to play for Coach Adolph Rupp and the University of Kentucky (#42 in the photo).

Corky drives around Berea's Don Mills in the Central City-Berea contest during the Louisville Invitational Tournament. Berea would win 72-64, with Mills Scoring 27, Corky 22. Both would later sign with the University of Kentucky.

Number #19, shooting from the top of the key, is Freddie Maggard, a guard for Carr Creek High. This shot was the dagger that ended Central City's Sweet 16 title hopes in overtime of their 1956 first-round contest. Carr Creek would go on to win the tourney that year. Number #24 in black is the Tide's Donnie Moore, while Corky, facing the camera, and near the goal, can only watch.

Corky and "King" Kelly relax in the Wayland Community Center in 2013. No doubt, there was probably a little "needling" going on, too.

Pictured left to right: Kelly Coleman, Howard "Howie" Crittenden (Cuba High 1952), Freddie Maggard (Carr Creek High 1956), and Corky Withrow. Photo by Bob Watkins.

This photo of the 1956 Kentucky Sweet 16 All-Tournament team is missing one of its main attractions..."King" Kelly Coleman of Wayland High. Accepting for him, and posing in the photo is his sister, Linda Carol Coleman. Standing to Linda Carol's left, in coat and tie, is Corky.

On November 11, 1998, Corky met with former Central City teammate Billy Duvall at a "Legends" Basketball Event in Central City. It was Billy who was unable to play against Carr Creek High in the State Tourney due to a previous injury.

Corky and Kelly—both Centennial Class inductees in the Kentucky High School Basketball of Fame in Elizabethtown—share good times at a "roast" of Corky at Charlie Thurman's Sonora Home in Hardin County in July, 2014.

Corky Withrow's 1956 Central City High senior class portrait.

Central City High School Class of 1956

Near Central City High School was this diner that served as a teen "hang out" for Golden Tide students. Corky and friends spent much time here, consuming large quantities of hamburgers and fries, as well as listening to Rock-N-Roll and country music on the juke box.

Chile Bowl

Withrow, Mills, Coleman Top All-State Team Named By Paducah Sun-Democrat

PADUCAH, Ky., March 24 (AP)—Two repeaters and Kentucky's all-time scoring champion dominated the Paducah Sun-Democrat's 1956 all-state high school basketball team announced today.

Corky Withrow of Central City won the Player-of-the-Year award for polling a record 301 votes of a possible 378. Close behind were Don Mills of Berea with 294 and Kelly Coleman of Wayland with 292.

Withrow and Mills are the only repeaters from the 1955 squad.

The fabulous Coleman, who wound up his high school career this year, shattered practically every Kentucky scoring record, both in season play and in the state tournament.

Also on the first 10 and their votes were Martin Holland of Heath (147), Roger Newman of Greenville (141), John Turner of Newport Public (132), Byron Pinson of Henderson (108), Mickey Kelly of Louisville Flaget (106), E. A. Couch of state champion Carr Creek (97) and David Denton of College High, Bowling Green (96).

All members of the team are seniors.

"Coach-of-the-Year" honors went to Bill Carter of Heath, whose team won 30 consecutive games before being upset in the semi-finals of the First Region tournament. Last year, with the same club, Heath had a 13-13 record.

Carter was a popular choice, receiving 110 votes. T. L. Plain of Henderson was second with 51 and John Campbell of Wayland third with 32.

Only coaches were eligible to vote on players nominated by the newspaper's all-state board. The team was based on regular season play and ballots were cast before the tournaments got under way.

The second team.

Billy Lickert, Lexington Lafayette; Calvin Bird, Corbin; Harry Todd, Earlington; Ken Cornelius, Mt. Vernon; Lowell Hughes, Prestonburg; Ken Meyer, Montgomery County; Dave Eakins, Henderson; Herby Kays, Shelbyville; Freddie Luigs, Paducah Tilghman, and Darrell Bicknell, Berea.

The third team:

Rex Story, Mayfield; Ronnie Bridewell, Newport Public; Dickie Baugh, Somerset; Bobby Shepherd, Carr Creek; Wally Johnson, Butler County; Fred Hynson, Lexington Henry Clay; Jerry Vest, Sedalia; Charles Osborne, Flat Gap, and Ned Jennings, Nicholas County.

Pinson, Shepherd Head Herald's All-Sta

By Billy Surface
Herald Sports Writer

The little man is rapidly being shoved out of the basketball picture—or at least that's what the results of The Herald's first annual All-State selections reveal.

Every member of the honor squad stands above the six-foot mark and the shortest cager picked on the first team is Flaget's Mickey Kelly, a 6-1 guard.

In fact, the 10-man team, which includes eight seniors, averages nearly 6-4, a pretty lofty bunch.

The Herald, in naming its first All-State selections, did away with the usual popularity system in which every coach in the state was entitled to vote, but instead compiled the choices of 32 veteran coaches and officials—two from each region. Thus the committee members, who voted only for the boys they'd seen in action, were in a position to compare the top athletes and make an unbiased decision.

Wayland's Kelly Coleman and Central City's Corky Withrow left little doubt as to their ability by being named on every ballot.

Coleman, whose fantastic scoring feats are somewhat legendary, and Withrow, good enough to merit the University of Kentucky's first cage scholarship this winter, also were named to the All-State Tournament team recently.

Third choice was Berea's ace pivotman, Don Mills, who was named on 30 of the 32 ballots. Touted by many as the best big man in the Commonwealth, the 6-7 flagpole led his team to the No. 1 ranking in the final regular-season poll.

Byron Pinson, classy Henderson performer, was the pick of 28 voters and his recent State tourney play verified his right to be accorded the high position, just ahead of Carr Creek's Bobby Shepherd, who finished fifth with 24 votes.

Sixth position went to Richard Newman of Greenville, a Fourth Region quintet. The Fourth incidently, was the only region to land two players on the first team.

Charlie Osborne, 6-5 junior from Flat Gap was the choice of 19 voters, while Kelly was eighth and College High's David Denton, ninth. Tenth place went to Earlington's Harry Todd, the only sophomore selected.

Carr Creek's affable pilot, Morton Combs, is the recipient of the "Coach of The Year" accolade, although his selection wasn't a runaway by any means. Combs received backing from nine of the 31 voters, while the runner-up spot ended up in a tie between Heath's Bill Carter and Cooper John Campbell of Wayland. Carter piloted his team to 30 straight victories, while Campbell's team finished third in the State tourney.

T. L. Plain of Henderson and Elmer (Baldy) Gilb of Henry Clay each received two votes, while the following had one backer each: Jim Riffey, Manual; Henderson Wilson, Sonora; Charles Finnell, Nicholas County, and Jim Connor, Newport Catholic.

Montgomery County's Kenny Meyer was the top second-team choice, winning in a narrow race over Lafayette's Billy Lickert, Ken Cornelius of Mount Vernon and Martin Holland of Heath.

Here are thumbnail descriptions of the "Top Ten":

Coleman: Shattered virtually every scoring record in posting the highest average ever compiled in Kentucky prep circles. The Wayland wonder had a four-year average of 33 points a game and a 48-point average for his senior season. Broke State tourney four-game total with 185, and made 68 in third-place game. A fine rebounder for his size (6-2) Coleman can practically name his college, although his coach says he's narrowed his choice to Kentucky and West Virginia.

Withrow: Led his team to State tourney berths for three straight years and in so doing, achieved all-tourney honors each time. Broke the 1,000-point barrier two straight seasons and accumulated 3,036 points during his four-year career. Season high was 53 points recorded against Bremen. Already accepted a grant-in-aid at UK.

Mills: Posted a 24-point average this season with Berea and his rebounding and defense was equally brilliant. Tied the Louisville Invitational Tournament scoring mark with 38 points while leading his team to the title. His steady improvement each season is a point that has impressed college coaches. Like Coleman, he can almost name his own meal ticket.

Pinson: Probably the most evasive center in the State for his 6-2 frame, a factor that has lured college scouts to Henderson like a magnet. An All-State Tournament choice two straight years, Pinson has received scholarship offers from Kentucky, Vanderbilt, Illinois, Murray and Western, according to his coach.

Shepherd: A husky mountain lad whose rebounding is his most valuable asset. Shepherd virtually swept the boards clean in pacing Carr Creek to the State title. Owns a 24-point average and has Dayton, Furman, Morehead, and West Virginia bidding for his services but will probably attend Kentucky.

Newman: Any time a boy receives a scholarship from Adolph Rupp as early as Newman did, he's bound to be outstanding. Touted by many as even a better cager than Withrow and outscored him during the last two meetings, despite having been sidelined with a chipped ankle bone.

Osborne: Only a junior but he rivalled Coleman for the mountain scoring mark by posting a 35-point average and swished in 64 in a regional skirmish. His coach, Francis Stapleton, claims that Morehead, Furman, West Virginia, South Carolina and several other colleges are already after him.

Kelly: Shortest member of the honor squad at 6-1, but nevertheless is rated as a fine guard. Led all Louisville prepsters with a 22-point average. Will attend either Louisville or Xavier.

Denton: Even though he played on the Western campus (College High) this 6-2 sharpshooter is expected to follow his high school coach, Ed Diddle Jr., to Middle Tennessee. Relies on a one-hand shot as his most valuable weapon.

Todd: This 6-7 pivotman should undoubtedly develop into one of Kentucky's finest centers. Is only a *sophomore* now but already has college coaches drooling for his services. Has an effective hook shot and is equally dangerous with his jump shot.

Herald's All-S

FIRST TEA

Player	Pos.	Class
Corky Withrow	G	Sr.
Kelly Coleman	G	Sr.
Don Mills	C	Sr.
Byron Pinson	C-F	Sr.
Bob Shepherd	C	Sr.
Richard Newman	C	Sr.
Charles Osborne	C	Jr.
Mickey Kelly	G	Sr.
David Denton	G	Sr.
Harry Todd	C	Soph.

SECOND TEA

Player	Pos.	Class
Kenny Meyer	G	Sr.
Billy Lickert	C	Jr.
Ken Cornelius	G	Sr.
Martin Holland	C	Sr.
E. A. Couch	G	Sr.
Fred Hynson	C	Sr.
John Turner	C	Sr.
Calvin Bird	F	Jr.
Ned Jennings	C	Jr.
Lowell Hughes	F	Sr.

THIRD TEAM

Dave Eakins (Henderson)
Jim Mitchell (Valley)
Billy Gilley (Carlisle)
Gene Herndon (Alamo)
Darrell Bicknell (Berea)
George Carroll (Ashland)
Herbie Kays (Shelbyville)
Ralph Davis (Vanceburg)
Louie Crigler (Boone County)
Rex Story (Mayfield)

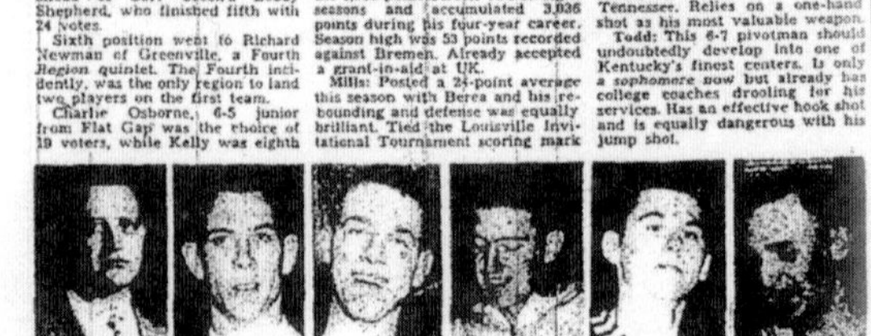

Combs — Withrow — Coleman — Mills — Pinson — Shepherd

Withrow Named On Tourney Team

Lexington—Corky Withrow of Central City was selected on the all-state tourney team of the KHSAA tournament Saturday night in Lexington.

Others included Kelly Coleman of Wayland, Byron Pinson, Pascal Benson and Dave Eakins, Henderson; Bobby Shepherd and E. A. Couch of Carr Creek; Harry Todd, Earlington; Rex Story of Mayfield; Billy Ray Lickert of Lexington Lafayette.

Corky Withrow Named Player of the Year

Lexington—Corky Withrow of Central City and Roger Newman of Greenville were named Tuesday on the Lexington Herald's first annual all-state high school cage team. As in the case of the Paducah Sun-Democrat team Muhlenberg County was the only county, the 16th District was the only district and the Fourth Region was the only region to place two men on the team.

Withrow tied with Kelly Coleman of Wayland with 32 votes for first place. Newman was sixth.

Billy Surface of the Herald staff wrote:

"The little man is rapidly being shoved out of the basketball picture—or at least that's what the results of the Herald's first annual all-state selections reveal.

"Every member of the honor squad stands above the six-foot mark and the shortest cager picked on the team is Flaget's Mickey Kelly, a 6-1 guard.

"In fact, the 10-man team, which includes eight seniors, averages nearly 6-4, a pretty lofty bunch.

"The Herald, in naming its selections did away with the usual popularity system in which every coach in the state was entitled to vote, but instead compiled the choices of 32 veteran coaches and officials — two from each region. Thus the committee members, who voted only for the boys they'd seen in action, were in a position to compare the top athletes and make an unbiased decision.

"Wayland's Kelly Coleman and Central City's Corky Withrow left little doubt as to their ability by being named on every ballot.

Coleman, whose fantastic scoring feats are somewhat legendary, and Withrow, good enough to merit the University of Kentucky's first cage scholarship this winter, also were named to the All-State Tournament team recently.

Corky Is No. 1 and Roger Is No. 2 On Paducah Sun-Democrat All-State

Paducah—Raymond (Corky) Withrow of Central City won the "player of the year" award of the Paducah Sun-Democrat by leading the balloting with a record 301 votes. He was second to Ken Kuhn of Louisville Male in the poll last year.

Muhlenberg was the only county, the 16th District was the only district and the Fourth Region was the only region to place two players on the first team. Roger Newman of Greenville was the fifth man on the Sun-Democrat's 1956 all-state high school basketball team.

Robie Harper of Hughes-Kirk received honorable mention.

Sports Editor Bill Carter in announcing the winners wrote:

The only other repeater was Don Mills of Berea, who received 294 votes, two more than Wayland's fabulous "King Kelly" Coleman.

Martin Holland finishes up fourth with 147 votes. Others on the first team are Roger Newman of Greenville (141), John Turner of Newport Public (132), Byron Pinson of Henderson City (108), Mickey Kelley of Louisville Flaget (106), E. A. Couch of state champion Carr Creek (97) and David Denton of College High, Bowling Green, (96).

Corky Withrow

Withrow, a 6-4, 190-pounder has been terrorizing the Fourth Region and surrounding area for 3 years, winning every honor possible. With the exception of the single game record, he holds all major scoring records in both the region and the county. Withrow became one of Kentucky's top high school cagers when only a sophomore. For his career, Corky scored 3,136 points, surpassing the 1,000-mark for two straight years. He amassed 1,058 points in 34 games this season for a 31-point average and collected 1,086 last year. His single game high was 53 against Bremen. An all-stater for two straight years, Withrow is also an outstanding baseball player and will turn professional after his college career is completed, if not before. A "B" student, Withrow has signed a grant-in-aid at Kentucky.

All-Americans: 500 top high

NOMINATED BY COACHES AND SPORTS EDITORS . . . . players in bold type are preseason choices as

Dave Denton (College of Bowling Green) 6-2; Roger Newman (Greenville) 6-2.

LOUISIANA

Jack Moreland (Minden) 6-7; Harriman Morgan (New Orleans De La Salle) 6-4; Jon Peebles (New Orleans Fortier) 6-4; Dave Corson (Fortier) 6-5; Billy Castilaw (Baton Rouge Istrouma) 6-5; Bobby James (Ruston) 6-5; Eddie Burt (Shreveport Byrd) 6-1; Fred Holt (Jena) 6-9; Carey Guglielmo (Baton Rouge Catholic) 6-1; Joe Scaffi (New Orleans) 6-0; George Kell (New Orleans Holy Cross) 6-2

MAINE

Danny Drinon (Bangor) 6-0; Carl Daigle (Bangor) 6-3; Ricgard Bishop (Morse of Bath) 6-1; Paul Davenport (Houlton) 6-2; Ed Marchetti (Morse) 6-1; Roland Gagne (Lewiston) 6-1; Don Sturgeon (Old Town) 6-0; Brian Murray (Bangor John Bapst) 5-11; Wayne Rogers (Ellsworth) 5-10; Carlo Cimino (Portland Cheverus) 6-1; Bob Fallon

MICHIGAN

Herb Wood (River Rouge) 5-8; Dan Potter (Hazel Park) 6-4; Bob Skrzycki (Detroit Catholic) 6-4; Chester Hicks (Inkster) 5-8; Bob Zimmerman (Jackson) 5-10; Ed Burton (Muskegon Heights) 6-4; Ed Reynolds (Benton Harbor) 6-1.

MINNESOTA

Ron Johnson (New Prague) 6-7; Tom Idstrom (Fairmont) 5-9; Ken Excel (Minneapolis Roosevelt) 5-11; Roger Plantikon (St. Louis Park) 6-2; Skip Fointaine (Proctor) 6-0; Paul Mortella (Hibbing) 6-3; Tom Moe (Edina) 6-2; John Wage (Aurora) 6-1; Dave Dragotis (Hopkins) 6-1.

MISSISSIPPI

Bobby Kitchens (Natchez) 5-10; Denton Ducker (Roxie) 6-1; Shelby Watts (Brookhaven) 5-9; Bobby Avant (Greenwood) 6-2; Jack Mitchell (Corinth) 5-10; Tommy Alexander (Laurel) 5-10; Charles Parson (West Lincoln) Jimmy

Smith (Omaha Tech) 5-7; Lynn Nelson (Ord) 6-4; Dan Arnold (Minden) 5-11; Bob Moore (Clarkson) 6-3; Dennis Mullins (Omaha Central) 6-3; Larry Feaster (Grand Island) 6-3; Dick Haggerty (Omaha Holy Name) 6-3.

NEW HAMPSHIRE

Bob Dickson (Manchester Central) 5-8; Dick Loiselle (Manchester Bradley) 6-0; Bill Smith (Berlin) 6-6; Bob Maloney (Dover) 6-0; Mike Pendergast (Portsmouth) 6-0; R. Hanson (Concord) 6-2; R. Breen (Nashua) 5-11; L. Harper (Laconia) 5-10.

NEW JERSEY

George Ramming (Union Hill) 6-5; Art Matson (North Arlington) 6-4; John Crotty (Jersey City St. Peter's) 6-0; Myron Magarro (Lodi) 6-4; Harp Junta (Pompton Lakes) 6-7; John Purcell (Bayonne) 6-2; Cliff Ehrlich (Teaneck) 6-4; Joe Russo (Paterson Bosco) 5-7; John Saxenmeyer (Belmar St. Rose) 6-4; Frank Michener (Passaic Valley) 6-0; Bill Collier (Newark West Side) 5-10.

NEVADA

Chub Quilici (Smith Valley) 5-8; Jim Rice (Panaca Lincoln County) 5-8; Do[n] Ashworth (Las Vegas) 6-2; George Allison (Carson City) 6-1; Bob Brad[…] (Panaca Fernley) 6-1; Don Helm (Las Vegas) 6-4.

NORTH CAROLINA

Grey Poole (Raleigh) 6-5; Dann[y] Casteen (Wilmington New Hanover) 6-0; Charles Wilson (Asheville Le[e] Edwards) 5-10; Poe Rochelle (Kingston Grainger) 6-0; Hal Edwards (Greenville) 6-3; Hal Gilbert (Rocky Mountain) 5-6; Ray Bender (Burlington Williams) 6-1; Rick McDonough (Charlotte Central) 6-4; Carroll Younkin (North Davidson) 6-5; Bradley Anderson (Greensboro Senior) 6-0; Reggie Heavener (Gastonia) 6-1; Winston Wiggins (Youngsville) 6-5.

NORTH DAKOTA

Ronald Schiff (Sherwood) 6-1; Maurice Railing (Lansford) 5-10; Otto Riel[…]

THE HIGH SCHOOL ALL-AMERICA SQUAD

1955-56 FIRST TEAM:

A. C. Black (Crozier Tech of Dallas, Tex.) 6-9; Corky Withrow (Central City, Ky.) 6-4; Horace Walker (Chester, Pa.) 6-3; Oscar Robertson (Crispus Attucks of Indianapolis, Ind.) 6-5; George Ramming (Union Hill of Union City, N. J.) 6-5.

1955-56 SECOND TEAM:

Jack Moreland (Minden, La.) 6-7; Albert Ellison (Linden, Tenn.) 6-4; Dennis Price (Norman, Okla.) 6-1; Fred LaCour (St. Ignatius of San Francisco, Cal.) 6-4; Earl Nau (Mt. Pleasant, Iowa) 6-2.

(Rumford Stephens) 6-1; Bill Bragdon (Westbrook) 6-0.

MARYLAND

Barry Shetrone (Baltimore Southern) 6-1; Dick Brown (Silver Spring Montgomery-Blair) 6-2; Carl Pakulski (Baltimore Patterson) 6-1; Charles Keller (Frederick) 6-2; Howard Beeman (Frostburg Beall) 6-6; George Miller (Baltimore Calvert) 5-10; Al Budnichuck (Towson Catholic) 6-1; Phil Kulinski (Baltimore Poly) 6-2; Dick Marshall (Easton) 6-3; Barrie Lindenbaum (Franklin) 6-2; Johnny Hoerr (Kenwood) 5-11.

MASSACHUSETTS

Charles Chevalier (Charlestown) 5-10; Al Attar (Fall River Durfee) 6-1; Don McGillicudy (Reading) 6-0; Joe Bellino (Winchester) 5-8; Peter Clarey (Malden) 6-1; Joe Lane (Worcester St. John's) 6-2; Rudy Williams (Cambridge Rindge Tech) 6-3; Dick Whalen (Somerville St. Clement's) 6-2; Jack Tierney (Cambridge Latin) 6-2; Bernie Sidman (Lynn Classical) 6-5.

Whetstone (Natchez) 6-3; Paul Jones (Goodman) 6-4; Louis Griffin (Meridian) 6-6.

MISSOURI

Jim Hoffman (Kansas City Northeast) 6-4; Jack Pirrie (Maplewood) 6-5; Geore Burkel (St. Louis Cleveland) 6-7; Jim Daily (Joplin) 5-10; Dick Chartrand (St. Louis U.H.S.) 6-0; Don Costello (St. Louis Beaumont) 6-4; Ivan Richmann (Fisk) 6-6; Gene Jordan (Malden) 6-3; Jack Wolff (Webster) 6-1.

MONTANA

Dennis Reber (Missoula) 6-3; Dan Balko (Great Falls) 5-9; Dan Burns (Missoula Loyola) 6-0; Bob Hurley (Anaconda Public) 6-3; Jack Watson (Helena Public) 6-1; Floyd Henderson (Bozeman) 6-0; Mike Freeboorn (Butte) 6-1; Dave Johanson (Sidney) 5-8.

NEBRASKA

Dick Harvey (Omaha Creighton Prep) 6-6; Keith Ozanne (Cozad) 6-5; Jim

NEW MEXICO

Kim Nash (Hobbs) 6-1; Sulo Mattson (Carlsbad) 6-2; Barry Stone (Portales) 6-5; Dare Miller (Roswell) 6-2; Doug Anderson (Los Alamos) 6-0; Ed Loper (Santa Fe St. Michael's) 6-3; Billy Cates (Lovington) 6-5; Floyd Donham (Hobbs) 6-0; Clyde Chaney (Antesia) 6-6.

NEW YORK

STATE: **Hugh Gallagher** (Mineola) 5-10; Al Siegel (Long Beach) 6-0; George Bird (Freeport) 6-0; Bob Ketzner (Valley Stream) 6-1; Monty Stickles (Poughkeepsie) 6-4; Richard Kenney (Binghamton Central) 5-11; Pete Corbett (Syracuse CBA) 6-10; Ray Mossey (Schenectady Mott Terrace) 6-4; Al Handley (Syracuse Assumption) 5-10.

CITY: **Bernard Cabey** (De Witt Clinton) 6-4; Ira Sussman (Taft) 6-0; Alfred Paine (Commerce) 6-0; Tommy Smith (St. Francis) 6-2; Tommy McNamara (St. Agnes) 6-3; Dick Rodin (Jamaica) 6-3; Robert Jones (Lane) 6-4; Gerald Kaufman (New Utrecht) 5-11.

(Ashley) 6-3; Al Roisum (Grand Fork[s] Central) 6-1; Ray Smith (Enderlin) 6-4; Jack Bergene (Fargo Central) 6-0; Sy Vermillion (Ft. Yates) 6-1; Dal[e] Leathers (Lansford) 6-3.

OHIO

Roland Boldz (Lockland Wayne) 6-0; Lee Patrone (Bellaire) 6-0; Ron Dykes (Middletown) 6-2; Gary Kessler (Wilshire) 6-9; Ray Apple (Cincinnati Hughes) 6-2; Earl Frederick (Lockland Wayne) 6-3; Spud Hornsby (Hamilton) 6-4; Bill Ralich (Steubenville) 6-7; Ron Godfrey (Martins Ferry) 6-5; Henry Josefczyk (Yorkville) 6-5; Joe Roberts (Columbus East) 6-6; Jim Parfitt (East Liverpool) 6-3; Mallie McCarthy (Milford) 6-3; Verlyn Witte (Reading) 6-6; Willie White (Springfield) 6-0; John Middendorf (Cincinnati McNicholas) 6-2.

OKLAHOMA

Dennis Price (Norman) 6-2; Bill Gary (Putnam City) 6-3; Dick Urban (Blackwell) 6-6; Dick Soergel (Oklahoma City Capitol Hill) 6-4; Floyd

Dell Sports selected Corky as one of its First-Team All-American Performers.

Today, a glass-enclosed display case—one containing the All-Star uniforms worn by Corky in the '56—can be viewed in the Central City Gymnasium. Photo taken by Glenn Braden in 2015.

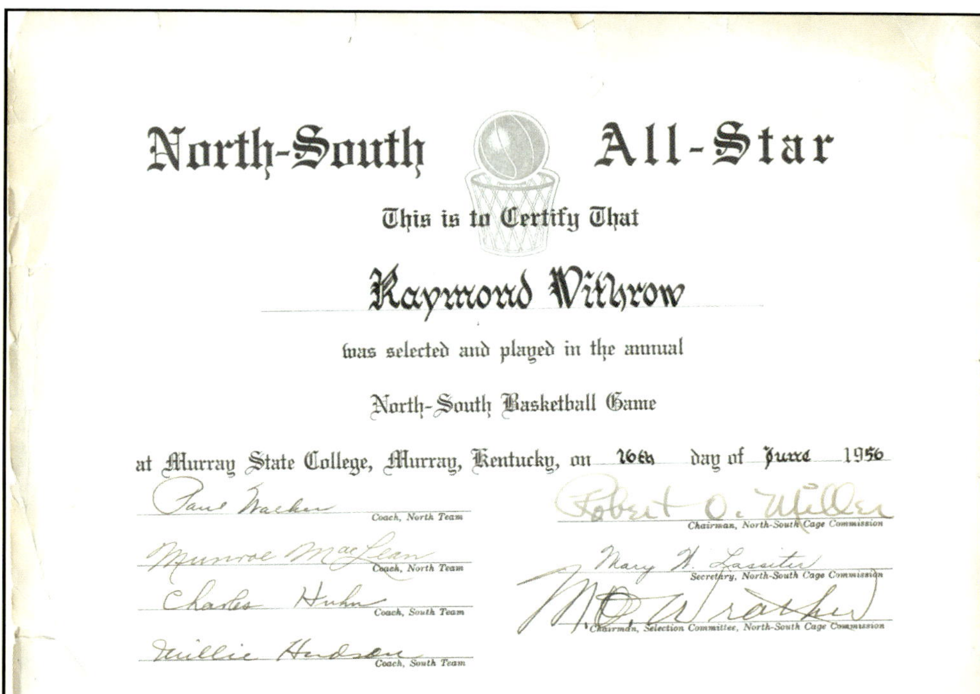

North-South All-Star

This is to Certify That

Raymond Withrow

was selected and played in the annual

North-South Basketball Game

at Murray State College, Murray, Kentucky, on 16th day of June 1956

Paul Walker — Coach, North Team

Munroe MacLean — Coach, North Team

Charles Huhn — Coach, South Team

Millie Hudson — Coach, South Team

Robert O. Miller — Chairman, North-South Cage Commission

Mary W. Lassiter — Secretary, North-South Cage Commission

M. O. Wrather — Chairman, Selection Committee, North-South Cage Commission

Certificate naming Corky to the North-South All-Star game in 1956.

The 1956 West (Kentucky) All Stars: Those identified are #30 Corky Withrow (Central City), #31 David Denton (Bowling Green), #35 Martin Holland (Heath), #40 Pascal Benson (Henderson Holy Name), #45 Roger Newman (Greenville), Rex Story (Mayfield), Coach Truman Layton "T. L." Plain.

The 1956 East (Kentucky) All-Stars: Kneeling, left-right, team Manager, George Carroll, Everett Varney, Charles Hall, Kenny Cornelius, Kenny Mayer. Standing, left-right: E. A. Couch, Lowell Hughes, Ralph Davis, Don Mills, Bobby Shepherd, Kelly Coleman, Rex Polley, Coach John Bill Trivette.

Withrow, Gish added to Hall of Fame

Messenger-Inquirer

Two former Central City High School greats have been added to John McGill's Sweet 16 Hall of Fame.

Raymond "Corky" Withrow of Owensboro, an outstanding player at Central City in the mid-'50s, and Delmas Gish of Central City, coach of the Golden Tide during the team's glory years in the '40s and '50s and later a referee, join the exclusive club.

Withrow was named as a player while Gish made the list as an official. Six other players, including Clem Haskins, three other officials and seven coaches were also named to the Hall of Fame. The latest additions were released during last week's state tournament.

Withrow led Central City to the Boys State Tournament Tournament in 1955 and 1956 and was also on the 1954 team that went to state. Although Central City lost in the first round all three years, Withrow nevertheless was named to the All-Tournament team in 1955 and 1956.

Withrow is tied for third in the state tournament record book with 12 field goals in a half.

Gish's 1945 Golden Tide team lost the championship game to Male, which was led by Ralph Beard.

McGill, the former sports editor of the Lexington Herald, has been attending the Boys State Tournament for 51 years. He covered 27 state tournaments for the Herald and the Ashland Independent. Each year he publishes the Sweet 16 Record Book.

Corky Withrow, Golden Tide Senior, 1956

Pictured here is the 1956 South squad that defeated the North squad in the "Chuck Taylor North-South All-Star Classic" held on the campus of the Murray State that summer. The South won 103-95. Corky scored 4 in this game, and Greenville's Roger Newman scored 6. Fred LaCour with 18, was named "Mr. Basketball" at the conclusion. Jackie Moreland, a U. of K. signee,as was Corky and Roger, led the South with 21. Kelly Coleman, although selected to the South's squad, was a no-show. In this photo, in no particular order, are the following players and the colleges each would eventually play for: Gene Arrington (Texas Tech), Carney Crisler (Utah), Albert Ellison (Western Kentucky), Howard Hunt (Duke), Fred LaCour (San Francisco), Jackie Moreland #33 (Louisiana Tech), Roger Newman #20 ((Kentucky), Jack Pirrie (Vanderbilt), Dick Soergel (Oklahoma State), Dennis Walker (Oklahoma A&M), Corky Withrow #31 (Georgetown College), The coaches for the South were Willis Hudson and Charles Huhn.

Mr. and Mrs. Delmas Gish, center front, are applauded at a Central City High Class of '56 reunion. Directly behind Mr. Gish is Corky, and to Corky's left is his former teammate, Billy Mason.

The 1959 Georgetown College Tigers. Seated at front: Tom Chaney, manager. Front row: Phillips, Dunnivan, Otis, Goode, Carter, Mitchell, Duvall. Second row: Coach Bob Davis, Grote, Gering, Westerfield, Wilson, Smith, Jones, Richert, Brown, Craig, Withrow, Farris, Williams, Assistant Coach David Cotrell.

The 1959 Georgetown College Tigers. The starting five: Withrow, Grote, Jones, Williams, Smith.

Corky, #22, shoots over a Bellarmine defender at Georgetown.

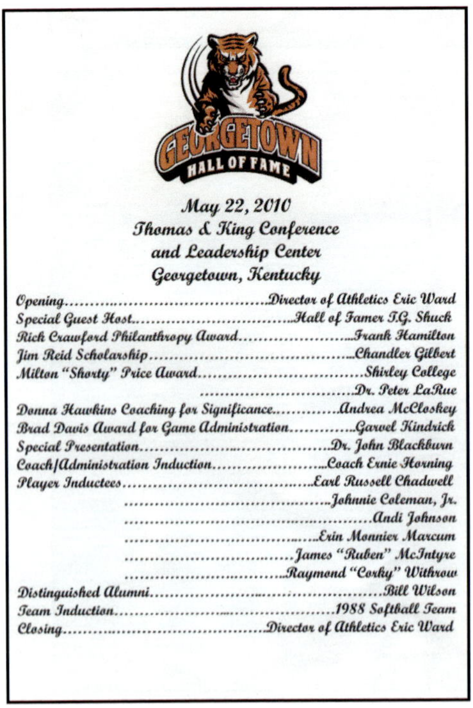

GEORGETOWN
HALL OF FAME

May 22, 2010
Thomas & King Conference
and Leadership Center
Georgetown, Kentucky

Opening..........Director of Athletics Eric Ward
Special Guest Host..........Hall of Famer T.G. Shuck
Rick Crawford Philanthropy Award..........Frank Hamilton
Jim Reid Scholarship..........Chandler Gilbert
Milton "Shorty" Price Award..........Shirley College
..........Dr. Peter LaRue
Donna Hawkins Coaching for Significance..........Andrea McCloskey
Brad Davis Award for Game Administration..........Garvel Kindrick
Special Presentation..........Dr. John Blackburn
Coach/Administration Induction..........Coach Ernie Horning
Player Inductees..........Earl Russell Chadwell
..........Johnnie Coleman, Jr.
..........Andi Johnson
..........Erin Monnier Marcum
..........James "Ruben" McIntyre
..........Raymond "Corky" Withrow
Distinguished Alumni..........Bill Wilson
Team Induction..........1988 Softball Team
Closing..........Director of Athletics Eric Ward

Georgetown College Hall of Fame Class of 2010

Dr. Bob Davis was Corky's basketball coach at Georgetown during his two seasons of college ball ('58 and '59). Coach Davis's success at the small Scott County School included a fourth-place NAIA National Tournament finish in '58, and a runner-up trophy in the same Tournament in '61. Coach Davis would go on to coach at Auburn University, as well as later being inducted into both the NAIA Hall of Fame and Georgetown College Hall of Fame.

Corky with the ball vs. Louisville at Freedom Hall in 1959. Georgetown won the game.

Chapter 13

Waycross to Wellsville

Amidst the turbulence and turmoil that always seemed to swirl around his college basketball days, Corky had baseball to anticipate. His first professional season (1956) could hardly be counted as a step forward, as there had been only a few weeks with Evansville late that summer. Then, to his great disappointment, came the eligibility issues that voided any chances to play basketball at Kentucky, Murray, and Kentucky Wesleyan. But still, through it all, there was a ray of sunshine, and that was baseball.

Corky's instructions for spring training '57 included reporting to the Milwaukee's minor league training facility near Waycross, Georgia. Here, near the headwaters of the Okefonokee Swamp in Ware County, he would join 300 or so other baseball hopefuls, each vying for a spot on the roster of one of Milwaukee's Class A to Class D teams.

For anyone having been associated with the Braves organization, Waycross memories are plentiful. When the Boston Braves moved to Milwaukee in March, 1953, they brought with them this training facility located near the swamp and about ten miles from the city of Waycross. This camp was specifically for the lower echelon of the Braves farm system and would remain as such throughout the entire history of the organization (1953-65). In an article titled "The Red Clay of Waycross: Spring Training in Georgia with the Milwaukee Braves" by Daniel Papillon and Bill Young (published in *2010 The National Pastime)*, a detailed description of baseball in Waycross is provided. Much of the following material about the Braves' Waycross days is summarized from Papillon and Young's article, but with Corky's memories and experiences added.

The town of Waycross had a long history with professional baseball. In 1898, the Chicago Colts, forerunners of the Cubs, began training here, but soon found the town to be "too temperant" to suit the appetites of thirsty players and team officials. A lack of entertainment and a sub-par "podunk hotel"—one with two bathtubs for eighteen men—added to the decision to abandon the town. Efforts were made to bring baseball here again in 1906 and 1913, but these also failed.

Semi-professional ball did return with more success in the mid-twenties when "Shoeless Joe" Jackson managed the Waycross Coastliners to a Georgia State Championship in 1924. Jackson, reputed to have been involved in the 1919 "Black Sox" scandal, had been banned from big league baseball in 1920, but continued managing and playing ball throughout Georgia and South Carolina after this. He maintained his innocence until his death in 1951. An often-told story, one connected with Jackson's life after baseball, spread after he opened a liquor store in Greenville, South Carolina, in 1933. Ty Cobb and Grantland Rice entered his store, the story goes, with Joe making no indications of knowing either man. Cobb and Rice made their purchases with nothing said. Cobb, choosing to remain quiet no longer, asked Jackson, "Don't you know who I am, Joe?" Jackson replied, "Sure I know you, Ty, but I wasn't sure you wanted to know me."

During Milwaukee's first season in 1953, teams representing five cities from five different leagues trained at the Waycross facility. This many clubs training at one site certainly wasn't the norm, but was part of the Braves' philosophy of placing all their young players together and under the close scrutiny of a multitude of managers, coaches, and scouts. With this "mass production" system, it was intended that players would progress faster than otherwise might be expected. To a degree it worked, at least in the earliest years.

Corky arrived in Waycross for his initial training experience after driving from Central City in his 1950 "James Dean-looking" Mercury. Issued a standard gray uniform after signing the register in the camp's administration building, Corky was handed a cloth number with instructions to sew it on his uniform shirt. Corky can't recall any numbers issued to him, but can laughingly narrow it down to somewhere between 1 and 350!

It was the responsibility of each player to furnish his own glove and cleats, but, if needed, the major sporting good companies always had salesmen with ample stock on hand. This wasn't necessary for Corky, however, as he had brought his own cleats and Nokona brand fielder's mitt from home. Later during his career, his gloves and cleats would come from MacGregor, a company—along with Louisville Slugger—with which he had signed a contract.

The Waycross training facility was fairly remote, and Corky remembers a tar surfaced road that wound through pines and swamplands before coming to an isolated opening. Here, in this clearing, were nine buildings and five baseball diamonds.

The history of the Waycross facility predates its baseball days, once serving our nation as an Air Force base during World War II. After the war, a one-half mile section was purchased and cut out for the training site of the Boston Braves. The Braves organization considered it a perfect site, as it was spacious and remote enough to eliminate any distractions that might interfere with their trainees' progress.

When the Boston Braves moved to Milwaukee in '53, the training camp included four diamonds laid out in a cloverleaf fashion. A fifth diamond, one separate from these, was soon added. In the center of the cloverleaf was a two-story cylindrical brick rotunda that served as an observation point for the many managers, scouts, and coaches that oversaw the training. All five diamonds were in constant use, and the shape of the tower allowed easy observation on all but the newest diamond.

The camp had nine buildings for use by the team and its officials. All nine were wooden vintage World War II and located in wooded areas away from the diamonds. A large building to the north served as a clubhouse, while another served as private offices for managers and administrators. A recreation room complete with a television and card table was also available in this building.

Shuffleboard, horseshoe pits, ping-pong, and a juke box were available for player use during free time, and there were movies shown three nights a week. But there was also an 11:00 p.m. curfew.

North of the administration building were six barracks where the players bunked. These long, narrow, wooden buildings had once served the Air Force in the same capacity, and little had changed in the decade since. The beds were bunk-style, and nearby were "very basic" bathroom facilities.

For meals the players reported to the cafeteria located in an old army mess hall. This was a square room complete with picnic-style tables. An open kitchen provided three meals a day, including a substantial breakfast and a light lunch of soup, milk, a Hershey bar, an orange, and an apple. A much more substantial dinner was served in the evening.

Each morning players were up and dressed before dawn. All would gather around a bulletin board to receive their individual daily assignments, listed with the name of the manager to whom each was assigned that day. The list was changed daily, so players were moved from manager to manager throughout their weeks in camp.

Morning workouts consisted of light calisthenics, infield and outfield drills, and, according to Corky, "plenty of batting practice." During the first three weeks of training there were afternoon games, usually against "in-house" teams, but on occasion an outside team would provide the competition. There would be morning games added to the agenda later in the spring, but Sunday mornings were always free for church services, rest, or whatever leisure activities the players chose. Sunday afternoon games always followed, however.

After several weeks of training, the players would learn their fate. This happened on the final day of camp and, like the daily assignments, would come via the barracks bulletin board. This time managerial assignments weren't just for the day, but instead, for the entire season. At least, that was the plan!

Sadly, not everyone would find their name on a manager's list on that final day of camp. "If you didn't, you looked on a pink sheet," Corky explains. "If you saw your name on that sheet, you knew you were being cut and would report to the administration building to receive your unconditional release. I saw guys brought to tears when this happened."

Corky attended spring training at Waycross three times during his career. He never read his name from the pink sheet, and when he left baseball in 1966, it was his decision to do so and, for the most part, on his own terms. Relatively few stay in minor league baseball as long as Corky, and even fewer can say it was their decision to leave. Corky can.

On the final day of the '57 spring training, Corky found his name listed on the managerial roster of Alex "Al" Monchak. Monchak was to be the manager of the Wellsville Braves, Milwaukee's Class D affiliate in the New York-Pennsylvania League. This league had formerly been the Pennsylvania-Ontario-New York League, so folks still called it the "PONY."

With his assignment to Wellsville and the conclusion of training that day, Corky packed his gear and headed to Central City in preparation for the drive to Wellsville. The distance to Wellsville was over 800 miles, and his plans called for driving straight through. Once there, he would be far from family and friends and truly on his own. But the excitement and anticipation that came from playing baseball on a daily basis far outweighed any thoughts of homesickness. Life didn't get any better than this!

Wellsville was a town of "maybe 4,000," Corky estimates, and was located in south-central New York, not far from the Pennsylvania border. It was quaintly picturesque with fine Victorian homes and a main street that wouldn't have been out of place in a Norman Rockwell painting. The surrounding countryside, nestled near the foothills of the Appalachians, was highly fertile farmland, but was also rich with oil, although not as much as during a past oil boom. If one could substitute coal for oil, Wellsville wasn't unlike Central City. All in all, it was a good fit for Corky, but his plans certainly didn't include an extended stay.

For those old enough to remember him, Wellsville was the hometown of George "Gabby" Hayes. Hayes was born in 1885 in Stannards, New York, a community located on the outskirts of Wellsville. Gabby's father owned and managed a small hotel there.

While still a high school student, Gabby played semi-pro baseball with some promise of a future in the game. But this future never materialized, as he chose to drop out of school and run away with a circus in 1902. From here, Hayes went on to become a successful vaudeville performer, prospered, but then lost everything when the stock market crashed in '29. Not one to give up, Gabby ventured to Hollywood to try the movies. His plans panned out in a big way, and many movie and television roles followed. Hayes died in Hollywood in 1969.

Many times Corky had seen Gabby Hayes on the big screen at the State in Central City. His Saturdays were often filled with matinee movies featuring Hayes as the grizzled and bearded side-kick of Roy Rogers, Tom Mix, Gene Autry, "Hopalong" Cassidy, and even John Wayne. But now, in 1957, he wasn't in Wellsville to pay homage to any movie star—Corky was here to play baseball.

Corky reported to Tullar Field on arrival in Wellsville. Here, along the banks of the Genesse River (a tributary of Lake Ontario), the Braves played ball and team management had their offices. Old Tullar Field is gone now, replaced by a Wellsville city park.

Corky had no plans for lodging when he walked into the office that day, but was informed by an office staffer that several of his teammates roomed at a house owned and managed by an elderly woman. Following this lead, he soon had a room at "Mrs. Buering's Boarding House." Since he was willing to share this room with a teammate, his part of the weekly rent was only $15, but the deal came with both a "no cooking" and "no women" clause. Corky had no problem with the no-cooking rule—there were plenty of diners in town—but the "no women" clause was a bit more problematic. And as for his landlord's ability to enforce these rules, "Mrs. Buering had a real keen sense of hearing for an old woman," Corky assures.

Each of the Wellsville players was provided meal money when the team was on the road, but otherwise paid their own food, rent, and entertainment expenses... not that there was much entertainment to be found in Wellsville! There was a drive-in movie, a couple of movie theatres, some diners and carhops, of course, but more importantly, at least to Corky, there were pool rooms. It was the pool halls that he and his teammates frequented when practice or a game wasn't in progress. Here, they gathered to kill time and, if skilled enough, earn a few extra dimes and quarters from the pockets of those less proficient. For Corky, this meant all the time spent honing his skills in the pool palaces of Central City would now pay dividends.

Corky enjoyed the '57 season in Wellsville. In most of the games he was a starting outfielder, the position he most enjoyed, but occasionally would play first. In his team's opening game, at home, he collected his first hit as a professional. It was in his second at-bat and, to his great satisfaction, was a homerun. "It was a feeling of exuberance I can't start to explain," he proclaims, "and words can't describe how I felt rounding the bases that day."

For Corky, this homerun marked the beginning of a career that would generally follow the same pattern throughout. At age nineteen he was built for power at 6'4", 197 lbs., and had, even as a boy, been bigger, stronger, and faster than others his age. Now it was still so, and with big arms, big hands, and a powerful batting stride, the sky was the limit, literally!

The Class D Wellsville Braves played in the eight-team PONY with the Erie Sailors, Corning Red Sox, Batavia Indians, Jamestown Falcons, Olean Oilers, Elmira Pioneers, and Hornell Redlegs. All these were within a two hour travel distance, so all team travel was by bus. Because of the close proximity of the teams, overnight stays were rare, but Corky does recall a three game overnight series when the team traveled to Erie, Pennsylvania, to take on the Sailors.

Wellsville won the regular season pennant with a 74-43 record that summer and followed this with a playoff title earned by defeating both Hornell and Olean in a four team league tournament.

Things went great individually for Corky, too. He played in 116 of the team's 117 games, most as a starter, and amassed 115 hits in 446 at-bats for a solid .258 average. Records show he had 19 homeruns to lead the team, but Corky insists he had 20! There were also 4 triples and 20 doubles. His 200 total bases ranked him as the team's second highest in this category.

The manager of Wellsville, forty year old Alex "Al" Monchak, was a career baseball man who had played a short stint with the

Phillies in 1940, served our nation in World War II, and would then spend the rest of his baseball years as a scout, coach, and manager.

Corky wasn't fond of Monchak's coaching, but the two somehow managed to make it through the season with no major flare-ups. "He was what I call a rah-rah type coach," Corky explains. "I never cared for that at all. We were supposed to be professionals now and motivated on our own without all that back-slapping stuff."

Other than his distain for Monchak's coaching style, most things about Wellsville were to Corky's liking. Otis and Flo Eva even made the long drive to New York to watch him play ball a few days, and Corky enjoyed the time they spent together.

But not all things went smoothly on the diamond, and one scary incident came close to ending his career early on. Explains Corky:

> I had just stepped in the batter's box to hit. While I was diggin' in, and before I looked up, something hit me in the side of the head. I dropped to the ground in terrible pain, but had no idea what had happened, or what had hit me at first. But I do remember thinking I had hit myself with my bat while taking a practice swing. It knocked me to the ground and everything was a haze. What had happened was their pitcher had quick-pitched me. I don't remember the pitcher's name, but he hit me in the side of my head, in front of my ear. It bent the frame of my glasses into a v-shape, and I really believe those glass frames were the only thing that saved my life. They had to carry me off the field that day, and I'm lucky to be alive.

With his first full season of pro baseball over, Corky headed back to Central City, confident he wouldn't be returning to Wellsville and Class D ball the following season.

At the conclusion of Georgetown College's fourth place finish in the 1958 NAIA National Tournament, Corky headed to Waycross for the second of his three spring training camps at "Bravesville." It was his belief that a good spring, added to his fine performance with Wellsville the previous summer, would solidify his chances of climbing a wrung or more up the ladder of Milwaukee's farm system.

He did have the great spring he desired, and friendships made there lasted long after his baseball days ended. One new teammate, Merritt Ranew, would come to be one of his closest friends throughout his time in baseball.

Merritt Ranew was born in Albany, Georgia, in 1937, and in 1957 was signed by the Milwaukee organization. The two, Merritt and Corky, became close friends while at Waycross, and their paths frequently crossed over the next few years. Merritt would have considerably more major league success than Corky, playing for the expansion Colt.45s in '62, the Cubs in '63, the Braves in '65, and later the Giants and Angels.

A horrendous baseball incident in 1966 came close to ending Ranew's career, however, and was one that would surely rate as one of the ugliest and bloodiest moments ever in professional sports history. This happened in Vancouver, Canada, while Merritt was catching for the Seattle Angels, an affiliate of the California Angels. On the mound for Seattle in this game was Jim Coates.

When Coates hit Ricardo Joseph on the shoulder with a pitch, Joseph charged the mound to retaliate. But before he could reach Coates, Joseph was tackled from behind by Ranew, who was running to the aid of his pitcher. With Merritt's tackle of Joseph, both benches emptied, and a wide-spread fight ensued. Joseph's chin was bloodied during the brawl.

After a measure of order was restored, Vancouver's next batter, Tom Reynolds, bunted the ball down the first base line. Coates, charging to field the ball, collided with Reynolds, who had made no effort to get out of Coates' path. Ranew, in an effort to aid Coates once again, stormed from the plate. Again, both benches emptied.

Waiting in the Vancouver on-deck circle was the Mounties' Santiago Rosario. With bat in hand, Rosario charged from the circle to deliver a powerful and skull-rattling blow to Ranew's head. The blow was hard enough to cause a three inch gash, internal bleeding, and paralysis of the left side of Merritt's head.

Corky's friend underwent surgery to remove a blood clot, followed by seventy-two hours of unconsciousness and a three week stay in the hospital. There was constant fear of his death throughout. Corky, although far away in Syracuse, New York, kept closely informed concerning his friend's struggle for life during this dark time.

Amazingly, Merritt recovered. But perhaps even more amazing was his return to baseball during the '69 season. A lawsuit was filed against the Vancouver Mounties and Santiago Rosario, and Ranew won the case in court.

After his retirement from baseball, Merritt returned to Georgia, becoming a highly respected trainer of championship horses near Valdosta. He also co-owned an Albany nightclub called the Jolly Fox. This club hosted several famous entertainers over the years, including the off-beat comedian Tiny Tim.

The close friendship between Corky and Merritt lasted far beyond their playing days, but as often happens as years pass, contact became less frequent. Merritt Ranew passed away on October 18, 2011, in Valdosta without Corky's knowledge. Deeply saddened when told later, Corky found it hard to understand why he hadn't been contacted with the news.

On the final day of training at Waycross in 1958, Corky was stunned to learn of his reassignment to the Wellsville Braves. "I felt cheated," he recalls. "When I saw my name on that list, I knew immediately I wasn't going back there. I told them I was going home... and I meant it! I didn't have my car with me that spring, but I found a ride back to Central City."

For this ride back to Kentucky, Corky turned to another new acquaintance, Em Lindbeck. Emerit Lindbeck was a former star baseball player and All-American quarterback at the University of Illinios and was drafted by the Los Angeles Rams. But, like Corky, Em had options. He chose to play baseball.

Lindbeck was married, and the couple still resided in their hometown of Kewanee, Illinois. When training camp ended, Em would be headed to Kewanee to pick up his wife and then report to his assigned team. Em wasn't assigned to Wellsville that season, but he and Corky would be teammates later. Fortunately for Corky, Em's route back to Illinois would pass directly through Madisonville, a half hour drive from Central City.

Corky's mother picked him up when he arrived in Madisonville, but was not particularly happy with Corky's decision to come home under those circumstances. But, like any good mother, Flo Eva finally accepted it. For the next few days Corky pondered his future, sometimes mad at Braves management, at other times mad at himself.

It didn't take long for the phone to start ringing, however. The calls were from Braves management with requests to reconsider his decision. He rejected their pleas at first, but when one appeal included an offer of increased pay, he agreed. Corky's unintentional holdout had, at least in his mind, brought Braves management to their knees. Corky had won, and now his ego could rest.

This time there would be no "yappin, clappin" Al Monchak, as Wellsville had a new manager, Harry Minor. Minor had been drafted by Pittsburgh after his graduation from high school in 1946, and for a decade played with the Pirates and Athletics, following this with minor league managing at Wellsville for three straight seasons. The '58 season was the first of these three. His greatest achievements would come later as a scout for the Braves and then the Mets. His scouting career stretched over a forty-four year period and included discovering several outstanding major leaguers, including Dwight Gooden, Darrell Strawberry, Lenny Dykstra, and Mookie Wilson.

Harry Minor was only thirty in 1958, and although managing Wellsville, was one of the team's day-to-day players as well. In 402 at-bats that season, he hit for a .289 batting average while hammering out 17 homeruns.

When Corky arrived in Wellsville for his second full season, he again rented a room at the boarding establishment of Ms. Buering.

This time he roomed with Wally Lozano, a married ballplayer from Albany, New York. Wally would play only one year in the minors, but would move on to have a highly successful baseball career with the Brantford Red Sox of the Canadian Professional League. Lozano passed away in 2010, but his baseball legacy lives on in Canada's Baseball Hall of Fame in St. Mary's, Ontario.

Corky's second season at Wellsville proved even better than his first. His individual stats rose significantly, and the Braves again won the regular season pennant, this time with a 70-56 record. However, the team failed to repeat as the leagues' playoff champs.

The records show Corky played in all of his team's 117 games and had 132 hits in 447 at-bats for an impressive .295 batting average. He also had 3 triples, 24 doubles, and 258 total bases. His 32 homeruns led the league and were 15 more than Wellsville's second leading homerun hitter, Manager Harry Minor. Corky also had 8 stolen bases, a .577 slugging percentage, 142 RBIs, and 81 base-on-balls. He struck out 123 times.

Statistically, this season would prove one of his best in pro ball, and this didn't go unnoticed by league officials and fans. Many felt he was the strongest candidate to be named the league's MVP, an honor officially labeled the Robert C. Stedier Award. This was given to the player deemed, somewhat awkwardly, "most-likely to go the furtherest in baseball."

Corky admits to having expected this award that season and was disappointed when he learned it had been presented to Bob Risenhoover, a pitcher with the Geneva Redlegs. Risenhoover would follow with five more seasons of minor league ball, but that was at far as he would get. If going the "furtherest in baseball" was the criteria for this award, Corky would have, indeed, been the better choice.

Corky, asked for other specific memories from this season, offered one involving a competitor. That competitor was a brash and cocky young player named Joe Pepitone. Pepitone, a first baseman with the Auburn Yankees, was already a "dandy" in every sense of the word. "He thought very highly of himself and wasn't easy to like," Corky bluntly explains.

Pepitone was just beginning his career in baseball that season, but already had a reputation as potential trouble. Most of this reputation evolved from his high school days, including one incident in which he was shot in the stomach during a schoolyard brawl.

As expected, trouble and mischief followed Pepitone throughout his baseball days, with most of this resulting from his fun loving, "devil-may-care" attitude. His self-destructive ways could be blamed for his failure to reach his immense potential, as he became more of a bad boy celebrity than the consistent top-notch performer he might have been. Still, the talent was there, proven with his three Gold Gloves and three All-Star game appearances.

As a final note on Joe, something should be said about his well-reputed vanity. A story is told that Pepitone often carried with him a bag of hair products, one that included two toupees. One of these toupees was his so-called game hair, worn under his Yankee cap during games, while the other was his town hair, worn for those frequent nights on the town.

Chapter 14

Corky's Got a Ticket to Ride

In the late winter/early spring of 1959 Corky headed to Waycross for his third and final time. This would mark the beginning of his fourth season as a professional ballplayer.

Again things went well, and with his impressive showing at Wellsville the previous two seasons, he wasn't surprised with his assignment to the Class A Jacksonville Braves of the South Atlantic League. The jump from Class D to Class A baseball was a significant one.

Jacksonville competed against seven teams spread across the southeast. The seven "SALLY" teams were the Knoxville Smokies, Macon Dodgers, Charlotte Hornets, Charleston Chasox, Columbus Pirates, Asheville Tourists, and Savannah Reds. Corky especially enjoyed playing in the ballpark at Charlotte, as he hit three homeruns in his team's first series visit there that season.

Prior to their affiliation with Milwaukee, Jacksonville had fielded a largely unsuccessful minor league team called the Tars, a team affiliated with the New York Giants. In '53 the club became the Braves, and was soon the first in their league to integrate when they acquired Hank Aaron, Felix Mantilla, and Horace Garner. By the time Corky was playing for Jacksonville, the team was owned by Texas millionaire Craig F. Cullinan, Jr. and was playing ball at Wolfson Park. Jacksonville's ownership changed in '59, and with the change became the Jets. One year later it changed again, this time becoming the Suns—a St. Louis farm-affiliate Corky would play for in early '64.

The quality of the players at this level was significantly higher than that of Wellsville, and Corky found himself playing on a team with several future big leaguers. Among these were Denny Lemaster, Manny Jimenez, Cecil Butler, Bob Botz, John DeMerit, Daryl Robertson, Bob Uecker, and Merritt Ranew, his close friend and former teammate from Waycross and Wellsville.

Bob Uecker would make it to the majors as a catcher, but his less-than-spectacular baseball career would be followed by a much more successful run as a baseball broadcaster, comedian, and television personality. His numerous appearances with Johnny Carson on latenight television prompted Carson to label him "Mr. Baseball."

Among the many comical stories told about Uecker is one concerning his inept attempts to catch the knuckleball-throwing Phil Niekro when both were with Milwaukee. Uecker accumulated a record-breaking number of passed balls due to Niekro's tricky and unpredictable pitches during this time. Rather than offer excuses for his failures, however, the self-effacing catcher offered the following advice to anyone with the responsibility of catching a knuckleballer. "The best way to catch a knuckleball," Uecker explained, "is to wait until it stops rolling, and then pick it up."

Corky enjoyed his time as a teammate of Uecker at Jacksonville—and later at Denver—and still laughs when his name comes up. "He was an average catcher and hitter, but lots of fun to be around," Corky recalls. "He was the clown prince of the locker room, but most of the stories I could tell about him shouldn't be in print."

Corky was now making "about $900 a month," and with this could afford to share rent for a small house on the beach near Jacksonville. Sharing rent with him was his teammate Daryl Robertson. "We spent a lot of time on the beach watching the pretty girls," Corky admits, "and I can assure you it was a whole lot more fun than living in Buering's boarding house."

Jacksonville's manager, Sebastian "Sibby" Sisti, was a gravel-voiced, sad-eyed, self-effacing man who had served as a utility player for the Boston Braves and, during the '53-'54 seasons, the Milwaukee Braves. His baseball career included playing every position except pitcher and catcher, as well as accumulating so many baseball injuries requiring stitches that teammates tagged him "The Embroidered Man."

Sisti would follow his managing days with a role as a movie technical advisor for *The Natural*, as his expertise at most every baseball position more than qualified him for the job. The movie even came with an acting role for Sibby, this as the manager of the Pittsburgh Pirates.

"Sibby enjoyed people, and people loved Sibby," explains Corky. "He was a delight to be around and could get the most out of his players for that same reason." But even with his admiration and respect for Manager Sisti, things were happening in Milwaukee's front office that would cause Corky's time in Jacksonville to sour. It had nothing to do with his manager, however, and Corky admits the end results could mostly be traced to his own stubbornness.

According to Corky, the roots of the ensuing disagreement with Milwaukee management stems from their decision to have Sisti play him at first base on a daily basis. Corky had played first with teams before, but not every day. "I wanted to play in the outfield, but someone in the Braves's front office decided to turn me into a full time first baseman," he complains. Corky assumes the order came from Birdie Tebbetts, the former Cincinnati Reds manager who, in October of '58, was hired by the Milwaukee Braves to serve as their Executive Vice-President.

Corky, after reading an article in Sports Illustrated that summer, concluded that Tebbetts was preparing him to fill the shoes of the aging Milwaukee first-baseman, Joe Adcock. Corky explains:

> They were wanting a power hitter to replace Adcock, and I guess they figured I might be the one. Joe had been with them for several years, and they knew his playing days were about over. Understand... this is just a possibility, but when I read Tebbetts' quote in the magazine where he said he "could see Corky Withrow playing first base for the Braves," I couldn't help but come to that conclusion. I was my own worst enemy by letting it bother me so much, but I just didn't want to play first every day.

It's hard to understand why Corky resisted the move from outfield to first as much as he did. Most young players would have been happy with the opportunity to replace a veteran on any major league roster, regardless of the position involved. But not Corky Withrow!

There was certainly a chance Corky's theory was right, but perhaps the Braves were simply thinking a few years down the road in Corky's case. Joe Adcock would be with the Braves through the '62 season, at which time he was dealt to Cleveland. Adcock finished his career with the Angels after the '66 season and died in Louisiana in May of 1999.

Regardless of the specifics, Corky allowed this disagreement over his role with the team to affect his performance. After starting the season strong with 8 homeruns in the first three weeks, his production declined, and no homeruns followed. In the fifty-seven games he played with Jacksonville that year, sixteen found him in the outfield, and forty-one at first base. Statistically, there were 41 hits in 186 at-bats for a .220 average, 8 homeruns, no triples, 8 doubles, and 33 base-on-balls. He "whiffed" 57 times.

After only fifty-seven games with Jacksonville, Corky was informed by Sisti that he was to report to Milwaukee's Class B team in Cedar Rapids. It was now Goodbye sunny beaches of Florida... Hello cornfields of Iowa! He blames none of this on Sisti, of course, realizing his manager did only what he was told to do. Along with his uncompromising stubbornness over the first base issue, Corky admits his love of the beach lifestyle hurt, too. Still, when told to report to Cedar Rapids, he claims he wasn't upset.

It was in late June, the best Corky can recall, when Sisti had told him of his demotion to Class B ball at Cedar Rapids. This club played in the Triple I and, once again, he would be playing on a team managed by Alex Monchak. The two had no fondness for each other while at Wellsville, but they had managed to avoid any real problems. But this time the shaky relationship would end in shambles.

Even with Monchak as his manager, Corky admits to having enjoyed most of his time at Cedar Rapids. "We played in Veterans Memorial Stadium... a nice park... 325 down the lines, with a constant wind blowing in from left," he notes. Even with this wind, his first trip to the plate resulted in a long, towering grand slam over the light pole in left field. This was a refreshing start to his time here, especially after the homerun drought he had experienced at Jacksonville previously.

The grand slam that night was truly a thing of beauty. It was hit so high and so far that the umpires lost sight of the ball in the darkness of an approaching electrical storm. Having lost sight, the umps—unsure as to fair or foul—debated the issue for several minutes before ruling it a homerun. Claims Corky, "The crowd would have rioted if the umpires had declared that one foul!"

There was another hit he vividly recalls from that same first game in Cedar Rapids, this one, Corky describes, "between the hat and the head!" After hitting the grand slam previously, the opponent's pitcher was in a bad mood. "He threw at me the next time and hit me in the head," Corky groans. "But I was too woosey and wobbly to retaliate. I was just thankful to be alive!"

It was a good season for grand slams, as it turned out. Corky clobbered three more in Veterans that season, and then added another when the club traveled to Lincoln, Nebraska, to play the Chiefs. Five grand slams in one season was impressive in any league and on any level!

Corky shared a Cedar Rapids apartment with Wynton Overstreet. "Wynton was real laid-back, but real tight with his money," Corky chuckles. "He was married with a wife back in his hometown and sent whatever money he made to her." When the team was on the road, Corky roomed with his pal, Merritt Ranew. Others of note on the Cedar Rapid roster were Dick Kelley, Tony Cloninger, Larry Maxie, and Denis Menke, all big leaguers at one time or another.

As the season progressed, Corky's relationship with Monchak regressed. There were several run-ins, including one that ultimately destroyed what was never more than a seemingly peaceful coexistence between the two. This incident happened when the team was in Burlington, Iowa, to play the Bees.

When the Braves's team bus arrived at the hotel to drive them the short distance to the ballpark, Corky was there, on time and ready to go. But his roommate, Merritt Ranew, wasn't to be found. No one on the team had seen or heard from Merritt, nor were his whereabouts known.

Corky, good buddy that he was, stepped off the bus to return to their hotel room in hopes of finding him there. Finding this to not be the case, Corky headed back outside to re-board the bus, but the bus was gone! "I was mad as hell," Corky fumes. "All I had done was to go back looking for Merritt, and Monchak knew that!" Corky continues:

> I remember thinking that if they couldn't wait a couple more minutes for me, then I must not be very important or needed. If they didn't need me, then why should I bother going to the ballpark at all? The hotel wasn't that far from the stadium, and I could have walked there, but I was in no mood to do that. I decided to go back to my room.
>
> After a little while in my room, I decided to go down to the hotel's bar and drink a beer. While I was sitting at the bar some women came in and sat down. We started talking, but it wasn't too long before I could tell that someone was standing right behind me. I turned around, and there was Monchak. What could I say? It wasn't a good situation for me, and there wasn't much I could do or say to defend myself. He wasn't happy that I hadn't come on to the ballpark, and there I sat in the hotel bar.

The following day brought a $50 fine for Corky. That doesn't seem much today, but that was a hefty amount for a minor leaguer then. But more importantly, the already tense relationship between the two had reached a boiling point. "I remember Monchak telling me that the Milwaukee front office already had a file 'this thick' on me," Corky laughs. "But I can't confirm they did."

Even with the tumultuous situation between the two, the season in Cedar Rapids was good for Corky statistically. The team finished with a losing record, but he had hit for an impressive .323 batting average, a result of having 80 hits in 248 at-bats in seventy-five games. There were 19 homeruns, 61 RBIs, 13 doubles, and a .621 slugging percentage. He struck out 79 times.

It was during this season that Corky was drafted into the military. Oddly, his enlistment would be with a Reserve unit from Wisconsin—a state Corky had never visited! But since he had signed a Milwaukee baseball contract, Wisconsin law required his enlistment.

Monchak—no surprise to Corky—had a problem with his leaving the team to travel to Wisconsin for the required physical and other tests, but, as Corky points out, "There wasn't an option; I was told to report there." Monchak's argument was based on his belief that all exams and paper work could be handled in Cedar Rapids rather than Wisconsin. But the U.S. Army wasn't interested in Al's opinion, so, despite Monchak's rantings and ravings, Corky reported to Wisconsin as instructed.

Corky's military stint began that October when he traveled to Rolla, Missouri, the site of Ft. Leonard Wood. Here, in what had once been a WWII prison camp for captured German and Italian soldiers, he underwent six weeks of basic-training and began his six months enlistment period.

Camp Wood had a basketball "base team," one that would play teams from other army bases, but that squad would accept no six month enlistees like Corky. Since Corky was not eligible for this squad, he had to settle for a spot on his "company team," a squad limited to games played only at Camp Wood. Corky had no problems making the roster of his company squad that fall, and in the team's first game, burned the opposition with a 51 point performance. This impressive total didn't go unnoticed.

The following morning Corky was out of the barracks early with his company and on a strenuous hike to a bivouac. An army truck soon pulled alongside, he noticed, and his company's sergeant was seen talking with the driver. "I didn't know what was going on, but my sergeant walked over and told me to get in the truck," he explains. "I didn't mind that at all." Once in the truck, Corky was driven back to the barracks where he was met by the coach of the Ft. Wood base team. The coach explained that the eligibility rules had been changed that morning, and six-month enlistees were now eligible for his squad. After being offered a spot on this squad, Corky, without hesitation, accepted. For once, a change in eligibility rules worked in his favor, and his 51 point performance had been the catalyst for that change.

With his inclusion on this roster, Corky was free to play basketball with, in his words, "almost no real, regular army duties to interfere." The team was often at other bases playing ball, and he can recall trips to St. Louis, Peoria, and several other Midwest cities and military installations—all while serving to protect the good people of Wisconsin! It was a sacrifice Corky felt compelled to make.

With the arrival of the new decade, twenty year old Corky Withrow was entering his fifth season of minor league ball, still under contract with the Milwaukee Braves. But this time he was pleased to learn he would be reporting to Lakeland, Florida, to train with the Detroit Tigers. This opportunity was a welcomed change. "It was great to be with players like Norm Cash, Al Kaline, Dick McAuliffe, and Jim Bunning, and I really wanted to stay," he says. "I guess the Tigers had an interest in acquiring my contract and had worked out a deal with Milwaukee to give me a look. But it didn't work out."

Corky had been to Detroit previously, and that trip had been back in the summer of '56 when he and Bobby Lee Foster had traveled there to attend a Tigers tryout at Briggs Stadium. The two had missed their flight from Louisville as a result of not hearing the departure announcement, but were able to catch a later flight. Corky did well enough to earn a contract offer from Detroit while there, and perhaps their interest in him traced back to that tryout. "They wanted me to sign with them then, but I guess I wasn't ready. It was a few weeks before I signed with Dick Keely and Milwaukee, and I wasn't sure what I wanted to do. Maybe it would have been better had I signed with them then, but I guess everyone has things they second-guess. I sure did enjoy playing in Briggs, though."

After three weeks of training in Lakeland, Jimmy Dykes, the Tigers' manager, informed Corky he was to leave camp and report to the Braves's Jacksonville club when that team finished their spring training. Along with the disappointment of not making Detroit's roster was the fact that his spring training had now been cut short, and he was heading back to Class A Jacksonville and the SALLY League.

With the frequent moves from team to team, manager to manager, and even teammates to teammates, one can legitimately question how minor leaguers dealt with the uncertainty and insecurity of a baseball career. Corky, in an effort to explain his thoughts on this, gave a shrug of the shoulders and a blunt "whatever," but after a moment of contemplation, added:

> I became pretty complacent about the moving and where I was at. The rosters were always different, and the managers, more times than not, were as interested in enhancing their own position in the organization as they were helping the players. Maybe that was okay, though. They moved as frequently as the players, so you never had much consistency or stability on a team. You could never predict what you would be facing from season to season, so if you liked a particular manager, coach, or teammate, there was no use expecting to be with him the next season. It was a revolving door all the time; in a sense, every man for himself.

The 1960 season would again find Corky on a roster with Merritt Ranew. The Jacksonville squad included a few other future big leaguers as well, and among these were Tommy Aaron (brother of Hank), Jim Hay (another close friend of Corky), and an up-and-coming pitcher and future Hall of Famer named Phil Niekro.

Corky remembers Niekro as "a strange little fellow who really didn't try to socialize much..., and just didn't try to fit in at all." Niekro, known to teammates as "Knucksie," was born in Blaine, Ohio, in 1939. His father, like Corky's, had been a coal miner and baseball player, but unlike Otis, Phil's father had the opportunity to play some semi-pro baseball.

Niekro was originally signed by the Braves in '59, but with only a $500 bonus. Phil would win 318 games during his career, a total that currently ranks 16th all time.

Niekro's "knuckler" was a thing of beauty to fans and teammates, but an absolute nightmare for the batters facing him. Pete Rose is said to have once remarked, "I work for three weeks to get my swing down pat, and Phil messes it up in one night." Phil's sometimes battery-mate, Bob Uecker, often had the unenviable task of catching these knucklers and described an incident in one game this way: "Phil struck out a hitter once, and I never touched the ball. The third strike hit me in the shin guard, bounced out to Clete Boyer at third base, and he threw out the runner at first. Talk about a weird assist... 1-5-3 on a strikeout!"

Jacksonville would win 70 and lose 69 that season, finishing in the middle of the league standings. Corky's stats show he played in 112 of their games, but failed to appear in twenty-seven others, a fact resulting from the poor relationship he had developed with the team's manager, Red Murff. Corky's homerun total here would reach only 13, and his .242 batting average was only so-so.

In thirty-one of these 112 games he had played first base—a sore spot during his previous stint in Jacksonville—but that wasn't the cause for his discontent this time around. The likable Sibby Sisti was no longer here, and in his place was John Robert "Red" Murff. "Murff didn't like me, and I sure didn't like Red Murff," Corky grumbles.

Red Murff (1921-2008) had played minor league ball throughout the fifties and was still playing during this '60 season at Jacksonville. He had even been named "Minor League Player of the Year" in '55 and followed this with two years of big league ball when he pitched a few games for Milwaukee in '56 and '57. He finished his playing days with the Louisville Colonels in '59 and then as player/manager with the Jacksonville team in 1960.

Murff's greatest success would come later when, as a scout for the New York Mets, he discovered several talented ballplayers, the most noted being Nolan Ryan and Jerry Koosman. Murff is also credited as being the man who convinced Phil Niekro to throw the knuckleball as his primary pitch—a skill that would carry Niekro into the Hall of Fame in Cooperstown.

Regardless of Murff's many successes, getting along with Corky Withrow wouldn't be one of them. There would be no middle ground in their ongoing mutual dislike, and the two avoided each other as much as possible.

Corky admits to spending excessive time at the beach again, this time headquartered in a beach front apartment he rented with Walt Matthews, the team's first baseman. Looking back, he's sure his beach activities had a negative effect on his game, and with the ongoing problems with his manager, his playing time gradually dwindled. Although it was obvious Murff was holding him out of games due to their personal conflicts, Corky sat quietly at the end of the dugout, watching his teammates play ball and ignoring Murff as much as possible. Obviously, something had to give.

Everything eventually came to a head when the team was in Asheville to play the Tourists. Corky had been held out of the starting lineup for the last few games, and so it was again. However, in the bottom of the eighth, with the Tourists about to bat, Murff yelled down the bench for Corky, instructing him to report to the outfield in place of his teammate, Len Gabrielson. Corky did as he was instructed.

Jacksonville quickly got the three outs to retire the Asheville batters, so the Braves returned to the dugout. As fate would have it, Corky was due up first in the top of the ninth. After pulling a bat from the rack, he walked to the on-deck circle to await his turn at the plate. But now Murff ordered him back to the dugout, as Jim Hay was being inserted to pinch hit in his place. This, needless to say, didn't sit well with Corky.

"I was as mad as I'd ever been," Corky claims. "When I stepped back in the dugout, I grabbed some bats from the rack, ran back out on the field, and slung the bats on top of a twenty foot high screen behind home plate." The hometown crowd, not sure of the reason for Corky's rage, reacted with both shock and delight at the spectacle unfolding on the field.

Murff, not sharing the crowd's delight with Corky's antics, darted from the dugout to confront him. With tempers flaring, Corky ripped off his uniform shirt and cap, slinging both at his charging manager. With both men finally spilling out weeks of built-up animosity, Corky briskly made his way through the dugout, into the clubhouse, and on to the team's hotel a few blocks from the ballpark.

Back in his hotel room now, Corky listened to the post-game report on the radio. The Braves were scheduled for another game against the Tourists the next afternoon, but Corky, realizing he had crossed the line, had already decided he wasn't playing another game for Red Murff. After all that had just transpired, he wasn't sure what the following day would bring, but was pretty sure it wouldn't be good. He was right.

Now, knowing the team would be leaving Asheville and heading to Knoxville following a game the next day, Corky devised a plan. "I called some friends in Central City and told them to bring my car to Knoxville to pick me up when the bus arrived at the ballpark the next day," he explains. "I was going home, but I wasn't telling Murff or anyone on the team this."

After a restless night, Corky arrived at the Asheville ballpark with the team about 10 that Sunday morning. There had been nothing said to him about his explosive episode the previous day, but the atmosphere was tense, to say the least. After going through the team's calisthenics and warm-up drills in a less-than-enthusiastic manner, Corky jogged to the outfield to shag fly balls hit by Manager Murff.

Making no effort to catch anything hit in his direction, Corky allowed baseballs to drop to his right, to his left, and at his feet. "I didn't move at all," he laughs. Murff saw no humor in this insubordination, of course, and grew angrier with each ball that plopped to the ground around Corky. Finally reaching his Corky Withrow-toleration limit, Murff yelled, "You sick Withrow?" "Playing for you, I might as well be," Corky replied. With this sarcastic and contemptuous response, Corky's day at the ballpark was over.

With Buddy Lear, Bobby Lee Foster, Joe Pruitt, and Larry Ray on the way from Central City, Corky's plan to go home was now fully in motion. Once the game against Asheville was over, the team would return to the hotel, board their bus, and then travel across the mountains to Knoxville. Still, he couldn't help but wonder what lay ahead. Was this the right decision? How would this action affect his future in baseball? Both were good questions that only time could answer, but his ego and youthful confidence had again won out. "I'm not the same person today that I was then," Corky confesses, "but with all the attention and adoration you received as a professional athlete at that age, it was real easy to overrate your own importance."

After boarding the team bus for Knoxville, and only a few miles down the road, the bus slowed, turning into the parking lot of the Asheville bus station. Nothing had been said about this stop until the team's trainer, Bill Cooper, rose from his seat to walk back to where Corky was seated. "Corky," Cooper said, "Red wants you to get off the bus here and says there's a ticket back to Jacksonville waiting for you in the terminal."

Corky hadn't seen this coming and wasn't sure what to do next. He had no choice but to exit the bus, of course, but what about his buddies driving from Central City to meet him? He had no way to contact them, and what would they do when they couldn't find him in Knoxville?

After considering his limited options, Corky chose to use the ticket to return to Jacksonville despite the inconvenience he had caused his Central City buddies. For the next few days Corky strolled the beach at his apartment, pondering his future and wondering what fines and punishment would come his way once Murff and the team returned.

Days later, with the return of his team for a home series, Corky grimly reported back, unsure as to what might happen. Nothing much was said as it turned out, "but the silence just about killed me," he acknowledges.

For the remaining few weeks of the season Corky spent most of his time watching baseball from the bench, as his relationship with Red Murff was way beyond repair. "I just wanted the season to end, and then get out of there," he claims.

Chapter 15

The Miserable Misfits of Mobile Bay

With the disastrous events of the '60 season at Jacksonville behind him, Corky looked to get his career back on track when spring training began in '61. He did just that! "It was a helluva spring, one of my best," he explains. "I played in every game and absolutely enjoyed every minute of my time there."

"There" was Riverside, California. Corky actually began his spring training in Palm Springs with the new expansion American League club, the California Angels, but after only a few days was sent to Riverside to train with the Angels' Class AAA affiliate, the Dallas/Ft. Worth Rangers. The Angels had been added to the American League in response to the recent addition of the New York Mets and Houston Colt.45s to the National League in October of 1960.

The Dallas/Ft. Worth club was a member of the American Association and had a working agreement with the Angels. Since California was a new team in need of players, and not one loaded with veterans, it seemed a prime opportunity for Corky to make a significant career move. This hadn't been the case when he trained with the Detroit Tigers previously.

Corky has no explanation for Milwaukee's decision to send him to the Rangers training that spring, but it may have been due to the efforts of Ray Johnston, the Rangers' owner. Johnston had previously worked in the front office of the Milwaukee organization, and as a result, would have been very familiar with Corky's potential as a power hitter. Since the Rangers had an agreement with California, perhaps Bill Rigney, the owner of the Angels, was also interested in Corky.

The Angels had only two minor league affiliates that season. One was the Rangers and the other was the Statesville (NC) Owls, a Class D team. Minor league clubs of that era could sign their own players, own their contracts, and generally operate independently of major league clubs if they desired. With this also came the power to affiliate with more than one major league team. In some ways this was good for the players, but in other ways hurt. More than once, Corky feels, minor league clubs holding his contract prevented him from having opportunities with big league clubs. "If you were a big draw for a minor league team and they owned you, they didn't have to sell your contract," he points out. There was also no "free agency" at this time.

Most of the Dallas/Ft. Worth players at Riverside had been assigned there by the California Angels. But there were also some sent to Riverside from the Philadelphia Phillies organization. Still, others were property of the Dallas/Ft. Worth club with no ties to any major league organization at all. This arrangement even applied to Rangers Manager Walker Cooper. Cooper, a former catcher for St. Louis, was strictly an employee of the Dallas/Ft. Worth organization, and as such had no ties with the Angels, the Phillies, the Braves, or any other major league club.

Corky unashamedly describes his training performance with Cooper and the Rangers as "tremendous." The team trained and played their games at Evans Park against other AAA teams, but also played a few games against the Angels' B team squad.

Corky's Ranger teammates included several future major leaguers, and among these were Dean Chance, Jack Hiatt, Hugh Pepper, Bob "Buck" Rogers, Ken Toothman, Bob Rous, Tom Burgess, and Jim Fregosi. Corky remembers Jim Fregosi as "a nice guy... straight and serious, and a real hard worker."

Corky roomed by himself while in Riverside, but had "fine" quarters in a nice hotel in town. There was plenty to do in Riverside and, according to him, "the California girls were real pretty."

Regardless of his outstanding spring, the stay with the Rangers would be short once the season began. After only four games, and with one hit in only one at-bat—a triple—Corky was told by Rangers management of Milwaukee's decision to send him to Mobile Bay, Alabama, to play for their Class AA farm club, the Mobile

Bears. It would seem that Milwaukee, due to his impressive spring performance, was now having second thoughts about dealing his contract to the California Angels organization.

Such was life in the minors. Here today. Gone tomorrow.

Mobile was a medium-size city located on the Gulf of Mexico, and its baseball club was a member of the eight team Southern Association. The other seven clubs were the Nashville Volunteers, Macon Peaches, Chattanooga Lookouts, Atlanta Crackers, Birmingham Barons, Little Rock Travelers, and Shreveport Sports.

The Bears played their home games at Hartwell Field, and the season included a 152 game schedule. According to Corky, in what could pass as a Mobile tourist brochure ad, "Mobile fans were great, and the team provided real nice living accommodations in a nearby Travel Lodge motel, all at significantly-reduced rates." "But," he added, "the season was a mess, and the team was a bunch of total misfits, myself included."

There was turmoil on the Bears' squad that summer, and Corky lays much of the blame at the feet of the team's manager, Ernie White. Corky describes White as having been "an arrogant and self-indulgent man," and one who was more concerned with his own advancement and wellbeing than that of his players. "White," Corky continues, "was always telling stories about his own accomplishments in the major leagues, and it got old hearing him brag."

Ernest Daniel "Ernie" White was born in 1916 in Pacolet Mills, South Carolina. A left-handed pitcher, he broke into the majors with the Cardinals in 1941 and had considerable success in his first three seasons playing on a roster with star performers, such as Harry "The Hat" Walker and others. His professional career was interrupted, however, as he was one of ten St. Louis pitchers called to war in 1944-45. Ernie saw action in the Battle of the Bulge, and it was during this time he suffered from extended exposure to icy water. Once home after the war, his "dead arm" resulted in his trade to the Boston Braves, but he could never regain his pre-war form. In 1948, after numerous comeback attempts, White switched from playing to coaching. Ernie White, as a result of all that happened, might fairly be labeled the consummate "what if" player.

But no matter that Ernie White had once been an up-and-coming star ball player, as well as one who sacrificed his career for our country in World War II, Corky didn't like the man and could never get past Ernie's braggadocio! With this in the way, the two men's distaste for each other grew and festered that season, and for reasons not worthy of discussion here, Corky describes his time with Ernie White and the Bears as "a soap opera-like atmosphere, one played out all season long."

Along with the drama off the field, Mobile struggled on the diamond, too, finishing with a most unbearable 61-92 record. Corky was not around for most of these games, however, as he would be sent to Austin, Texas, after only fifty-eight games with the "Bay Bears."

Since Mobile played their games in the deep south, and it was during the turbulent early sixties, Corky observed racial bigotry and prejudice up close. "There were several Hispanic and black players on our roster, and I still feel bad about things they had to deal with that the rest of us didn't," he notes.

Even though baseball was several years integrated by this time, there were still many unwilling to accept it outside the sport. "More than once we refused to eat at places where we were told they couldn't serve our teammates," Corky explains. "But sometimes we had no choice. We'd eat in the restaurant and take food to them on the bus. It was hard enough just trying to stay in baseball, much less moving up to the majors, but they had all this other stuff to deal with on top of that. It had to be hard for them."

When Corky received word that he was to leave Mobile and report to the Austin Senators, it was with great jubilation. "I was happy to be gone," he states. Ernie White was probably happy, too.

In his fifty-eight games with the misfit Bears, Corky had 53 hits in 213 at-bats, 7 homeruns, 9 triples, and 2 doubles. Along with his .249 batting average, there were 32 RBIs, 38 strikeouts, and 17 base-on-balls.

Chapter 16

A Bus Load of Spam, Billy Graham, and the Southside Bar and Grill

Leaving behind the turmoil in Mobile, Corky headed west to Texas. Here he would be playing for the Austin Senators, a Class AA team in the Texas League. The Senators were managed by Bill Adair.

Marion D. "Bill" Adair (1913-2002) was first signed by the Brooklyn Dodgers in 1935. By 1942 he was still in the minors, playing second base for the Memphis Chicks. With the U.S. involvement in World War II, Adair enlisted in the Army in '43 and eventually rose to the rank of Technical Sergeant serving in the European Theatre. He returned to the minors after the war, but despite playing through the '56 season, never made a major league roster.

Among Adair's best minor league seasons was 1949 when he was the player/manager for the Owensboro Oilers of the Kentucky-Illinois-Tennessee League, or, as most called it, the "KITTY." Owensboro was the Class D affiliate of the Boston Braves at that time, and the team played its games at Miller Field, a park Joe Dimaggio once described as "the best minor league ballpark in the United States."

The favorable impression the Oilers' facilities had made on "Jumpin Joe" probably could be traced to the years between 1953-55 when Owensboro was the Class D affiliate of the New York Yankees. Corky recalls attending several games the Oilers played during this time and especially enjoyed the 1954 season when an eighteen year old rookie named Tony Kubek played shortstop for Owensboro. Kubek hit .344 that season, and had 7 homeruns for the Oilers during his one season here. He would later go on to become one of the New York Yankees' all-time greats.

Corky hadn't seen many Owensboro games prior to the time of the team's affiliation with the Yankees and was unaware Bill Adair had played and managed there previously. But his interest in the KITTY's last few years of existence is ongoing, primarily due to this Owensboro connection, and the fact that Central City actually fielded a KITTY team during the latter part of that same '54 season.

The KITTY was originally formed in 1903 and would have an on-and-off existence through the '55 season when it permanently disbanded. Usually the league was comprised of teams from Kentucky, Illinois, and Tennessee, but there would be infrequent exceptions. Near the end of its fifty-two year run, the league's teams included the Cairo Dodgers, the Hopkinsville Hoppers, the Madisonville Miners, the Union City Greyhounds, the Fulton Railroaders, the Clarksville Cats, the Mayfield Clothiers, the Jackson Generals, and the Owensboro Oilers.

In the early 1900s team monikers, as often as not, were tagged on teams by local journalists and included colorful and locally related ones such as the Cairo Mud-Wallopers, the Hopkinsville Lunatics (a reference to the state mental institution located nearby), and the Mayfield Clothiers. Some of these monikers stuck; some didn't.

As interesting as KITTY history is, the stories told about the players are equally colorful. League researcher Kevin McCann, in an article published in the June-July 2005 issue of "The Bull Pen Kitty League Newsletter" tells of several, one involving a "mean-spirited" first baseman named William "Buster" Brown.

Brown, playing for the Hopkinsville Hoppers in a 1922 game in Paris, Tennessee, hit what he thought was a homerun, but the umpire ruled it foul. When the game ended, Buster was still mad, and after spitting tobacco juice in his hand, walked over and rubbed the juice in the unsuspecting umpire's eyes. With his eyes on fire, the ump yelled for water. Brown, responding to his victim's plea, dumped a full bucket of the liquid over his head.

The following day Buster was arrested on the charge of disturbing the peace and was fined $20 in the Paris city police court. Since Brown had no money to pay the fine, the Hoppers' manager, Art Wilson, paid the $20 fine for him. Case settled, right? Wrong! No sooner had the fine been paid than a second warrant was handed to Brown. "Half that ballpark is in the county," the officer reportedly told Buster, and with this Buster was instructed to go upstairs—this time to county court. Here, once again, Brown was ordered to pay a $20 fine and, once again, Wilson paid the fine for him. Brown, according to writer McCann, remarked, "Fined on the first floor, fined on the second floor. Boss, ain't you glad this building don't have 20 stories?"

Central City's brief time in the KITTY began on July 5, 1954, the result of the withdrawal of the Jackson Generals on June 1 of that season. The Generals record at the time of their disbanding was 1-44, including a 36-game losing streak. Taking advantage of this opportunity was Billy Dennis of Central City. Dennis, with financial assistance from several other local baseball fans, pieced together a team to complete Jackson's schedule. The Central City Reds, managed by Joe Richardson and Hayden Ray, would play their games at the City Park's baseball field—"a nice, well-lit field," according to Corky—and would finish the season with 13 victories. However, the budget was tight (an old push-mower was used to cut the grass), and the following season, the league's last, Central City fielded no team.

Corky has nothing but fond memories of his days with Austin and Bill Adair, a man he credits with giving his career a fresh start after all his previous struggles with Monchak, Murff, and White. "It was the right team at the right time in my career," Corky claims. "I was pretty frustrated with baseball at that time, but Austin changed all that."

The Senators played in the six team Texas League with the Amarillo Gold Sox, the Tulsa Oilers, the San Antonio Missions, the Rio Grande Giants, and the Victoria Rosebuds—a moniker that surely struck fear in the hearts of their opponents. All were Texas-based teams with the exception of Tulsa.

With his late season arrival in Austin, Corky would be with the Senators for only their final fifty-two games, and records show he played in fifty of these. The team finished fourth in the league standings with a 69-71 record, but he managed to belt out 47 hits in 175 plate appearances for a respectable .269 average. There were 8 homeruns, 11 doubles, 2 triples, and 32 RBIs.

All travel in the Texas League was by bus. This had been the case everywhere he had been so far, but here, with greater distances between the competing teams, the trips were unlike any he had experienced previously. "We had to travel all night in some cases," Corky recalls, "and sometimes there would be nowhere to stop for hours."

One such trip involved an unusually long amount of time and travel, as it was a twelve game road swing through Mexico. Along the way Austin played Mexican teams in what the league called the Pan-American Games. The Senators weren't alone in this endeavor, however, as each of the other league teams had a similar trip scheduled across Mexico.

Corky remembers departing Austin with a bus full of players and coaches, as well as luggage, equipment, and "all the canned foods we could cram on." This included spam, vienna sausages, deviled ham, and anything else that was canned and remotely passed as meat. It wasn't that the players were all that fond of spam and such, but, instead, was due to management's warnings against eating Mexican meat products, and, of course, drinking the water. The team's officials may have been a bit overly cautious regarding this, but as Corky explains, "They didn't want a bus full of sick ballplayers with food poisoning stuck out in the middle of some remote Mexican desert." The players heeded their management's advice for the most part, and by the time they returned to Austin two weeks later, the canned food had been completely consumed.

Austin's first two Pan-Am games were played in Mexico City. These were followed by games in Monterrey, Vera Cruz (Acapulco), and Posa Rica. There were other games played in other cities, but Corky can't remember where.

Among his most memorable experiences from this trip was one involving an injury he suffered and the resulting hospital visit that followed. Corky explains:

> We were playing Posa Rica in a night game. The lighting on the field was bad, and it was almost impossible to see any fly balls hit to the outfield. I was playing

> left, and a Posa Rica batter hit a fly down the left field line. I didn't get a good jump since I couldn't see it, but I ended up making a running, backhanded catch in foul territory. My momentum carried me into a chain-link fence that was set in a low concrete wall. When I collided with the fence, my foot rammed into the concrete. That yanked my toes out of joint. I looked down and saw my spikes sticking up through my shoes. I sat down and pulled my right spike off. Three of my toes were sticking straight up, and they're not supposed to do that! I remember the pain was awful. They drove me to what they called a hospital. The hospital was a little building in Posa Rica, and when we got to the front door, I noticed three red neck buzzards eating out of the garbage can by the door. I thought to myself... this can't be good, but still it was the only place around to find a doctor. Once we were inside, I realized it wasn't going to get much better after they told me they had nothing to use for the pain while the doctor was yanking my toes back in joint. Instead, they handed me the corner of a sheet to chew on while they yanked. It's a wonder I didn't catch some disease from the sheet, but I guess I was lucky just to get out of there alive, and with all ten toes intact.

When the two week tour ended with the last game in Posa Rica, the team boarded the bus the following morning to begin the thirty-seven hour bus ride back to Austin. The long drive across the barren landscape was bad enough, but with the added misery from his ailing foot, it proved almost unbearable. "I was never so glad to get out of a vehicle in my whole life and felt like kissing the ground when I stepped off the bus in Austin," Corky reports.

Even with two weeks of living on canned foods, primitive medical treatment, and miserably long bus rides, Corky's partial season with Bill Adair in Austin had salvaged his sputtering career. It was with renewed optimism that he returned to Central City that fall, and the next two years ahead would prove to be even better.

With every new year came exciting new places and adventures for Corky. Some were good, and some not so good, but were, nevertheless, exciting. The combination of professional baseball and college basketball had brought him opportunities that few ever experience, and in the fall of 1961, another such adventure came knocking at his door.

This new opportunity was a chance to play professional basketball, and the invitation came in the form of a phone call from Chuck Taylor in the spring of '61. Corky was training with the Dallas/Ft. Worth Rangers in Riverside at the time, and Taylor was well aware Corky was five years into his baseball career. But he also knew of his potential as a NBA basketball player. The call was made to determine if Corky would be willing to attend fall training with the Philadelphia Warriors in Hershey, Pennsylvania, if that organization selected him in the upcoming NBA draft in March. Taylor, a man better known for his association with Converse shoes, was acting on behalf of the Warriors.

Corky was surprised to get this call, but knew Taylor from the North-South High School Classic at Murray a few years prior. Since Corky was now eligible for the NBA draft—his college class officially graduating in '61—Taylor and the Warriors were inquiring as to any interest he may have in returning to basketball. Corky admits he had no special desire to do so, but any new experience sounded exciting, and since the Warriors' camp was in Hershey, not far from New York City, this would give him an opportunity to visit a friend living in The Big Apple once camp ended. Of course, the NBA season was months away, and there was still an entire baseball season to be played first.

The 1961 NBA draft was held in New York City on the 27th of March. The league had nine teams (compared to thirty today) and consisted of two divisions. The Boston Celtics, Philadelphia Warriors, Syracuse Nationals, and New York Knicks made up the Eastern Division, while the Los Angeles Lakers, Cincinnati Royals, Detroit Pistons, St. Louis Hawks, and Chicago Packers comprised the Western Division. The Packers, a recently formed franchise, would have the first draft selection.

With the #1 pick, Chicago selected Walt Bellamy from Indiana University. His selection proved wise, as Bellamy would be named "Rookie of the Year" at the end of the season. The following season Chicago's moniker would be changed to Zephyrs, and even that was short-lived, as the team left Chicago, moving to Baltimore where they became the Bullets.

Of the 107 players drafted in fifteen rounds in '61, Corky's name would be called with the ninety-seventh pick in the eleventh. Philadelphia's other picks were Tom Meschery at number seven, Ted Luckenbill at number fifteen, and Bob McNeil in a later round. It is also of interest to note that Roger Newman was picked as the sixty-fourth pick by Boston. Other Kentuckians drafted in '61 were Donnis Butcher, Ned Jennings, John Turner, Fred Sawyer, Howard Stacy, Carl Cole, Charlie Osborne, and Billy Ray Lickert.

At the conclusion of the '61 baseball season with Austin, Corky fulfilled his promise to the Warriors by flying to Philadelphia for training camp. Here, he was met at the airport by Warriors Coach Frank McQuire and Eddie Gottlieb, the team's owner. Also meeting McQuire and Gottlieb that day was another Warriors' pick, Tom Meschery. Together, this quartet traveled by car to the basketball camp at Hershey.

It was with excitement and anticipation that Corky began practice with Philadelphia that fall, but in some ways the reality fell short of the anticipation. "It was nothing like I expected," Corky admits. "It was still exciting, but I expected more." First on the list of surprises was the fact that the Warriors roomed at the local YMCA. The accommodations were "okay," according to Corky, but not at all what he expected. Even the team's biggest star, Wilt Chamberlain, bunked here—certainly something few modern era athletes would consider doing. Team meals, adequate but far short of fine dining, were served buffet-style on the bottom floor of the same building. "It wasn't luxury by any means, but to my knowledge, no one complained," Corky explains. "They were just nice, normal guys like everybody else, and I think everybody was just happy to have the opportunity to be there."

Corky, by his own decision, wasn't in camp long enough to have that many stories to tell, but there are a few. There was a Billy Graham Crusade he attended in Philadelphia with a friend one evening, and he especially enjoyed his time with the Warriors' Guy Rodgers. "Guy took a special interest in me because I was a baseball player," he explains. "He was a huge baseball fan and was always asking me questions about the game and what life was like in baseball. We both enjoyed talking about baseball."

There was another friendship made, this one with Wilt Chamberlain. "Wilt took a liking to me, too," Corky brags. "I'm not sure why, but he even took time to drive me around town in his pink Cadillac convertible." He describes Wilt as "a down to earth guy with a great sense of humor" and tells of going into bars together, with Wilt buying everyone there a beer but never drinking one himself. "He always drank orange juice, everywhere he went."

Even though Guy Rodgers and Wilt Chamberlain "took a liking" to Corky, that didn't prevent them from emptying his pockets at the poker table. "Al Attles, Guy Rodgers, and Wilt cleaned me out of everything I had in a poker game one night," he laughs. "I lost $20 to them, and to me that was a good amount." This is not to say that Chamberlain needed what little money he could rid Corky Withrow of, as the "Big Dipper" was earning $75,000 a year at a time when the average American worker was making less than $5,000.

With this kind of salary, Wilt could afford a lavish lifestyle that included a luxury apartment near Central Park in New York. He lived here throughout the year and commuted daily between New York and Philadelphia during the basketball season.

How dominant could Wilt be on the basketball court? To answer this, one can point to his first game encounter with Walt Bellamy, the top draft pick. When tip-off time came, Bellamy met Chamberlain at center court for the jump. "Hello Mr. Chamberlain, I'm Walter Bellamy," the rookie said. "Hello Walter. You won't get a shot off in the first half," Chamberlain said in response.

Wilt, backing his words, proceeded to hold Bellamy to zero points that half, this by blocking his first nine shots. When halftime arrived, Bellamy had failed to get a shot to the rim and was, it is said, totally shell-shocked from the experience.

When the second half began, Bellamy was met by Wilt with a handshake, and an "Okay Walter, now you can play" greeting. Bellamy, thanks to Wilt's generosity, scored 14 that half, but Wilt had outscored him 51-14 for the game.

Corky spent about two weeks in camp with the Warriors that fall. He enjoyed his time in Hershey, but his heart just wasn't in basketball. There was also the injured foot acquired during the Mexican trip to consider, and he certainly didn't want a re-injury to slow his baseball career. So, with these things in mind, he told Coach McQuire of his intentions to leave camp. "I may have made the roster if I'd stayed," Corky speculates. "Both McQuire and Gottlieb tried convincing me."

Looking back, Corky is proud of his time spent with the Warriors. "Now I can tell people I'm probably the only person on the planet who played professional basketball with Wilt Chamberlain and professional baseball with Stan Musial," he explains. "It doesn't get much better than that!"

Although not on the NBA level, Corky did play some basketball that fall and winter. "I played for the Adams Texaco team in an Owensboro league," he proudly proclaims. "I think I did pretty good, too."

In late October, after returning from Pennsylvania, Corky and a buddy were playing pinball in the Southside Bar and Grill on the outskirts of Owensboro when he noticed a couple of girls enter the room. One, he claims, "was the sharpest-looking woman I'd ever seen." After introducing himself to Barbara Yewell, Corky was shocked to find out she had no idea who he was. How could this be possible? he asked himself. "Don't you ever read the newspapers?" he asked Barbara Yewell.

Barbara Helen Yewell, born on the 21st of April, 1940, at Southerland in Daviess County, was the daughter of Frank Lloyd and Gladie V. Flener Yewell. Raised on a farm with five siblings, Barbara had graduated from Utica High, a small school south of Owensboro in Daviess County. Although Utica fielded baseball and basketball teams, she wasn't involved and, by her own admission, had absolutely no interest in those or any other sports. To Barbara Yewell, Corky Withrow was "just another guy," something he found hard to understand. Barbara explains:

> I went to the Southside Grill with a girlfriend. We enjoyed going there to dance, and we were both learning a new dance called The Twist. When we walked in, my friend saw Corky with some other boy, and I remember her saying 'Oh my goodness... that's Corky Withrow!' She couldn't believe it when I told her I didn't know who he was, so she explained to me he was a big baseball player. But that really didn't impress me at all. Later he asked me to dance, and at some point asked for my phone number, but I didn't give him my number. I told him it was in the phone book.
>
> He called the house a lot during the next few weeks, and when I left town with a girlfriend for a few days, he went 'nuts' trying to find me. I didn't act crazy about him, and I still accuse him of being attracted to me for that reason. I didn't really care who he was, and that was a big challenge for his ego.

Corky doesn't dispute any part of Barbara's version, and although it took some serious convincing on his part, the two dated throughout that winter. When Corky returned to Austin to play the '62 season with the Senators, he missed her more than even he expected, and after placing a call to her back in Owensboro, asked Barbara to come to Texas to marry him. She did just that.

On April 16, 1962, Corky and Barbara were married by an Austin Justice of the Peace at the Williamson County Courthouse. "It was a pretty informal affair," Corky recalls. "I didn't even have a necktie to wear, so I stopped at a Five and Dime on the way to the courthouse. A friend drove me there, and we arrived at the courthouse about fifteen minutes before they closed. I'm sure the judge wasn't real happy about that."

Barbara would eventually learn the game of baseball under the expert tutelage of her husband. She grew to love the trips to the ballpark to watch him play baseball, and the two shared many good times and experiences in their travels to various cities across the United States and South America over the next few years. And to think it all began at the Southside Bar and Grill!

Chapter 17

DEAD GOATS AND ARMED GUARDS

Corky reported to Daytona Beach, Florida, for spring training in 1962. This time he would be training with the Toronto Maple Leafs, an unaffiliated AAA club with a work agreement with the Milwaukee Braves.

His time with the Leafs in Daytona would be short, and again, the team's manager was one Corky could find no middle ground upon which to agree. This man was Charlie "Chuck" Dressen, someone who, according to Corky, "was a micro-manager who absolutely tried to control every situation that happened during a game and with his players."

Charlie Dressen, born in 1898 in Decatur, Illinois, first broke into baseball in 1919 as a second baseman for the Moline Plowboys of the Triple I, and then the Peoria Tractors in 1920. In that same winter of '20, George Halas recruited Dressen to play football for the A. E. Staley Food Starch Company of Chicago. While playing for the "Staleys," Dressen was the quarterback, something that may explain, as Corky points out, his need to "control every situation." In 1921, under Halas's leadership, the Staleys joined the newly-formed National Football League, but with the name Chicago Bears.

By 1924 Dressen was in the Cincinnati Reds organization, playing in an infield with Edd Roush, Eppa Rixey, and Carl Mays. Although Dressen has been described as "whip smart," he never had enough talent to become a baseball star, relying instead on "playing the percentages." Following his days with the Reds, he played for the Baltimore Orioles and Minneapolis Millers, but by 1932, his days as a player had ended, at which time Dressen accepted a managing position with the Class A Nashville Volunteers of the Southern League.

In 1939, Dressen's managing career took a major leap when Larry McPhail hired him to join the staff of Leo Durocher, the manager of the Brooklyn Dodgers. Durocher had been a teammate of Dressen at Cincinnati in the mid-20s, and under these two, "dem Bums of Brooklyn" developed into a baseball power with the likes of Joe Medwick, Dixie Walker, Pete Reiser, and Harold "Pee Wee" Reese, a native of the Ekron community of Meade County, Kentucky. The Dodgers won the National League pennant in '41, but followed this with the first of several losses to the Yankees in World Series play.

Although many considered Dressen to be the brains behind the Dodgers' success, their straight-laced owner, Branch Rickey, fired Chuck in 1942 due to his habit of betting the horses. When the Dodgers faltered, Rickey offered to rehire him, but only on condition the gambling would stop. To this Dressen agreed, remaining with the club through the '46 season before jumping ship to the Yankees as a coach.

By 1960, Dressen was managing the Milwaukee Braves, but their failing farm system had left them short of talent. In '61 Chuck was fired by Birdie Tebbetts, but ended up with the Toronto Maple Leafs, a minor league team with a work agreement with the Braves. Now, with the Maple Leafs at Daytona Beach, Chuck Dressen and Corky Withrow would cross paths.

Dressen was self-confident with a "sunny" disposition, but one whose "win with brains" strategy often translated to a "just hold them 'til I think of something" philosophy when his team faced a dire situation during a game.

Corky's main problem with Dressen's leadership was his insistence on playing the percentages in every situation, rather than allowing players to do whatever they felt was a strong suit. For Corky, this was hitting the long ball, of course, but with the extremely deep center field wall at Daytona, most deep drives turned into long outs. Explains Corky, "I was really hitting good that spring, but most of my hits were deep to center. Dressen and Sparky Anderson, his assistant manager, didn't like this. Someone told me later that this probably kept me from moving up that season."

Corky wouldn't finish spring training with the Maple Leafs but was told to report back to the Austin Senators for another season in Texas. He had no problems with this assignment, and the upcoming season would be one of his finest.

In 1962 Corky's baseball salary was $7,500, the minimum major league baseball amount at that time. With Corky and Barbara's marriage in April, the couple settled into a nice apartment in Austin. Corky had lifestyle adjustments to make, of course, some of which involved finances. "My paycheck was stretched pretty thin by month's end," he says, "but it was a fun summer, and Barbara and I couldn't wait to get to the ballpark every day."

Barbara, Corky explains, knew absolutely nothing about baseball when the two married, but she still accompanied him to the games and quickly came to enjoy baseball, even with her limited insight into the game's complexities. "I spent the first summer explaining all that went on during the games," Corky says, "but she would still say some pretty funny things to the other players' wives. Sometimes I'd suggest she just sit and watch the game but to keep her mouth shut and not say anything about baseball to them!"

The newlyweds loved the city of Austin, and the season, unlike several of his previous ones, went without a hitch. Manager Bill Adair was gone by this time, but Jimmy Brown, his replacement, was another manager Corky could work with.

Jimmy Brown (1910-1977) had played eight seasons of big league ball after his debut with the St. Louis Cardinals in 1932. As an infielder for the Cards, Brown was in the running for MVP honors three times, and was a National League All-Star in 1942. That season he hit .330, leading St. Louis to a World Series Championship over the Yankees. After serving in the Air Force during the last three years of WWII, Brown finished his playing days with the Pirates in '46—another example of a player who sacrificed prime years to serve our country. But Corky remembers Jimmy Brown, not for his playing days and military service, but simply as "a good manager... an older fellow... who drank gin mixed with Pepsi-Cola." That really seemed like an odd combination to Corky.

Although Jimmy Brown's Senators could muster only a 69-71 record and fourth place finish in a league with the El Paso Sunkings, Tulsa Oilers, Albuquerque Dukes, San Antonio Missions, and Amarillo Gold Sox, Corky was at the top of his game with a league-leading 36 homeruns. This total smashed the old Austin high mark of 22, and to go with this impressive total was a .291 average and 102 RBIs. With these accomplishments can be added an appearance in the Texas League All-Star game, followed by "Player of The Month" honors in August—an award primarily earned by blasting 13 homeruns that month. All this, it should be added, led to some notice in a national sports publication as well. Corky's stock was definitely on the rise!

Corky loved hitting at Austin's Disch Field, and certainly his homerun total is verification. Among his proudest achievements was hitting a ball over the deep center field fence in a game—the first time for this feat in Disch's fifteen year history! "That fence was deep, and with a constant wind blowing in, I surprised myself when I hit it out," he acknowledges.

But his homeruns didn't end with games at Austin's Disch Field. "I absolutely loved hitting in the ballpark at Tulsa, and I wore their pitchers out there," he claims. Tulsa was a Class AA farm club of St. Louis, and Corky feels his domination of Tulsa pitching that season was a determining factor in the Cardinals' decision to purchase his contract from Milwaukee in September of '63. Says Corky: "I hit Tulsa pitching so hard in Tulsa... and Austin... that I had, I figure, probably drawn the attention of St. Louis. Then, with Stan Musial retiring in '63, the Cardinals needed a power hitter to replace him. After seeing what I had done to Tulsa pitching in '62, they probably thought I could help fill the void."

The ballpark in Tulsa was Oiler Park, an old stadium that had been recently renovated by new team owner, A. Ray Smith. Smith, due to the lack of public and private funding, would move the Oilers to New Orleans in '76 and then to Springfield, Illinois, from '77-'81. In '82 the team was moved again, this time to Louisville, where they set minor league attendance records as the Louisville Redbirds. In 1985, after failing to outbid Marge Schott for the Cincinnati Reds, Smith sold the Redbirds. They, in turn, became the Riverbats, and then finally, the Bats.

Among his teammates at Austin was a familiar face from training camp days at Waycross. This was Em Lindbeck, the provider of Corky's ride to Madisonville following Corky's early-on decision not to return to Wellsville for a second season. Em, like Corky, would spend nearly his entire baseball career in the minors, with only a two game appearance in the majors. After his playing days ended, Em returned to his home in Kewanee, Illinois, and eventually served a term as that town's mayor.

With every season came new friends and acquaintances, and one Corky recalls from this season was Wade Blasingame. The two would be teammates the following season, too, as both would make the roster of the Denver Bears in '63. Corky has a few stories about his time with Blasingame—a $125,000 "bonus-baby" signed by Milwaukee at age seventeen in 1961—and most of these, as one might expect, involved Wade's lifestyle as a "privileged" and highly paid athlete at such a young age.

There were certainly high expectations when Milwaukee signed Wade after his high school graduation in '61. As a star high school pitcher in Fresno, California, he had amassed a perfect 26-0 win-loss record in three seasons at Roosevelt High. Due to his tremendous talent and potential, only four major league teams felt they could afford the price it would take to sign him. Of these four suitors, it would be the Braves acquiring his signature.

Milwaukee viewed Blasingame as the future replacement for their forty year old pitching star Warren Spahn, and the Austin journalists dubbed him "Baby Spahn" as a result. Spahn's shoes would be big ones to fill, but the $125,000 bonus was a clear indication Milwaukee thought him up to the task. After his inking, the Braves sent Wade to their Class C affiliate of the Pioneer League in Boise, Idaho, but by '62 he was already in Austin with Corky and the Senators.

It probably comes as no surprise that Wade was the highest paid player on the Austin roster. With money to burn, and no shame in displaying his recently acquired wealth, Wade maintained a lavish, playboy lifestyle, one complete with fine, but rather outlandish clothing and other material possessions reflecting the image of a privileged athlete.

Blasingame would have only a 10-win, 14-loss record that season, but this was viewed, at least by management, as a successful effort since the team had a sub-.500 season in, what most considered, a hitter's league. To most in Austin, including the papers, Wade was a sensation.

Corky describes Wade as having been a "showoff with a California attitude," but also as one who was always fun, a "nice guy," and "one who, if you needed a little money, would hand it to you." But there was also a mischievous side to Wade, and Corky offers this example:

> We were on our way back to Austin after a game one evening. It was a long drive back that night, and we were tired and hungry. We stopped somewhere, and some of the team got something to eat. Others, including myself, had already spent our money on food, card games, whatever, and didn't have enough left to buy much to eat here. Wade was trying to be funny and pulled out a big roll of money in front of us. He pulled out a $5 bill from the roll, lit it with a lighter, and then lit his cigar with the bill. Some of us didn't see the humor in this, but that was Wade for you.

Blasingame would go on to play several years of major league ball, but had control issues throughout that time. This, along with several injuries, prevented him from reaching his full potential. Still, Wade Blasingame has to be considered one of the greatest prospects of all times.

Another Austin teammate that season was Dennis Ribant. Ribant, a native of Detroit, is said to have been so good at baseball as a teen he didn't bother playing high school ball.

Eventually choosing baseball over a professional hockey career with the Red Wings, Ribant signed with Milwaukee in '61, and by the end of that same season was with the Senators in Austin. In '62 he was back with Austin, and in '63 would join both Corky and Wade Blasingame on the roster of the Denver Bears. In '64 the New York Mets purchased his contract, and a major league career followed through the '71 season. After baseball,

Dennis found his way into the insurance business in his hometown, but trouble found him in 1999 when he was indicted for one count of bribery, and felony state income tax evasion for filing false returns. In 2004 he pleaded guilty and was forced to pay $102,000 in restitution as well as serve five years of probation.

In a season crammed full of great memories there were some not-so-great moments as well. Racial discrimination against the Senators' Hispanic and black players brought situations to be dealt with frequently, and Corky got up close and personal insights into a world he never imagined as a boy back in Central City. "But," as Corky reasons, "those incidents brought us close together, especially when we saw teammates face some of the awful things they had to deal with." Corky, describing one such incident, explains:

> It was late at night, and we were out in the middle of nowhere. Our bus stopped at some little diner, the only one in miles, and we got off to go in. When we got to the door, the manager told us the black and Hispanic players couldn't be served, and they would have to go back and wait on the bus while the rest of us ate in the diner. This had happened to us before, and usually we would just leave and go somewhere else to eat. But this time there wasn't anywhere else around to eat. Everyone was hungry, so we agreed to bring food back to them at the bus after we ate in the diner. We didn't like having to do this, but we went ahead and sat down. Every table had one of those little individual jukeboxes where you put money in and played a song. When we finished eating, we picked up the carry outs for our teammates on the bus, and then left the diner. I can guarantee you that not one of those jukeboxes was working when we left. We had pulled all the cords loose from the wall!

When asked for any other thoughts on his final season with the Austin Senators, Corky added, "I still don't know why, but I remember our team had a hard time getting any new bats that year. I had a contract with Louisville Slugger throughout my career and would order five or six at a time, but for some reason they were real slow in coming that season."

At the conclusion of the '62 season, and after returning to Owensboro, Corky received a phone call from Les Moss, the manager of the Chicago White Sox. Together with White Sox shortstop Luis Aparicio, Moss was putting together a team to play in a winter ball league in Venezuela. This team would be playing in the Liga Occidental de Beisol and would be representing the city of Rapinos as the Western Raptors. The Raptors would be comprised of both major and minor leaguers from the United States and would be managed by Moss and Aparicio.

Although there were only four teams in this league, and it was far from home, the pay would be good at $1,200 a month, and a nice, rent-free apartment would be provided in Maracaibo. With virtually no expense to the players, plus the fact the pay would be considerably better than that of any part-time job Corky or Barbara could hope to find in the Owensboro area, the offer was too good to refuse.

The Rapinos Western Raptors had been playing in this league since 1957, but this season would be the last for both the team and league, as financial problems couldn't be resolved. During the league's six year history, Rapinos would prove the most successful franchise with five league titles, including the one they would earn this season. Of these five, Les Moss would manage the team to three. Luis Aparicio, along with an uncle, were co-owners of the Raptors for all six seasons of the team's existence.

The team that Moss and Aparicio put together that season included Don Buford, Fritz Ackley, Ken Berry, Angel Bravo, Lewis Joyce, Taylor "T-Bone" Phillips, J. C. Martin, Deacon Jones, and, of course, Corky Withrow. Both Moss and Aparicio also played as well as managed the squad. The other three teams in the league had rosters containing mostly American born players as well, and one of those teams (Lara) was managed by Earl Weaver, who would go on to have great success as an American League manager.

Travel arrangements to Venezuela were provided by Moss and the team, but it was necessary for Corky and Barbara to arrange their own flight to Miami to meet the provided transportation. For this leg of the journey they took an Ozark flight from Owensboro. On arrival at the airport in Miami, and despite carefully made preparations by the team, the Withrows were informed of problems with their paperwork. This, as it turned out, would necessitate an overnight stay and rescheduled flight.

Security at the Miami airport was extra tight that October of '62 due to the fear and near-panic caused by the recent discovery of Russian missile silos and sites on the island of Cuba, only ninety miles away. The missiles, armed with atomic warheads, were directly pointed at targets in the United States. Matters quickly escalated after this discovery, and then reached crisis level when President Kennedy demanded that Soviet Premier Khrushchev remove the missiles or face the consequences that would follow. With this line drawn in the sand, the world held its collective breath.

Nerves were on edge everywhere in the U.S. that fall, but in Miami—only missile-time minutes from Cuba—it was closer to panic! Odd as it seems today, many Miamians were fleeing the city out of fear it would be the first target of the Soviets. Corky, recalling the night spent there, claims he and Barbara "pretty-much" had the city to themselves, since the whole town seemed to be deserted. "It was eerie in one way," he added, "but I don't remember being scared. Barbara was nervous, though." Corky, it seems, had somehow managed to find himself in the middle of a major world crisis!

The following day, with paperwork approved, they were cleared for flight out of Miami. The original flight plan would have taken them directly over Cuba, but the "October Crisis" required a re-routing around, and away from, Fidel Castro's communist-ruled island. Still, at least in the mind of most aboard, there was danger.

The route to Caracas, Venezuela, even in normal times, was long. But now, with the necessary re-routing, a refueling stop in Santo Domingo was required. As the plane touched down in Santo Domingo, Corky and Barbara, glancing out the window, were shocked when heavily armed security guards ran to the plane, quickly encircling it. This was not what anyone aboard expected—and was certainly unnerving—but with all that had happened that week, it was comforting to know protection was a priority. With the plane refueled, it was on to Caracas where, once again, heavily armed guards encircled their plane.

Warnings of possible danger continued throughout their time in Venezuela, and this was especially true when traveling to other cities and countries for games. Players, due to various drug cartels, were advised to travel only in large groups at night, if necessary at all, and to avoid talking to anyone on the streets for any length of time as large crowds might soon form around them. Even though these crowds may only have been adoring fans, there was always the danger of injuries.

The drug cartels operated in all the South American countries, but were especially dangerous in Colombia. The Raptors traveled to Bogota, Colombia, for a non-league game, but didn't travel together. Corky classifies this experience as one he would have been better off without. He explains:

> Automobile drivers in South America were crazy. They drove way too fast and wild for me, especially on those narrow mountain roads with steep drop-offs and no railings to prevent you from going over a cliff. There were even "spirit houses" built right next to the roads to honor some relative who had been killed in a wreck at that spot. These houses... shacks is a better word... were every few yards on these curvy roads, and it was unnerving to say the least. It didn't give you much confidence in your driver, I can assure you that! Anyway, I decided I wasn't riding to Bogota in a car with one of these crazy drivers, even though most of my teammates did. I thought it might be better to take a plane, so that's what I did, even though I had to pay for the ticket. But as it turned out, the plane ride was as scary as the cars, and when it came time to land, the plane had to drop almost straight down to the landing strip due to the high mountains and short runway. I was a nervous wreck the

> whole time. I was really glad to get the ball game over and get out of Colombia.
>
> The ball park was poorly lit, and I could barely see my own hands in front of of my face, much less the ball. With all the scary travel, drug cartels, and other things, I was real anxious to get back to Maracaibo.

The people in Venezuela loved baseball, and to them the Western Raptors were heroes with rock star status. Luis Aparicio had actually warned the team of this early on and even advised them to stay clear of large, adoring crowds. Corky, after hitting a walk-off homerun to win a game here, saw what Aparicio meant when the team was forced to wait in their locker room for hours after the game due to the large and excited mob that assembled outside the club house door. "It was nothing like I'd ever seen before or since," he laughs.

Another surprisingly bizarre incident happened in a contest in which the Raptors ran up an insurmountable lead in the early innings. Corky, noticing the fans in the stadium's upper deck standing up "wave-style," could only wonder what was happening when these same upper deck fans began pouring a liquid from paper cups onto the fans in the lower deck. As it turned out, the liquid poured on the lower deck fans was urine, and it was, as Corky found out, not all that uncommon for fans to do this when the game was decided early. Corky reasons "they became bored," and since the richer fans could afford the lower deck seats, this action was "some way the poorer class could strike out against the wealthier class."

Corky also has stories about impossible traffic jams at intersections, and how cab drivers, when at four-way intersections, would sit and blow their horns for several minutes before working up enough nerve to make a mad dash in hopes of surviving the crossing unscathed. And as for the food selections in restaurants? There were none! You ate meat and potatoes. That's all that was listed on the menus.

But there were goats! They were everywhere—the hills, the roadsides, the pastureland, even on the streets of cities. Everywhere one went! According to Corky, some of his teammates even made a sport of throwing rocks at the poor creatures. "If you hit one with a rock just right, it would fall over dead," he laughs. "I know animal support groups would throw a fit over this now, but Fritz Ackley would pile rocks by the roadside and try to kill all he could. Fritz had his own goat population control program, I guess you could say."

All things considered—revolutions, missile crisis, drug cartels, crazy fans, cab drivers, and goats—Corky and Barbara came home with a warehouse of memories from their time in South America. But they didn't come home together! Instead, due to rumors of a coming governmental coup d'etat with drug cartel backing, Barbara and the other players' wives were sent back to the United States before the Raptors' season ended.

When the season did end, Corky was ready to come home. As he boarded the plane, and while watching the heavily armed security guards out his window, he couldn't help but be reminded of just how good it was to be headed back to Kentucky.

Chapter 18

If Ya Ain't Strikin' out, Ya Ain't Swingin' the Bat

Without question, the most exciting year of Corky's ten year professional career was that of 1963. First, there was spring training with the Milwaukee Braves of the National League. This was followed by several productive months with the Class AAA Denver Bears of the Pacific Coast League. Then, in what was the fulfillment of a life-long dream, came a place on the roster of a major league baseball club. Although the stay in the majors was short, it was the chance he had worked for.

The year began with the promising news he would be training with the Milwaukee Braves at their training facility in West Palm Beach, Florida. The Braves had held Corky's contract since '56, and he had toiled in their farm system since. Now, after seven seasons, he would have his chance.

Corky and Barbara had just returned from Venezuela, and after a brief visit with her mother in Owensboro, the couple hitched their twenty foot travel trailer behind their '62 Impala and headed for sunny Florida. Here, they rented a trailer lot about three miles from the Braves' newly constructed West Palm Beach Municipal Stadium.

It was now mid-February, and for the next five weeks Corky found himself training with future Hall of Famers Warren Spahn, Hank Aaron, Eddie Matthews and Joe Torre, as well as other established stars, such as Joe Adcock and Lew Burdette. Spahn, their ace pitcher, was nearing the end of his brilliant career, but, as Corky is quick to point out, hadn't given up his habit of chain smoking Camel cigarettes.

Along with these notable stars, the Milwaukee roster also included Del Crandall, Tommy Aaron, Roy McMillan, Denis Menke,

Len Gabrielson, Lee Maye, Rico Carty, Tony Cloniger, Denny Lemaster, Bob Sadowski, Gus Bell, Bob Shaw, Wade Blasingame, and Bob Uecker. Several of these were former teammates of Corky, so he wasn't completely among strangers.

During the first two weeks of camp, the team did plenty of calisthenics, stretching exercises, sprints, batting practice, fungo, and fielding drills, and even the team's stars were expected to participate in these. As the weeks went on, the practices intensified. Around 4 each afternoon, the day was over for all except pitchers and catchers, who worked a while longer. After all this, the players usually met at a local bar to socialize, unwind and discuss the day's events.

As for meals at the Braves camp, there were breakfast and lunch provided at the team's facility, but dinner wasn't provided by the team. Corky and Barbara's place of choice for this meal was a nearby Morrison's Cafeteria, a chain franchise they searched for in other cities, too.

Milwaukee's manager was Bobby Bragan, but Corky has few memories of him. "I wasn't around him much," he explains, "and I honestly don't think he gave me a real chance of proving myself." A few years ago Corky and Barbara were in Florida on vacation and decided to visit the ball park at Jacksonville where he had played parts of three seasons. After talking to someone who was employed there, the man informed them he was Bobby Bragan's brother. Corky explained he had been with the Braves in early '63, so Bragan's brother dialed Bobby and then handed Corky the phone. "We had a nice conversation, and he remembered me," Corky says of Bobby, "but I couldn't resist asking why he didn't give me a better shot at making the roster." Bragan's answer, after a brief pause, was to the point. "Well, I had several good hitters," he explained.

Corky was neither surprised nor disappointed when told he would be leaving the Braves camp that spring. "I think I did good when I did play, but with a solid team like that, good wasn't good enough." Corky enjoyed his time with the Braves, but claims to having been awe-struck just knowing he was wearing the same uniform as Hank Aaron.

Equally memorable was the experience of meeting greats from other teams, including several players from the New York Yankees when the Braves played them in an exhibition game that spring. Among those he met were Yogi Berra and Mickey Mantle. "It was special just sitting in the dugout and watching the Yankees play," Corky reports.

After receiving word he was to leave camp and report to AAA Denver of the Pacific Coast League, he and Barbara headed to Bartow, Florida, for the remainder of spring training with the Bears. Although camp was nearly over, it was still crammed full of games, including ones against some big league clubs. Among these opponents were the Kansas City Athletics, the Minnesota Twins, the Chicago White Sox, and even one against the team he had just trained with, the Milwaukee Braves.

After finishing spring training with the Bears in Bartow, Corky and Barbara headed west to Denver for the '63 season. Here, Corky would be playing in one of the minor's biggest ball parks, Bears Stadium, a name later changed to "Mile-High." Denver was one of baseball's most successful minor league teams, and their attendance figures were usually high. Their July 4th Fireworks Night would sometimes draw 45,000 to the park. For minor league play, Denver was, indeed, one of the bigger stages.

The Withrows loved living in Denver. "It was a big city, but with no traffic jams," Corky notes. "I loved the cool evenings, and with the thin air, baseballs would travel a long way. There were lots of good restaurants there, too, and we lived in a real nice, air-conditioned apartment in a complex with a swimming pool. Several of my teammates lived in that complex, and we were like a big family. We had a great time around that pool."

The "family" Corky mentions was a mixture of new and old faces. Among these were Bob Uecker, Tommy Aaron, Wade Blasingame, Len Gabrielson, Eddie Haas, Lou Johnson, Dick Kelley, Jim McKnight, Chi Chi Olivo, Jay Porter, Dennis Ribant, Phil Roof, Chico Salmon, Woody Woodward, and Ethan Blackaby. Ethan, known as "Blackie" to his teammates, would room with Corky when the Bears were on the road, and both Lou Johnson and Phil Roof were fellow Kentuckians.

Along with a team photo, the Denver season program featured individual photos of McKnight and Corky, both with bats on shoulders, and an accompanying caption labeling them, "Possibly the most prolific one-two punch in the Pacific Coast League."

Another teammate, pitcher Clay Carroll, would later have a fine major league career with the Cincinnati Reds. Clay, Corky claims, "was a square peg in a round hole, but in a good way. Maybe not the smartest guy on the team," he laughs, "but Clay would do anything for you, a great guy."

Carroll, born in Clanton, Alabama, was one of nine children of a cotton mill worker. His father's salary of $45 a week was stretched thin, and Clay once told a reporter that his biggest thrill each week was getting enough money from his father to buy a popsicle every Friday—the same as his eight siblings. With a thick southern drawl when he spoke—and an "I'll get 'er done" attitude—Carroll became a mainstay with the "Big Red Machine" of the '70s. His greatest moment was probably his win over the Boston Red Sox in the seventh game of the '75 World Series.

The Bears manager that season was Jack Tighe. Tighe (1913-2002) was an easy-going type, with tons of good stories. Corky describes him glowingly, calling him a "soft spoken" man, but one the players respected greatly. "He had his rules, and you abided by them. I liked him as much as anyone I ever played for."

Tighe was in his first season with the Bears that year, having just departed from the Louisville Colonels of the American Association. As a player, Jack had never risen above Class A during a career with the Tigers organization. His playing days were short (1936-1939), but by 1940 he was managing in the minors. By the latter half of '42, however, he was managing the Detroit Tigers and would return as their manager during the '57 and '58 seasons. Following this, Tighe worked in the Milwaukee organization. His entire career lasted fifty-two years, and his death came at age 88 in Florida.

The Pacific Coast League in 1963 was comprised of two divisions—North and South—with Denver in the South. With them in this division were the Oklahoma City 89ers, the San Diego Padres, the Dallas/Ft. Worth Rangers, and the Salt Lake City Bees. This order was the same as the teams finished the division race that season, and Denver would finish below Salt Lake City. The North division, in order of their finish, included the Spokane Indians, the Hawaiian Islanders, the Tacoma Giants, the Portland Beavers, and the Seattle Rainiers.

A close look at the location of these PCL cities reveals the extensive amount of travel necessary for the league's teams. Due to these longer distances, air travel was necessary, and PCL series often included more games scheduled than in other leagues. In the case of travel to Hawaii to play the Islanders, these trips sometimes involved nearly week-long stays. Few ball players, we can assume, objected to a few extra days in Hawaii.

The Bears may have been "family," but on the diamond they struggled. "We were a good hitting team, but had no pitching," Corky explains. The team led the league in homeruns with 173, runs scored with 843, and team batting with a .281 average, but suspect pitching, and a league-leading 210 fielding miscues doomed them to a 71-87 record, and ninth place finish in the 10 team PCL pennant race.

The Bears began the season with a strong showing, but major league call-ups soon began to deplete their roster of top line performers. At mid-season their pitching began to falter, but still they managed to remain in pennant contention through July. The drop from contender to near-bottom of league standings followed.

Memorable moments and stories are plentiful from this season in Denver. In the team's first home game, Corky rocketed a ball over the left field wall, and by so doing, claimed a $50 dollar bonus offered by the owner to the player hitting the Bears's first homerun of the season. "Barbara was seven months pregnant, climbed over the wall by our dugout, and still beat me to home plate to grab that check," Corky laughs.

Another memorable homerun, one also at Bears Stadium, knocked a letter "L" out of the word "BALL" on the seventy-five foot high scoreboard beyond the left field wall, 385 feet from home plate. A few days after this, in its nationally published monthly edition, *Sporting News* magazine made mention of this homer in an article featuring Corky.

As the weeks passed, and with Corky and the team often away on road trips, Barbara, desiring to be with family when their first child was born, moved back to Owensboro. With her departure, Corky's teammate J. W. "Jay" Porter moved in with Corky, sharing the rent on the Withrow apartment.

Jay, a native of Shawnee, Oklahoma, was born in 1933, and at age seventeen had played on an American Legion team with Frank Robinson. In 1951 he was signed by the Chicago White Sox. Robinson was signed by the Cincinnati Reds that same year, but Porter's signing bonus of $65,000 was significantly higher than the amount paid to Robinson by the Reds.

Porter's major league debut came as a catcher with the St. Louis Browns in '52, and from '55-'58 he was with Detroit. Short stints with the Indians, Senators, and Cardinals followed, but by the end of '59 his big league days were over. The remainder of his playing days would be in the minors, and a managing career would follow. It is worth noting that in 2006, Jay Porter was named "One of the Ten Greatest Characters in Detroit Tigers History."

If Jay Porter could be classified a "character," so could Corky Withrow, and when together as roommates, the two found ways to prove it. Corky explains:

> When Jay and I shared the apartment in Denver, we would stop by the Coors Brewery every day. It wasn't far from the ballpark. The people there would give us two cases of beer to take to the park for our teammates to share after practices and games, every day of the season at no charge. We never told our teammates we were getting this beer free, and they never found out differently. We were great guys in their eyes! During a stretch of the season, we hit a really bad slump and lost several games in a row. Our manager, Jack Tighe, got pretty upset with us and banned beer from the clubhouse. Even though he banned the beer, for whatever reason, we never told the people at Coors, and kept picking up the two free cases every day. We'd take them to the apartment for ourselves. By the time I left there for the Cardinals in September, the cases of beer were stacked

to the ceiling, and it looked like a brewery in there. I don't know what Jay did with all that beer after I left.

Another story Corky tells on Porter also involved Ethan Blackaby, Corky's roommate on the road. Explains Corky:

> We were playing in Seattle and sitting in the dugout when Blackie spit a big wad of tobacco juice on Jay's white, sanitary socks. Jay stayed cool, though, and sat there without saying anything. Of course, everybody in the dugout, except Jay, thought that was hilarious. A couple of innings later, after everyone had forgotten about the spitting incident, Jay put a huge wad in his mouth, walked over to Blackie, grabbed both sides of his head, and spit tobacco juice in his ear. Everyone in the dugout was rolling with laughter!

Corky was with the Denver Bears for 145 of their 158 regular season games that summer of '63. His 29 homeruns led the team, and to go with these were 118 hits in 477 at-bats for a .247 average, 99 RBIs, 5 triples, 19 doubles, 79 runs scored, 51 base-on-balls, and even two stolen bases. He did, however, strike out 144 times.

Now, after seven seasons of professional baseball, and at age 25, Corky was still holding on to his dream of playing in the majors. But, still, he couldn't help feeling his window of opportunity was closing. Barbara, now nine months pregnant, was back in Owensboro awaiting the birth of their first child, and Corky, through hard lessons learned, realized that baseball couldn't offer a stable, secure, or long-lasting career for most. With this in mind, he had to wonder if the opportunity to play major league ball would come again, and would he have the ability to be successful if it did?

As the '63 season with Denver was winding down, Corky had several things on his mind outside of baseball. Barbara was hundreds of miles away with their baby due any day, and although she was with family and in good hands, he couldn't help but feel a bit of guilt for his absence.

On the 5th of September, Corky and the Bears were in Dallas for an overnight series with the Rangers. With the conclusion of the first of these two games, the team dressed, gathered for a team meal of ribs, salad, bread, and beer, and then returned to their hotel rooms sometime around 1 a.m.

Normally, players would sleep until late in the morning after a night game, but around 6 a.m. the phone in Ethan and Corky's room rang. Corky was groggy when he answered, and his first thought was that someone from Owensboro was calling with news concerning Barbara. This was not the case, however, as the call was from Jack Tighe, his manager.

Tighe informed him his contract had been purchased by the St. Louis Cardinals, and he was to pack his gear, catch a plane at the Dallas airport, and then join the Cardinals at Forbes Field in Pittsburgh that same evening. Of course, Corky could hardly believe what he was being told.

This call represented, he explains, "the culmination of all my efforts, frustrations, dreams, plans... everything." With only the clothes he had worn to Dallas, a shaving kit, a change of underwear, and his glove and cleats, Corky—after a quick call to Barbara—caught a cab to the airport.

After an all-day flight, one including several stops along the way, Corky arrived at the Pittsburgh airport around 8 that evening. From there he caught a cab, and while riding through downtown Pittsburgh, spent the entire time trying to decide what he would do and say once he joined his new teammates in the dugout at Forbes Field. Corky, battling a constant barrage of emotions that evening, recalls:

> It was intimidating to know you would be walking into a dugout with people like Stan Musial, Ken Boyer, Curt Flood, and on and on. These were guys I had grown up reading and hearing about, and St. Louis was one of the teams I had listened to on the radio when I was a boy. Who was I to walk in and say anything to them? It

> was pretty intimidating to tell the truth. I figured it was best to just sit down and say nothing.

When Corky stepped out of the cab at the ballpark, he was on his own. Unescorted, he found his way to the visitor's clubhouse and walked in. It was now around 9:30, and the second game of the double header was in the mid-innings. Corky continues:

> I walked in the clubhouse, but there wasn't anyone there. I looked around and noticed a uniform hanging on a locker with my name on it. The uniform was number 29, and I can't explain how I felt when I saw that uniform hanging there for me. Seeing the 'Birds on the Bat' on a uniform with my name on it was a dream come true, but I was so nervous I could barely get it buttoned!

By the time #29 found his way to the Cardinals dugout it was, best he can recall, the fifth inning, and St. Louis was trailing the Pirates by five. Corky, worn out from his short night's rest and full day of plane travel, was running only on nervous energy. "My mind was racing a hundred miles an hour. It was surreal that night," he claims.

Taking a seat on the bench, Corky said nothing. "I wasn't anything to these guys, and I didn't want them thinking that I thought I was anything special," he explains. Then, in what Corky considers one of his greatest career moments, a Cardinals player walked up to introduce himself. "Hello, I'm Stan Musial," the player said. Corky, now freed from his self-imposed silence, grabbed Stan's hand and replied: "You don't have to tell me who you are Mr. Musial. I'm Corky Withrow."

Corky is proud it was Musial who first welcomed him to the team, and following this, other Cardinals, including Curt Flood, Dick Groat, Mike Shannon, Curt Simmons, Tim McCarver, Julian Javier, and Ken Boyer did the same. "They sure do grow 'em big in Kentucky," Boyer said to Corky.

These warm welcomes certainly eased Corky's anxieties that night. "They couldn't have made it any easier or better for me.

They were great," he recalls. Now, feeling more relaxed than before, Corky returned to his seat, assuming he would remain there until the game's end. But he was wrong.

Minutes later, Johnny Keane, the Cards' manager, approached Corky with instructions to pinch hit for Ron Taylor, their pitcher. Corky, caught off guard by Keane's instructions, struggled to maintain his composure as he fumbled for a bat and helmet. At the plate he would be facing the hard throwing Bob Veale, a 6'6" "fireball" pitcher who, Corky groans, "threw little-bitty baseballs like a giant launching bbs off a mountain." Veale was a tough assignment for even the league's most experienced hitters, but sending a rookie like Corky Withrow to the plate bordered on insanity.

Corky remembers every pitch Veale threw him that night. Catching for the Pirates was Forrest "Smoky" Burgess, and Corky remembers Smoky laughing when, after a call strike fastball on the first pitch, he turned to Burgess and said, "I ain't seen it yet, but that one sounded high!" After a call second strike, Corky proceeded to foul off the next four pitches, but a third strike followed on a curveball.

After losing to the Pirates 5-0, the Cards returned to their hotel where Corky was assigned a room by himself. Exhausted from all that happened, he was still delighted beyond words when Julian Javier, Tim McCarver, Curt Flood, and Carl Sawatski asked him to join them for dinner at a nearby restaurant. It was an offer he couldn't refuse!

At the time of Corky's contract purchase and Cardinals call-up, St. Louis was involved in a tight National League pennant race with the Los Angeles Dodgers. The Cardinals had won nine straight and had an 81-60 record when he joined them. After losing to the Pirates in Corky's first game on Sept. 6, St. Louis would start another winning streak of 10 that would continue until the 16th. With these 19 victories in 20 games, the Cardinals narrowed the Dodgers' lead to one game. Corky couldn't have chosen a more exciting time to join the St. Louis roster.

On Saturday, Sept. 7, Corky's first full day with St. Louis, the team reported to Forbes Field around 10 a.m. to prepare for the third of their four game series with the Pirates. "I had gotten up early that morning and was so excited I couldn't wait to get to the ballpark," he recalls. "I had a hotel room by myself that weekend, but I couldn't sleep at all."

After team exercises, Corky, in another surreal experience, found himself throwing baseballs with Stan Musial during warm ups, and then posing with Stan in a photo arranged by a Central City *Times-Argus* reporter. The reporter wasn't at the ballpark that day, but had contacted a Pittsburgh photographer with the request after word reached Central City of Corky's call-up. This photo with Musial is the most treasured one from Corky's baseball days.

And as if all this wasn't enough, Corky also learned he would be starting in right field that day, batting fifth in the order behind Ken Boyer, the Cardinals' third baseman. Corky played six innings of this game, but in two at bats against Pirate hurlers Bob Gibbon and Earl Francis, had no hits. There was an RBI-producing ground out to third, however, and this RBI would prove to be the only one of his month-long major league career. St. Louis won the game 6-5. At least he has the satisfaction of knowing his RBI made a difference in the one run victory!

The fourth and final game of this series was a Sunday afternoon contest. Corky wouldn't be in the starting lineup this time, nor would he be inserted as a substitute. The Cardinals would win this one 3-2, and with the victory, see their record climb to 83-61. After this game, still trailing Los Angeles in the pennant race, the Cardinals headed home for a four game series with the Cubs. But Corky wasn't on this flight back to St. Louis. Instead, he had returned to his apartment in Denver to pack his clothes and bid farewell to his Denver teammates. He would then rejoin the Cardinals for their series against the Cubs in St. Louis.

Without question, the St. Louis Cardinals, owned by Gussie Busch at that time, was one of the most successful of all major league organizations. Dick Groat, an all-star performer for the

An old photo of Bosse Field, Evansville, Ind. Corky began his career here with the Evansville Braves in '56, and ended it here with the Evansville White Sox in 1966.

Bob Coleman coached the Evansville Braves durring Corky's first Pro-Season in '56.

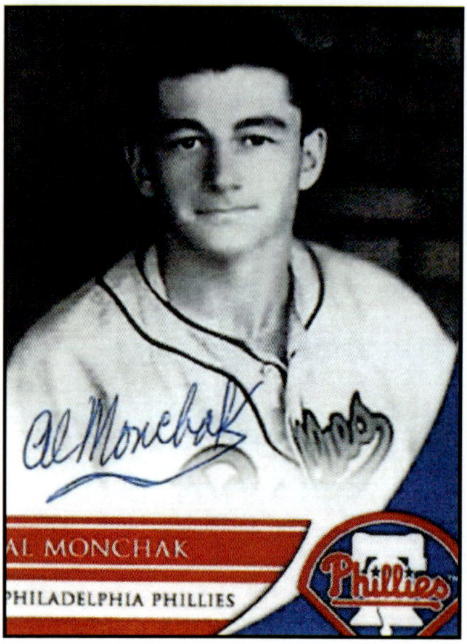

Al Monchak

Sibby Sisti

Harry Minor

Jimmy Dykes

Monchak, Sisti and Minor managed Corky at Wellsville, Cedar Rapids, and Jacksonville. Dykes was his manager for spring training in '60.

Corky's military stint with a Wisconsin Reserve Unit was served at Camp Leonard Wood, Missouri in '59-60. As a star-performer for the camp's "base team", he traveled around the Midwest playing basketball.

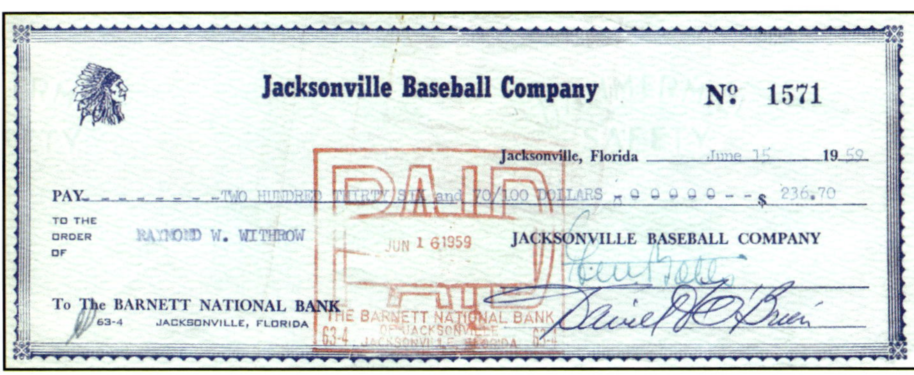

This check, cashed by Corky on June 16, 1959, was issued to him by the Jacksonville (Braves) Baseball Company for $236.70.

Among the many close friends Corky made throughout his baseball days were Emerit "Em" Lindbeck (seen above), Merritt Ranew, Jay Porter, and Ethan Blackaby. On several occasions these men were teammates—sometime roommates—and the friendships they built lasted long after their playing days ended.

Ethan Blackaby

Merritt Ranew with Corky in 2001.

Merritt Ranew during his Louisville Colonels days.

J.W. "Jay" Porter

Red Murff

Walker Cooper

Ernie White

Bill Adair

Murff, White and Adair managed Corky at Jacksonville, Mobile, and Austin, while Cooper was in charge at Dallas, Ft. Worth.

On October 11, 1962, Corky was honored with a hometown celebration after his very successful '62 season with the Austin Senators.

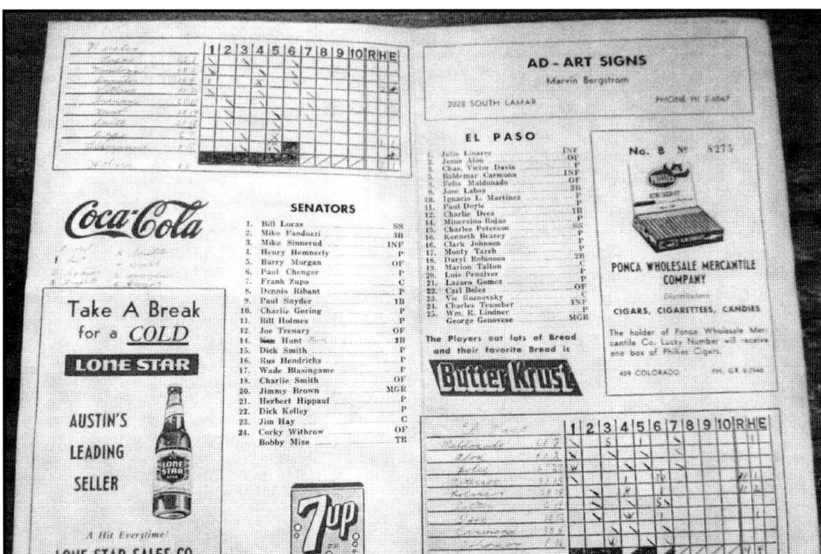

Corky is playing right field and batting "clean up" for the Austin Senators in this 1962 Austin vs El Paso program.

Chuck Dressen

Jimmy Brown

Bobby Bragan

Carl Sawatski, a Cardinals catcher, was Corky's roommate when the team was on the road.

Aug. 26, 1962

"Man to Fan"

By HERB PARKER
Sports Editor

If his current batting statistics hold up a boy from Central City will be playing major league baseball next season. Raymond "Corky" Withrow, the best all-around athlete ever produced by the sports-minded Muhlenberg County town, has been belting the cover off the baseball for Austin, Texas, and Austin is an AA club, just a hop-skip-and-jump from the majors.

Corky began gaining recognition almost as soon as he began playing for Austin last spring. His home run output began immediately and by the first of this month he was threatening the all-time Austin homer mark of 22.

Withrow not only broke that record several days ago but has now hit 30 round-trippers. His home runs have helped him accumulate a whipping 91 runs-batted-in and his batting average, as of last Sunday was a vert respectable .276.

Jimmy Brown, Withrow's manager at Austin, said recently that Corky "was doing a tremendous job" this season. Brown reports that "the 6-5 soft spoken kid from Kentucky has played five positions for Austin this year, third base, first base and all three outfield sports."

It supposedly affects a man's hitting when his fielding positions are constantly changed but Withrow has adjusted to each situation. He has been stationed in centerfield during the past several weeks.

Austin is a farm club of the Milwaukee Braves and Corky has been in the Braves' organization ever since he signed a bonus contract in 1956.

Corky did not play in '56 but went to the Class D Wellsville, N. Y., team in 1957 and played there for two seasons. He then began to move up quickly, playing for Braves' farm clubs at Cedar Rapids, Jacksonville, Fla., Mobile, Ala., and then Austin.

When Corky first signed he planned to spend the winters playing basketball for Kentucky Wesleyan but the NCAA, after it reportedly got some prodding from another state school that desired Withrow's services, ruled that he could not play pro baseball and also play ameteur basketball for Wesleyan. Other boys had done just that while performing for the Panthers but in Corky's case the NCAA said "no".

Withrow then enrolled at Georgetown College and played basketball for the Tigers. He eventually decided to devote his full time to baseball however and gave up his collegiate hoop career. Corky played with the Adams' Texaco Owensboro basketball team last year during the off season.

Withrow is 6-5 and weighs over 200 pounds. He is fast and has a good throwing arm. Corky should have over 100 runs-batted-in when Austin season ends on Sept. 3 and that, plus his home run total, will certainly cause the Braves to take a long look at the Kentucky product next spring.

With a couple of breaks and a good spring training performance, Corky will be on the Braves roster when the 1962 major league season gets underway.

Luis Aparicio

During the winter months of '62-'63 Corky played for the Rapinos Western Raptors in Venezuela. Les Moss and Luis Aparicio managed the team as well as playing.

This page, from the 1963 Denver Bears program, features Corky and teammate Jim McKnight. Denver was a member of the Pacific Coast League. "Bears One-Two Punch: Corky Withrow on the left, and Jim McKnight on the right, should give Denver the most prolific power punch in the PCL this season. Last Year Withrow hit 34 homers, with Austin, and McKnight, who played with the Chicago Cubs last season, mostly as a pinch-hitter, belted out 24 circuit smashes while with Houston in 1961."

RAYMOND W. WITHROW

First Baseman - Outfielder

Born Nov. 28, 1937, Highcoal, W. Va. 6'3½", 197 pounds. Bats and throws right. Resides in Central City, Kentucky. Married. 1962 Texas League All-Star Outfielder. Signed by Dick Keely.

Year	Club	G	AB	R	H	2B	3B	HR	SB	RBI	Pct.
1959	Cedar Rapids ...	75	248	49	80	13	2	19	0	61	.282
1960	Jacksonville	112	335	46	81	8	5	13	3	44	.241
1961	Mobile	58	213	24	53	9	2	7	0	32	.249
1961	Austin	50	175	20	47	11	2	8	0	29	.269
1962	Austin	131	486	92	141	22	6	34	0	105	.290

This photo comes from the 1963 Denver Bears Program.

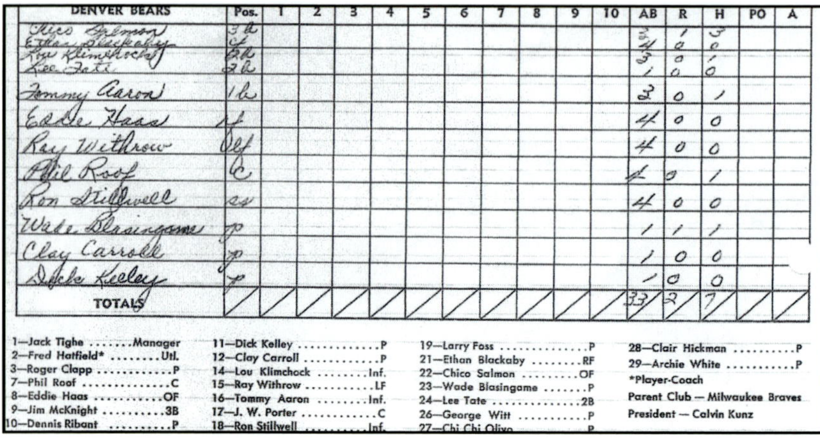

DENVER BEARS	Pos.	1	2	3	4	5	6	7	8	9	10	AB	R	H	PO	A
Chico Salmon	3b											3	1	3		
Ethan Blackaby	rf											4	0	0		
Lou Klimchock	2b											3	0	1		
Lee Tate	2b											1	0	0		
Tommy Aaron	1b											3	0	1		
Eddie Haas	lf											4	0	0		
Ray Withrow	[illegible]											4	0	0		
Phil Roof	c											4	0	1		
Ron Stillwell	ss											4	0	0		
Wade Blasingame	p											1	1	1		
Clay Carroll	p											1	0	0		
Dick Kelley	p											1	0	0		
TOTALS												33	2	7		

1—Jack Tighe ....Manager
2—Fred Hatfield* ....Utl.
3—Roger Clapp ....P
7—Phil Roof C
8—Eddie Haas ....OF
9—Jim McKnight 3B
10—Dennis Ribant ....P
11—Dick Kelley ....P
12—Clay Carroll ....P
14—Lou Klimchock ....Inf.
15—Ray Withrow ....LF
16—Tommy Aaron ....Inf.
17—J. W. Porter C
18—Ron Stillwell ....Inf.
19—Larry Foss ....P
21—Ethan Blackaby ....RF
22—Chico Salmon ....OF
23—Wade Blasingame ....P
24—Lee Tate 2B
26—George Witt ....P
27—Chi Chi Olivo ....P
28—Clair Hickman ....P
29—Archie White ....P
*Player-Coach
Parent Club — Milwaukee Braves
President — Calvin Kunz

This scorecard, from a '63 Denver Bears program, shows Corky listed as Ray Withrow. Among other Bears in the line-up that day were Clay Carroll, Tommy Aaron, Wade Blasingame, Ethan Blackaby and Paducah, Kentucky native, Phil Roof.

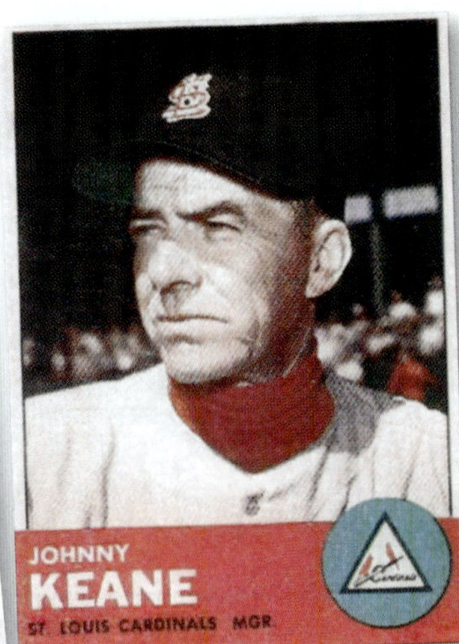

Without question, the '63 regular-season was Corky's most memorable. First came Spring training with the Milwaukee Braves, followed by Pacific Coast League play with the Denver Bears. The season then culminated with a month with the St. Louis Cardinals. Jack Tighe, left, managed Corky at Denver. Keane, right, managed Corky at St. Louis.

This was taken during spring training with the Milwaukee Braves in 1963. He failed to earn a spot on the Braves' roster, however.

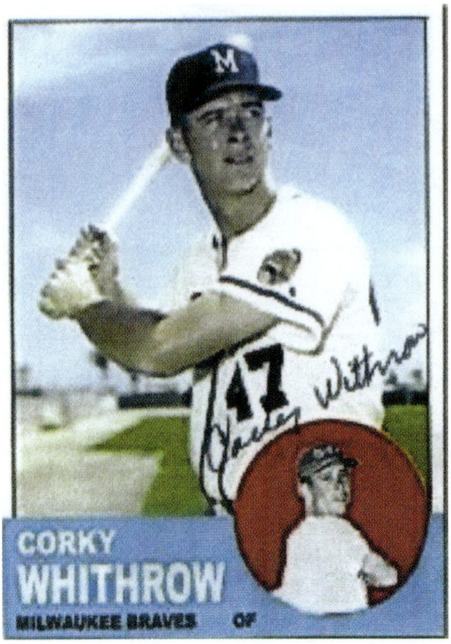

This baseball "trading card" shows Corky in a Milwaukee Braves uniform. It was taken during his spring-training days in Florida with the Braves. Take note of the fact that the name Withrow is misspelled.

Although this photo is autographed with the date showing 1963, it was actually taken at Spring training with the Cardinals in Florida in '64.

Although arriving much too late in the season to be included in the team's photo, Corky would join the St. Louis Cardinals in Sept. of '63. On the far right, front row (#6), is Stan Musial.

On the left is Stan Musial, on the right is Corky Withrow. This photo, taken at Forbes Field in Pittsburgh, was made by a Pittsburgh photographer at the request of the Central Times-Argus after hearing of his call-up to St. Louis the previous day. The date of this photo would have been on Sept. 7, '63.

Taken at Sportsman Park in St. Louis, this photo shows Corky in a pre-game pose. The right field bleachers are in the background.

Corky Withrow as a St. Louis Cardinal 1963 taken in the dugout at Crosley Field in Cincinnati, OH.

Sportsman Park, St. Louis, Missouri

This photo, taken at Crosley field in Cincinnati in September of '63, shows Corky with baseball and pen in hand before a game. To his right is Stan Musial, an unidentified boy, and Jerome "Dizzy" Dean, a former "Gashouse Gang" Cardinal, and television broadcaster.

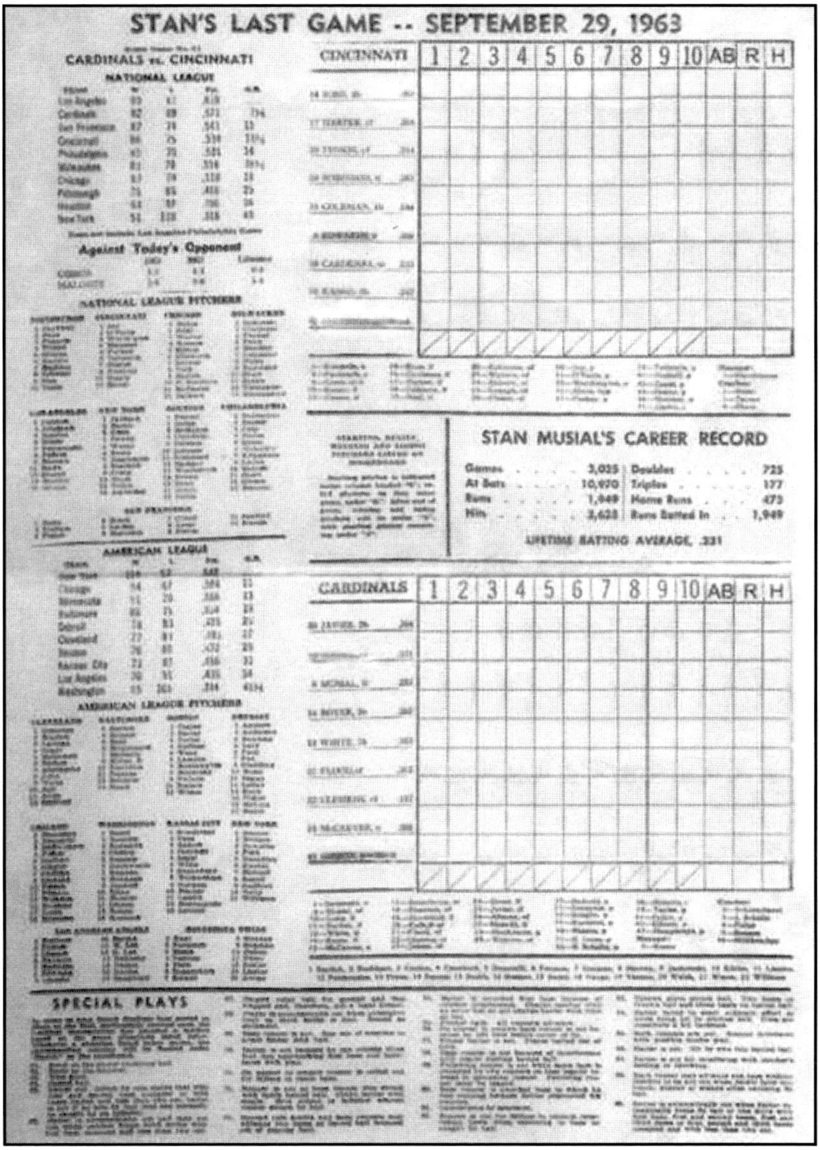

The scorecard from Stan Musial's final game as a Major Leaguer on Sept. 29, 1963. This was also Corky's final Major League game. Corky's name is listed on the roster below the scorecard, the third row, last name.

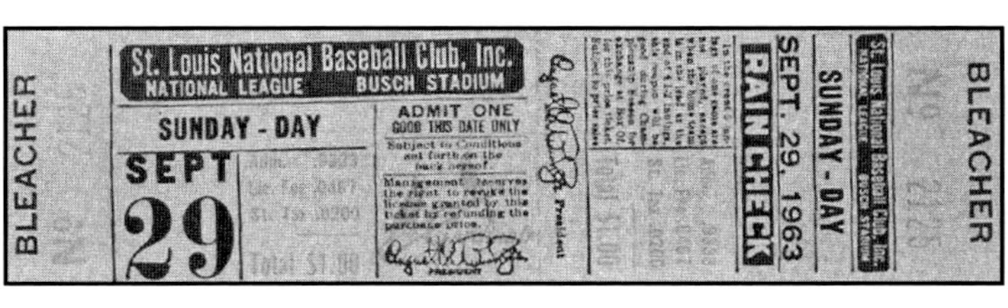

Corky poses for the camera prior to a game at Wrigley Field in Chicago.

✦ Player ✦ Transactions

MAJOR LEAGUES

Angels—Traded infielder Billy Moran in three-way deal that sent infielder Jerry Kindall from Indians to Twins and infielder Vic Power from Twins to Angels.

Athletics—Sent outfielder Manny Jimenez and pitcher Aurelio Monteagudo to Dallas; recalled pitcher Dan Pfister and outfielder John Wojcik from same team.

Braves—Optioned pitcher Dick Kelley to Denver.

Cubs—Sent catcher Merritt Ranew to Braves to complete deal for first baseman-outfielder Len Gabrielson.

Phillies — Recalled pitcher Dave Bennett from Chattanooga.

White Sox—Recalled pitcher Fred Talbot from Indianapolis.

CLASS AAA

Atlanta—Signed outfielder Ed Olivares.

Buffalo — Sent pitcher Ray Apple to Williamsport.

Columbus—Sent outfielder Dave Kwiatkowski to Asheville.

Rochester — Released shortstop Don Buddin, who signed with Indianapolis.

Toronto — Optioned pitcher Ed Hobaugh to Hawaii.

Denver — Sent first baseman George Kopacz to Austin.

Salt Lake City — Sent outfielder Bob Will to Jacksonville in exchange for outfielder Ray (Corky) Withrow, who was assigned to Fort Worth.

Seattle — Signed third baseman Tim Cullen.

Spokane—Sent pitcher Steve Anderson to Salem, Ore.

CLASS AA

Reading—Sent pitcher Charles Bunker to Winston-Salem.

Williamsport—Sent pitcher Jan Wall to Auburn; released pitcher Jay Meeks.

Lynchburg — Sent first baseman Dale (Skip) Rohde to Tidewater.

Fort Worth—Signed pitcher Jon Robisch.

Tulsa—Released outfielder Howie Bedell.

6-20-64

In June of '64 the Jacksonville Suns traded Corky to the Salt Lake City Bees. Due to the Chicago Cubs interest however, Corky was told to report to the Ft. Worth Cats, a Cubs affiliate. Corky would play for Salt Lake City in the following ('65) season.

Stan Hack "Smilin Stan" was Corky's manager at Salt Lake City.

Alex Grammas

Harry "The Hat" Walker

Grammas was Corky's manager at Ft. Worth, while Walker managed him at Jacksonville.

Corky began his final season of baseball with the Class AAA Syracuse Chiefs of the International League, but at his request was sent to the Evansville White Sox. Corky is pictured with the Chiefs in the second row, second from left, and in the same row, fifth from left, is Frank Carswell, his Manager.

Frank Carswell

CORKY WITHROW PROFESSIONAL BASEBALL STATISTICS:

*PLAYED BASEBALL BEGINNING IN THE SECOND HALF OF THE 1956 SEASON, LASTING UNTIL THE CONCLUSION OF THE 1966 SEASON.

*MINOR LEAGUE GAME APPEARANCES	1,128
*MINOR LEAGUE PLATE APPEARANCES	4,300
*MINOR LEAGUE OFFICIAL AT-BATS	3,816
*MINOR LEAGUE HITS	991
*MINOR LEAGUE STRIKEOUTS	884
*MINOR LEAGUE HOMERUNS	211
*MINOR LEAGUE RUNS-BATTED-IN	663
*MINOR LEAGUE LIFETIME BATTING AVG.	.266
*COMBINED LIFE TIME BATTING AVG.	.260

*MAJOR LEAGUE GAME APPEARANCES	6
*MAJOR LEAGUE OFFICIAL AT-BATS	9
*MAJOR LEAGUE HITS	0
*MAJOR LEAGUE STRIKEOUTS	2
*MAJOR LEAGUE HOMERUNS	0
*MAJOR LEAGUE RUNS-BATTED-IN	1
*MAJOR LEAGUE BASE ON BALLS	0
*MAJOR LEAGUE BATTING AVERAGE	.000

*MINOR LEAGUE STATISTICS BY LEVEL:

*CLASS D	(2 SEASONS)	BA-.277	HITS-247	HOMERUNS-51
*CLASS B	(2 SEASONS)	BA-.321	HITS-80	HOMERUNS-19
*CLASS A	(2 SEASONS)	BA-.234	HITS-122	HOMERUNS-21
*CLASS AA	(4 SEASONS)	BA-.266	HITS-327	HOMERUNS-67
*CLASS AAA	(5 SEASONS)	BA-.233	HITS-215	HOMERUNS-53

*TEAMS PLAYED FOR DURING REGULAR-SEASON:

*EVANSVILLE BRAVES
*WELLSVILLE BRAVES
*JACKSONVILLE BRAVES
*CEDAR RAPIDS BRAVES
*JACKSONVILLE BRAVES
*DALLAS/FT.WORTH RANGERS
*MOBILE BAY BEARS
*AUSTIN SENATORS
*AUSTIN SENATORS
*RAPINOS WESTERN RAPTORS
*DENVER BEARS
*ST.LOUIS CARDINALS
*JACKSONVILLE SUNS
*FT.WORTH CATS
*SALT LAKE CITY BEES
*ATLANTA CRACKERS/BRAVES
*SYRACUSE CHIEFS
*EVANSVILLE WHITE SOX

Chart with statistics

2198 Inubushi Kamicho,Sano
Tochigi 327-0806
JAPAN

Dear Mr. RAY WITHROW

How do you do?
I have been a biggest fan of you since I met you on baseball book. I love Baseball in my all of my life.
Baseball is the most beautiful game in the world.
I regret that I cannot watch your live play in ball parks.
I respect your play in the Ball parks and your human nature.And you are so great nice guy !!
I have been studying baseball history in my life also I love 60's Days.It's great decade,"The Golden Age".
And I hope that this letter will find you and your family in the very best of health and happiness.
I realy appreciate that you read my letter.
Please, May I have your autograph on my card?
I want to keep your biggest fan forever.
Thanks for your kindness.
Domo Arigato gozaimasu

レイ・ウィズローさん
どうもありがとうございます!

Sincerely yours
From
Kohei Nirengi
KOHEI NIRENGI
二連木 康平

This letter, although not a typical one, is an example of the hundreds of fan mail and autograph requests that Corky, even in 2015, still receives. This one, from Japan, is rather humorous due to its broken English.

Corky and Barbara Withrow

Corky and Barbara with son Keith, and daughter Kelly Lynn.

The Withrow Family. Back row, left to right: Kelly Lynn Burke, Carl Burke, Keith Withrow, Kim Withrow, Chad Pryor, Lester Cantrell. Second row, left to right: Jackson Burke, Alexa Burke, Barbara Withrow, Corky Withrow, Whitney Pryor, Hayley Cantrell. Front: Olivia Burke, Logan Cantrell.

ATHLETICS with Alexa

His powerful fist shattered the faces of the jukeboxes upon his exit, while his face twisted in rage and disgust. Surrounding him, teammates did the same as a torrent of uniforms stormed from the Texas establishment. A few minutes earlier, peaceful baseball players entered for a meal. Chaos began with just four words from the manager's lips, "You can't eat here."

When Tommy Aaron (brother to Hank Aaron) and Billy Lucas (brother-in-law to Aaron) entered the restaurant, they were asked to leave. So Aaron and Lucas left, followed by the rest of their team. In 1961, desegregation was only beginning. Black athletes still slept in separate hotels than whites, because the fight for equality was ongoing.

"[This incident] was disturbing to the whole team, because [to us] there was no black and white, no color barrier of any kind. We respected each other's abilities. We rooted for each other, and ... that was just a disgrace to the black players. From then on, we showed solidarity to each other," recalled Mr. Corky Withrow, a former St. Louis Cardinals outfielder and KHSAA Hall of Famer.

Withrow also remembers the All-American City basketball tournament at Kentucky Wesleyan College in 1957, when Mississippi State was pitted against Iona University, whose jersey was worn by several African Americans. Before game time, the governor of Mississippi called his athletes home because "black and white were not mixed at the time," Withrow explained.

Throughout his career, one athlete broke the color barrier. At the plate, he stood with pride, unaffected by the spitting remarks from the sidelines and field. He combatted racial slurs and discrimination. He completely altered the sports world, turning it upside down by mixing cultures, races and ideas.

"You have to respect a player that knows that he is going to get the abuse, the name calling and the cussing, ... but still you had him [in the] situation that changed the face of baseball forever," Withrow said. "Thank goodness for Jackie Robinson. The whole Major League should be thankful for a person like [him]."

Today, stadium lights illuminate fields on which black skin lines up next to white, on which Caucasian hands shake those of African Americans where equality reigns. The intense work of previous athletes should not be forgotten. The fact that rosters are filled with players of all ethnicities and backgrounds should be appreciated.

In sports, race doesn't matter. Ability does. Passion does. Hard work does. Talent knows no racial barrier. Thank you to all players who made that possible. Thank you for your sweat and willingness to work despite hate. Thank you for your tears, competing despite hurt. Thank you for your radical stance, continuing the fight to prove that all men are created equal, both on and off the field and court.

Corky's granddaughter, Alexa Burke, was a journalist for her Daviess County high school newspaper, "The Big Red Machine "In the paper's September 24, 2014 issue, Alexa provided this article on race and sports: One including a quote from her grandfather.

In 2010, Corky was honored with induction into the Dawahares/KHSAA Hall of Fame in Lexington. A medal was presented to Corky by his son Keith, and a plaque was presented by KHAA President, Julian Tackett, shown here with Corky.

Pictured left to right: Charlie Thurman, Corky Withrow, Coach Ron Bevars, and Sherrill Williams. The event is Corky's induction into the Dawahares/KHSAA Hall of Fame in 2010.

On Saturday night, July 12, 2014, Corky was inducted into the Kentucky High School Basketball Hall of Fame at the Historic State Theater in Elizabethtown. With each class, sixteen members are inducted, and Corky's represented the third of these groups to be honored.

This photo, taken on the front porch of the Wayland Community Center in Floyd County in September of 2015. Shown (left to right) Corky Withrow, Kelly Coleman, Charlie Thurman, Rick Whobrey, Sherrill Williams, and J.R. Van Hoose. J.R. is a former Kentucky "Mr. Basketball" like Kelly, and was also a 2013 inductee into the High School Basketball Hall of Fame in Elizabethtown. Photo by Kayla Moore.

Taken at the Wayland Community Center after a long day of filming for a documentary on the life and athletic career of Kelly Coleman, this photo by Harold Kelly features Corky and "King" Kelly surrounded by friends. Kneeling: Rick Whobrey. Right to left, standing: Serur Dawhare, J. R. VanHoose, Kayla Moore (J.R.'s fiancé), Sandra Turner, Tyanna Hansford, Ben Tackett Jr., Jerry Fultz (Mountain Sports Hall of Fame Executive Director), Stewart Hall, Charlie Thurman, King Fultz (Jerry's wife). Rear-Center: Sherrill Williams.

Cardinals that season, later described them as "the finest organization in all professional sports," and one that "treated players better, treated your kids and family better, paid you better, and made travel better." Although Corky's time with St. Louis wasn't long, he agrees with Groat's assessment, adding, "I can't even start to describe what it was like to be a St. Louis Cardinal. We were heroes and rock stars to those fans, and everywhere we went, people wanted autographs. Everyone from management to fans treated us great, and I wouldn't take anything for my time there." Even today, decades later, hardly a month passes without Corky receiving letters from a St. Louis fan, usually one requesting an autograph to add to a collection.

Gussie Busch had made great efforts to build a successful organization in St. Louis and had even recently hired Branch Rickey as a senior consultant. Along with others, these two had put together what many considered the best infield in baseball, one that would find all four of its starters in the July All-Star game. These four were Bill White, Julian Javier, Dick Groat, and Ken Boyer. To go with these, management had also added a potentially outstanding young catcher named Tim McCarver.

After Corky's first weekend with the Cardinals, the team returned to St. Louis for a four game series with the Cubs. These games, played on four consecutive days from Sept. 9 to 12, were all St. Louis victories, but Corky appeared in none. On Sept. 10, a day on which the Cards won 8-0, he received a phone call informing him of the birth of his and Barbara's child, a son they named Keith Earl. But with St. Louis in the thick of a pennant race, and the regular season conclusion only three weeks away, Corky felt it in his and Barbara's best long-term interest that he remain with the team.

Following the four game sweep of Chicago, Milwaukee came to Busch Stadium for another four game series from Sept. 13 to 15. The Cardinals won all four of these, pushing their record to 91-61. Although Corky saw no playing time in this series, he did have the opportunity to visit with several former teammates now on the Milwaukee roster.

Having won 19 of their last 20 games, but still one game out of first place, the Cardinals next played host to the league-leading Los Angeles Dodgers. The three game series (Sept. 16-18) would be the most crucial of the Cardinals' remaining ten games, and anything less than two victories—barring a total Dodger collapse—would destroy their pennant-winning hopes.

The first game in this series was of some historical note, as Dodger owner Walter O'Malley had arranged for three California television stations to broadcast the game in Los Angeles, the first time a Dodger road game was shown there. Behind the pitching of Johnny Podres, the Dodgers won this game 3-1. Corky, once again, saw no game action that day.

The following day, against Dodgers pitcher Sandy Koufax, St. Louis lost again, this time in a 4-0 shutout. Corky, as a pinch hitter in the ninth inning, batted once against this future Hall of Famer, but grounded out. St. Louis hopes for a pennant were dwindling away.

The final game of the Dodgers series was another loss for the Cardinals, this time 6-5. Corky played in the twelfth and thirteenth innings of this extra-inning classic, but in his only at-bat failed to get a hit. St. Louis held a 5-4 lead in the top of the ninth, but Dodger Dick Nen, a newly arrived call-up from Spokane, hit a game-tying homerun. Los Angeles would go on to win in the thirteenth, and with the series sweep, had increased their league lead from one game to four in just three days. Nen, by the way, would never have another hit while with the Dodgers, nor would he have another hit for any other big league club until 1965, this one with the Washington Senators.

The Cardinals were devastated after these three losses to the Dodgers, and with only seven games remaining, realized that all legitimate pennant hopes were gone. Mathematically, it was still possible, of course, but with absolutely no margin for error. It would require a miracle.

The next two games, at Cincinnati's Crosley Field against the Reds, were two more St. Louis losses. Blame it on the let down after the Dodgers series if you must, but only two teams—the Dodgers and Reds—had topped the Cards in their regular season series. It was while at Crosley Field that Corky had the opportunity to meet Jerome "Dizzy" Dean and Harold "Pee Wee" Reese, both in Cincinnati for the Game of the Week television broadcast. Among Corky's prized photos is one of him seated in the dugout, alongside his friend and teammate Stan Musial and very near the comical Dizzy Dean.

Corky had a road game roommate by this time, and he was Carl Sawatski, a chunky-built catcher who had played for the Milwaukee Braves during their World Series Championship season of 1957. Carl, born in Shickshinny, Pennsylvania, in 1927, had been a minor league "hitting terror" before his major league days and would later serve as president of the Texas League from 1976 until his death in 1991. Noted for his argumentative nature on the diamond, Carl was named to *Esquire* magazine's "Polish All-Time, All-Star, Argument-Starter Team" in 1976, but Corky only recalls him being a friendly and generous type, one who even loaned him the use of a Volkswagon whenever the Cardinals were playing at home.

On Sept. 24, the Cardinals dropped their sixth game in a row when they went to Wrigley Field to play the Cubs. The final score was 6-5. This game marked the first time Corky had been to Wrigley since 1944, the time when he and his brother had been unintentionally left behind by their parents. Corky saw no action in this game, however.

Of the nine St. Louis games Corky saw action in that season, none sticks in his memory more than the one on Sept. 25. The Cardinals won 5-2 that day, but that's not what made this game so memorable. He explains:

> Stan Musial was retiring, and this game marked his farewell appearance at Wrigley Field. After playing left field for three or four innings, Musial was taken out of the game so the fans could give him a standing ovation.
>
> Even though it was in Chicago, the fans had come to see his final game here. When Johnny Keane pulled Stan from left field, he substituted me in his place. The Cubs fans didn't appreciate this very much, and after Stan's ovation died down, they—the 'bleacher bums—began pelting me with bags of popcorn, half-eaten hot dogs, cups of Coca-Cola, and any obscenities you can think

> of. All I had done was go in for him, but they were there to see 'Stan the Man', not Corky Withrow."

Corky played most of the game that day and batted three times. He had no base hits in those three trips, but recalls hitting a "pop out" foul off the Cubs' pitcher, Freddie Burdette. Catching this foul ball was his friend and former teammate Merritt Ranew, the Cubs' catcher.

With the conclusion of the Cubs-Cards series, it was back to St. Louis to play their final three games. The visitors were the Reds, and these games would be the final ones for Stan Musial. Since Stan—a soon-to-be Hall of Famer—was retiring, it probably is worth noting that Cincinnati was starting a promising rookie named Pete Rose. Corky remembers Rose playing on this day, but certainly could never have imagined the impact Rose would later have in baseball. "He was just another good player then," Corky reports.

The now disheartened Cardinals lost the first two games of this series, 3-0 and 3-1. Corky played in their 3-1 loss on the 28th, but grounded out against Joe Nuxhall in his only at bat. The final game of the season, one played on Sept. 29, was overshadowed by Musial's retirement and all the celebrations that came with it. A home plate ceremony, attended by baseball Commissioner Ford Frick, owner Gussie Busch, and other dignitaries and former players, was held prior to the game, and Corky, with his 8mm film camera, recorded it all close-up.

Corky headed back to Owensboro at season's end. In several ways he regretted it was over, but knowing he would soon be with Barbara and their three-week-old son, more than made up for whatever emptiness came with the season's conclusion. "Keith," Corky explains, "was born on the very same day as Stan Musial's grandson. I know it sounds like an excuse, but the fact that my call-up to St. Louis happened at the same time as my son's birth definitely affected my play that month. I knew, when I reported to them, I was mentally unprepared at the time, but I couldn't control that. Had it been some other time, then maybe things might have been different. I was also so awed by all the people I was around, I never got comfortable enough to play my best."

Corky feels there was one more reason for his poor hitting performance with the Cardinals that month. "I didn't have my own bats with me," he says. "I used a K55, 36-ounce, 35-inch bat with a medium handle, but had left all of mine back in Denver and didn't have time to order new ones. Musial let me try his, and some others did, too, but I never found one I felt comfortable with. That was an important thing with professional ballplayers."

The 1963 baseball season had been Corky's most exciting without question, but what '64 might bring, he couldn't say. He hoped for another go-round with St. Louis, of course, but it was baseball and nothing was guaranteed. His stats—no hits in nine at-bats and 1 RBI in 12 innings played—would impress no one, he understood, but with a good attitude, hard work, and a chance to prove himself to Cardinals management at spring training, just maybe he could hang on.

Chapter 19

Rejection, Readjustment, Reality

When spring training rolled around in late February of '64, Corky found himself in St. Petersburg, Florida, with the St. Louis Cardinals. Again he had the opportunity he had hoped for and was living his big league dream. Still, though, he hadn't made the club's roster yet, and considering all the talent around him, there certainly was much to do to prove himself.

Even with the retirement of Musial, St. Louis was loaded with skilled players and, according to Corky, "likeable, but very serious, hard-working gentlemen." Glowing with compliments for these Cardinals, Corky claims "The Braves just didn't have the gentlemen the Cardinals had." Citing Bob Gibson as an example, Corky describes the big fireballer as a "perfect gentleman" off the diamond, but not so when he was on the mound. "He was an absolute beast on the diamond, and I didn't even want to face him in batting practice," he admits.

Gibson, born and raised in the inner city slums of Omaha, may have been, along with Ty Cobb, the fiercest competitor of any era and would earn the reputation of being a headhunter who often even scowled at his own teammates during games. Tim McCarver was often the recipient of Bob's harsh stares, but never questioned Gibson's competitive intentions in a game. "He's the luckiest pitcher I ever saw. He always pitches when the other team doesn't score any runs," McCarver is reported to have said.

Corky and Barbara, with infant son Keith, enjoyed that spring in their small travel-trailer, but things didn't go as well on the diamond. Corky feels his play was fine, but that their manager, Johnny Keane, didn't give him enough playing time to prove his worth.

"I worked hard and did well when I did play, but that didn't come very often," he complains. "It was really frustrating, and I was very disappointed. I don't know why Keane didn't let me play more that spring."

With a "terrible feeling of rejection," Corky was dismissed from the Cardinals' camp and given instructions to report to Bartow, Florida. Here, he would finish training with the Jacksonville Suns, the Class AAA affiliate of St. Louis. Even though the move wasn't totally unexpected, it was still a huge let-down after tasting life in the "bigs."

Three seasons had passed since Corky had been put off the Jacksonville Braves' team bus in Asheville by Red Murff, and much had changed there since. Red Murff was no longer manager, and Jacksonville, rather than Class A, was now a AAA St. Louis affiliate playing in the International League.

Corky and Barbara found a Jacksonville beachfront lot to rent for their trailer that summer, and although the living quarters were cramped, low overhead and an ocean view more than made up for any inconveniences. On the road, Corky roomed with Dale Long, a teammate who would go on to have a long and successful career as a major league umpire.

The Jacksonville Suns were coached by Harry William Walker (1918-1999), the son of Ewart "Dixie" Walker, a former Washington Senators pitcher. Harry was also a brother of Fred "Dixie" Walker, a former National League batting champion with the Brooklyn Dodgers. Baseball blood ran thick in the Walker family. Like both his father and brother, Harry also had a nickname, but in this case it wasn't "Dixie." Instead, due to his habit of constantly adjusting his cap between pitches while at the plate, teammates tagged him "The Hat."

Harry Walker had a long and successful career as an All-Star outfielder for the Cardinals from 1940-47, before being traded to the Phillies, the Cubs, the Reds, and then back to the Cardinals in '55 as player/manager. During this time he compiled an overall .296 batting average, including a .371 average in 1947. Without question, Harry "The Hat" understood the art of hitting, but the fact that his philosophy was based on the premise that anyone not capable of hitting 40 homeruns a season shouldn't try to hit homeruns at all, certainly didn't bode well for Corky Withrow.

"We started off on the wrong foot, and it only got worse," Corky groans. "He was determined to make a punch hitter out of me, punching the ball to right field, but it was ridiculous on his part to think I could do that." With only half-hearted attempts to carry out his manager's plans to change his batting habits, Corky soon found himself relegated to the Suns' bench. "It got to the point where, sometimes, I would leave the dugout around the fifth inning and go to the clubhouse and dress. I'd listen to the rest of the game on the radio."

Corky's time with Harry "The Hat" and the Suns would, for obvious reasons, be short. In only thirty games with the team, he produced only 14 hits in 73 trips to the plate. And to go with his anemic .192 batting average, there was only 1 homerun.

With little to show for his time with the Suns in Jacksonville, Corky was informed on June 18 that the Salt Lake City Bees of the Pacific Coast League had acquired his contract from St. Louis by sending Jacksonville a player named Bob Will. Salt Lake City, a AAA club with a work agreement with the Chicago Cubs, wouldn't be where Corky was heading, however. Instead, his latest assignment would be with the Ft. Worth Cats, the Cubs' AA farm club in the Texas League. Although Chicago didn't own his contract, it certainly appeared they had a keen interest in Corky's career.

Corky's summation of his time with the Suns in Jacksonville, and his trade from the St. Louis organization that followed, was much the same as several of his previous experiences and disappointments. "Up to that point the season had been a void," he says. "I was frustrated with Harry Walker, and I guess part of that frustration came from feeling rejected earlier by St. Louis during spring training. I really didn't mind being sent to Ft. Worth by that time."

The Ft. Worth Cats, a franchise new to the Texas League when Corky reported to them in June of '64, played their games at Lagrave Field, a park located north of town, but one with a great view of the Dallas/Ft. Worth skyline. Lamar Hunt and Tommy Mercer owned the club, but only during this initial season, as the Cats would be sold twice by 1965, at which time they became the Dallas/Ft. Worth Spurs. Lamar Hunt, it might be noted, would own the NFL's Kansas City Chiefs in 1966, the year they played the Green Bay Packers in the first AFL-NFL championship game. Although not called the "Super Bowl" in '66, Hunt is credited with coming up with the name two years later.

Managing the Cats was Alex Grammas. Grammas had just concluded a nine year big league playing career, mostly in a reserve role for the Cardinals, Reds, and Cubs. Beginning with Ft. Worth in '64, his managing career would eventually lead him back to Cincinnati, and then, in what would be the pinnacle of his career, the World Series Champion Pittsburgh Pirates in 1969.

Corky has nothing but high praise for Grammas. "He had a positive mental approach to the game and respected us as players," he notes. "He worked hard for our benefit and not for his own advancement. Chicago didn't have a good farm system at that time, but Alex was a sharp fellow who did all he could with what he was given."

Corky appeared in seventy-six games for the Cats that season, hitting .242 with 64 hits in 265 at-bats. Of these hits, 13 were doubles and 12 were homeruns. He earned 39 base-on-balls, but whiffed 84 times.

Two incidents stand out in Corky's memories from his time with Ft. Worth, the first of these happening in a game against the Oilers in Tulsa. On his first trip to the plate that day, Corky fanned on three pitches, all of which were, in his opinion, nowhere near the strike zone. After a few unflattering remarks to the plate umpire, he returned to the dugout.

A couple of innings later Corky was due up again. This time, to the amusement of teammates, opponents, and all in the stands, he emerged from the dugout with an altered uniform. His pants were rolled up to his knees, and across his shirt—at arm pit level—was a long strip of athletic tape. This was, of course, Corky's caustic way of reminding the umpire exactly where the strike zone boundaries lay. The umpire was not as amused as others at the park that day, and when Corky stepped in the box, time was called.

The umpire explained to Corky he wouldn't be allowed to bat with his uniform altered, but Alex Grammas—himself amused while trotting to the plate—requested that the umpire show him the rule stating a player was forbidden to do this. With no such rule in the book, the umpire conceded. Corky had made his point.

Another amusing story resulted from a road game the Cats played in Albuquerque, New Mexico. The team had traveled the long distance from Ft. Worth to play the Dukes in an afternoon and nighttime double header. With the team heading to El Paso for their next game, the bus ride after the contests with Albuquerque would take most of the following morning, as the last game wouldn't end until 11 p.m. or later.

When the team arrived at the Dukes' ballpark that afternoon, the Cats' bus driver, a man dealing with a divorce at the time, began drinking—either as a celebration or out of deep sorrow. He continued indulging in drink that entire evening.

As the team boarded the bus around 1 a.m., they couldn't help but notice that their driver was in no condition to drive the bus on to El Paso. Mgr. Grammas, desperate to find a quick replacement, asked if any among them could drive a bus. Corky, since no one else responded, held up his hand. "I told Alex I could, but what I didn't tell him was that it had been only one time... while in the Army... and I had driven the bus into a ditch and hit a light pole that time." Since Corky was the only volunteer, Grammas had no choice but to hand him the wheel. Corky, recalling that journey of long ago, explains:

> I did okay that night and actually had a good time driving. I made Ellis Burton my 'co-pilot,' and he sat in the seat right behind me. We both put the Greyhound bus driver hats on, backwards, and Ellis and I rode along waving out the window at the other trucks and cars we passed. We were going across New Mexico and Texas with a busload of ballplayers and acting like idiots. We made it to El Paso safely, but the bus driver got fired,

> I think. But they didn't bother to offer any permanent driving jobs to me and Ellis.

Corky's time with Alex Grammas and Ft. Worth was enjoyable, but like so many times before, short. The Cats would finish in last place, but minor league play was more about individual performance than team goals, anyway. And even if a team was in a pennant race, a player could never really count on being around when the season ended. "It was hard to get very excited about a pennant race," Corky admits, "...maybe a little...but it was more about getting yourself to the big leagues. It was dog-eat-dog, to tell the truth."

After eight full seasons of professional baseball, Corky knew the clock was ticking down on any chance of a significant major league career when he reported for spring training in early '65. Realizing this season might be his last real opportunity, it would be to his advantage to give his best effort. This opportunity would come with the AAA Salt Lake City Bees of the Pacific Coast League.

The Bees trained in Mesa, Arizona, at a facility Corky describes as "the poorest during my time in baseball. Chicago never did put much into their farm system," Corky says, "and in my opinion, that's what held them back for all those years."

Corky reported to Mesa totally committed to baseball, however, and was determined to do well regardless of the facilities. "I roomed with some young pitcher. I can't remember his name, but he was more interested in his social life than baseball," he says. "He always had people around our apartment, and it was hard to get much rest. But I kept my nose clean, worked hard, and had a good spring."

When training ended in Arizona, Corky flew to Salt Lake City where he was joined by Barbara and Keith. Barbara had driven their car from Owensboro, and the three would spend the summer in an apartment in the city. Corky, describing their time in Utah, recalls:

> We enjoyed Salt Lake as much as anywhere we'd been. It was like living in a bubble. The people were fabulous, there was almost no crime, we didn't need air-conditioning, and the city and mountains were beautiful. Their stadium was beautiful, too. Barbara would bring Keith to the games, and I was pretty proud when he was there. The fans there were great to us, and I had a good year with three or four walk-off homeruns.

In fact, Corky was doing so well that *Sporting News* magazine, in their June issue, named him their PCL "Player of the Month." He was also leading the league in homeruns. With these accomplishments, plus the local press coverage, Corky had emerged as the Bees' top attendance draw. However, this success had both positive and negative effects on his career—damned if you do, damned if you don't—if you will.

The Bees had purchased Corky's contract from St. Louis, and by so doing, would be most instrumental in determining his baseball future. This was still before free agency, and since Salt Lake City was independent of any major league organization—at least as a farm team—the club's female owner had the final say on any deals.

When Corky was told the Bees' owner had refused to sell his contract to the Cubs due to his drawing power, he was, to say the least, upset. "I felt like I was being punished for doing so well there," he explains. "I really think my chances with the Cubs in Wrigley would have been good, but this woman was blocking them for her own selfish reasons. There wasn't much I could do about it, though, and I really got frustrated with the situation."

Salt Lake City played in the Eastern Division of the PCL. This division was comprised of the Oklahoma City 89ers, Denver Bears, San Diego Padres, Indianapolis Indians, and Arkansas Travelers. In the Western Division were the Portland Beavers, Seattle Angels, Vancouver Mounties, Tacoma Giants, Hawaiian Islanders, and Spokane Indians. Salt Lake would finish the season with a 56-91 record, and by so doing, finished in last place.

The Bees' manager that season was Stan Hack, a former All-Star third baseman for the Cubs from 1932 to '47. Corky describes

"Smilin Stan" as being an "easy, laid-back, rather timid person," but one who had his players' best interests as his top priority. When Corky was read a quote from another of Hack's former players describing him as "the sweetest man in the world," Corky nodded his head in agreement.

Despite his frustration with the team's owner, Corky continued playing well. There were memorable moments as always, one of which ended with extremely painful, but rather humorous results. Corky recalls:

> We flew to Honolulu for a series with the Islanders, and I took my movie camera to take movies on the beach. Some of us stayed too long that day, and when we got back to the hotel, I was sunburned and sick. I told Stan Hack, our manager, that I was too sick to play that evening and asked that he not play me since I could barely walk. The game was tight that night, but I just watched from the dugout. In the late innings Stan came down the bench to me and told me to go in to pinch hit. It was the ninth inning, and we were one run down with the tying run at first. I was so sick, I honestly didn't care who won. I went to the plate thinking I would take three half-hearted swings, strikeout, and get back to the dugout with the least pain possible. But, wouldn't you know it, I swung at the first pitch and hit the ball off the right centerfield fence. I ran the best I could, but the crowd had to be thinking something was terribly wrong with that guy. I was hurting an awful lot, but I had to run on to second while the tying run scored. As I was rounding second, the coach at third signaled me to keep running. The outfielder threw to third, so I had to slide. That was the last thing I wanted to do. All I wanted was to get to a base and stop there. As I was sliding into third, the throw sailed over the base into the dugout. I was hurting badly from the slide, but had to get up and head for home now. The throw to the plate was close, so I had to slide again. I was safe, but in so much pain

> by that time that all I could do was lay there. We won the game with my run, but all I had wanted to do was strikeout and sit down.

Something else Corky remembers from his trips to Hawaii concerned Hollywood actor Richard Boone. Boone, says Corky, lived in Honolulu and was a big fan of the Islanders and baseball in general. Best known for his role as Wire Paladin in the television series *Have Gun-Will Travel*, he was always on the field during pre-game warm ups and made it a habit to meet all the visiting team's players. This, according to Corky, was enjoyed by all.

As the season progressed, Corky became more discouraged over the matter of his contract and the owner's refusal to deal him to the Cubs. "I had given my best effort, wanting to move up, but she wouldn't give in," he grumbles. "You really didn't have control of your own destiny then and [were] honestly a slave to the owners. I had a family to support and wanted some kind of future for them, but baseball was all I knew. I was really discouraged and ready to throw in the towel by that time."

Another point of contention between Corky and the Salt Lake City owner concerned a broken promise. When Corky first joined the team that spring, the owner had informed him that he would have to agree to accept a pay cut. However, if he could meet certain standards, statistically and otherwise, his paycheck would be restored to its previous amount. Reluctantly, Corky accepted this arrangement, but, even after performing up to these agreed standards, Bees' ownership never came through with any more money.

The incident that finally caused him to "throw in the towel"—at least with the Bees—happened as the team flew back from a road series with the Indians in Indianapolis. The flight had taken fourteen hours in the team's outdated DC-3 airplane and, as Corky explains, the wings had iced over as they neared the runway at the Salt Lake airport. "I looked out the window and could see ice on the plane's wing," he says. "I grabbed the arms of my seat and gripped them tight. I was sure we were going to crash, and all I could think about was Barbara and Keith. I never felt good about getting on that old plane anyway."

The plane landed safely, but Corky had reached a decision as a result of the terrifying experience. "Barbara was picking me up at the airport," he explains, "and while we were driving home, I told her I was never getting on that plane again." For the ten days after this icy-wing episode, Corky continued playing with the Bees, but these games were home ones in Salt Lake City. When the team reported to the airport for the next road series, Corky, remaining true to his words to Barbara, was a no-show. He, Barbara, and Keith were headed back to Owensboro.

Months later, in late November of '65, that same DC-3 plane crash landed, killing thirteen of BYU's biggest football boosters on their way to New Mexico for a game. The plane, leased by these wealthy boosters, was flying too low on a cold, snowy day and clipped Point of the Mountain, causing it to lose a wing and cartwheel several thousand yards before coming to a halt.

Corky had been with Salt Lake City for the first sixty-eight games of the season. His 16 homeruns in those games led the Bees, and his total still led the club at the conclusion of their 147 game season that September. Bobby Cox, a future big league manager of great ability and success, finished second in homeruns to Corky, but with only 12 in 136 games played. Corky's final batting average with Salt Lake City was a respectable .254.

Now, back in Owensboro, Corky bided his time, reasonably sure some team would eventually call. He was right. Bill Adair, his former manager during the '61 season in Austin, wanted Corky to finish the season playing for him and the Atlanta Crackers. Although very late in the baseball season, Corky accepted the offer since there were no other substantial job prospects in sight. And because the offer came from Bill Adair—the man he credits with salvaging his struggling career four years earlier—he just couldn't say no.

Atlanta, an affiliate of the Milwaukee Braves, was a Class AAA team playing in the International League. Although Milwaukee had sold Corky's contract to St. Louis in September of '63, they had re-acquired it from Salt Lake City after his decision to walk away from the Bees a few weeks prior.

With the offer to play for the Crackers accepted, Corky was instructed to join the squad in Columbus, Ohio, where they were playing a series against the league-leading Jets. After flying to Columbus for this series, he then would travel with his new team on their return to Atlanta. Barbara, now pregnant with their second child, remained in Owensboro with Keith.

The Atlanta Crackers had a storied past that dated back to the turn of the century. As a Class AA team in the Southern Association, the Crackers won enough games to be labeled, at least by Cracker fans, "The Yankees of the Minors." The club later made the move to the International League when the Miami Marlins left Florida, moving to Atlanta in '61. With this move, the Marlins changed their moniker to "Crackers," attempting to somehow connect their past with that of the former Southern Association's Crackers.

By the time of Corky's arrival in late '65, the Crackers were playing their final season in Atlanta, as the Milwaukee organization was preparing to move the Braves there the following season. When the Braves arrived in '66, the Crackers moved to Richmond, Virginia. Here, they became the Richmond Braves. Although records show the '65 Atlanta team as the "Crackers," Corky insists the players' uniform shirts actually read "Braves." If so—and he should certainly know—this was likely done in preparation for the Milwaukee Braves' arrival in Atlanta the following season.

The Crackers played their final season in a new stadium specifically built for the National League Braves' arrival in '66. Construction on this new Atlanta-Fulton County Stadium was completed a year early, however, and as a result, afforded the Crackers the opportunity to use the facility during the '65 season. Corky, although only with the team for their final thirty-two games, was "totally awed" upon entering this stadium the first time and is appreciative of the fact that he was among the first to have played baseball in this facility.

Since the Crackers' season was nearly over when he arrived, Corky roomed by himself at the Americana Hotel near the ballpark. "I was missing Barbara and Keith pretty bad," he recalls, "and was pretty discouraged by all that had happened at Salt Lake. I was just riding things out until I could figure out something else to do to support my family. I had pretty much given up on getting back to the majors, and it was all kind of scary, to be honest."

Corky had to keep playing ball for now, however. Barbara was now seven months pregnant and was still working as a filing secretary for a State Farm Insurance agent in Owensboro. She, like Corky, had grown tired from all the disappointments and frustrations that came with professional baseball.

In the thirty-two games with Atlanta, Corky went 15 for 88 for a career-low .172 average. However, 5 of his 15 hits were homeruns, and 2 of the remaining 10 hits were doubles. It was all-or-nothing when he went to the plate for the Crackers, it would seem.

At season's end, Corky returned to Owensboro. He was soon to complete his degree work at Kentucky Wesleyan, something he had worked at, on and off, for the past several years. Along with this, there would also be a new addition to the Withrow family that fall. Kelly Lynn Withrow, his daughter, was born on the 23rd of November.

Although Corky is unsure as to any details, the Detroit Tigers acquired his services during the winter months of '65-'66. "I can't tell you whether they bought my contract from Milwaukee, or I was just loaned to Detroit," he explains. "By then I was so discouraged, I didn't even bother asking. I was finishing classes at Wesleyan and didn't report to training camp that spring, either. They were okay with that."

Corky did report to his team once the season began, however. That team, the Syracuse Chiefs, was a Class AAA team in the International League, and a farm club of the Tigers. This season would mark his eleventh in pro ball, if the partial '56 season with Evansville is included. During this span he had been on the roster of fifteen minor league clubs, one Venezuelan pro team, three major league clubs during spring training, as well as the month with the Cardinals. There were also two seasons of college basketball and a fall training camp with an NBA team.

As had happened at several stops before, Corky would again have problems with the team's manager. This time that manager was Frank Carswell, a man Corky classifies as having been a "self-indulgent pretty boy."

Frank Carswell (1919-1988) had signed with Detroit in 1941, but after four years of WWII service with the Marine Corps, would spend most of his playing days as a power hitting minor leaguer. In 1957, his playing days ended, and a successful managing career from '57 through '70 would follow. He later would be inducted into the International League Hall of Fame, an entity existing only in the form of a traveling display in ballparks throughout the baseball season.

Hall of Famer or not, Carswell didn't impress Corky Withrow. "I didn't care for the way he handled his players," Corky explains, adding, "We were in Rochester and had lost a couple of games in a row. He came in the clubhouse and chewed us out like we were kids. You don't treat professionals that way." Corky, in no mood for the criticism Carswell was dishing out, picked up a bat, slamming it on a trunk in front of his manager. "I was so burned out with baseball by that time, I didn't care what Carswell did."

Not only did Carswell fail to meet with Corky's approval, but neither did the city of Syracuse. "Things were absolutely detestable there," he recalls. "That whole city was dirty and run-down, and when Barbara and the kids got there, I sent them back home. I didn't want them living there, and I didn't want to be there, either."

Things seemed to be falling down around Corky by this time. He was, he explains, "still earning the minimum big league salary of $8,000, paid with checks coming from St. Louis, Milwaukee, Detroit, and everywhere else." And now, with Barbara and his two children back home, he was keeping only that necessary to cover his basic needs, as most of his salary was sent home to them. "I really couldn't see the point of playing baseball anymore and finally had all I could take."

Reporting to the team's management, Corky told them he wanted to go home and, if possible, complete the season on the roster of the Evansville White Sox. This was, at best, a long shot, as Evansville was now an affiliate of the Chicago White Sox, and some dealings would be necessary to arrange this request. But days later, and to his surprise, Syracuse management informed him of just such a deal.

To show for his miserable time with the Chiefs, Corky had appeared in thirty-three games. During this time there were fifty-eight trips to the plate, resulting in 10 hits for a meager .172 average. Of these 10 hits, 2 were homeruns. Manager Carswell's Chiefs would fare poorly, too, finishing the season with a 54-93 record and a league standing last place finish.

With his arrival at Evansville, Corky knew his baseball days were numbered. He hadn't announced any plans concerning his decision yet, but he knew, in his heart, he couldn't continue. He was home now and sick of all the trials and tribulations that came with being a journeyman minor league ballplayer.

Although now back where his career had started a decade earlier, much had changed. Evansville was now a Class AA team playing in the Southern League and was a farm club of the Chicago White Sox organization. They officially were "White Sox"—like their parent club—but the locals dubbed them "E-Sox."

The team was managed by George Noga, one who, Corky claims, "understood how to handle both the younger and older players"—a skill not all managers possessed. "I was an 'old man' to the younger players by that time," Corky laughs, "and some managers just wanted to spend more of their time and effort working with the younger ones. But Noga was good with both, and I consider myself lucky to have ended my career on a good note with a manager like him."

Corky played most every day during his time with the E-Sox, and in ninety at bats collected 22 hits for a .244 average. There were 6 homeruns. In looking back on his final day in baseball, his only regret concerns the last of these 6 round-trippers. He explains:

> I batted in the seventh inning of the first game of a double header played at Bosse Field on the final day of the season. In that at-bat, I hit a grand slam homerun. I knew that day would be my final one in baseball, but with another game following, I also figured there would be more at bats for me. I batted twice more in the next

> game, but if I'd thought about it at the time I hit the grand slam, I would have rounded third, doffed my cap to the crowd, crossed home plate, and just ran right on out of the stadium and into the sunset. That would have been a perfect way to end my career.

With his final games in the record book at Bosse that day, Corky drove home knowing he wasn't returning to baseball. Although teams would continue sending contracts to his Owensboro home for the next few years, he never once was tempted to sign, claiming, "I didn't want to start over. I'd had enough of baseball."

Chapter 20

Is There Life After Baseball?

Near the conclusion of the '66 season, Corky and Barbara purchased a small house located on 3rd Street in Central City. It was the first they would own and one only blocks from Corky's parents. The house required some remodeling, but with this accomplished, they moved in that October.

A new phase of their life was starting now, and for Corky, it wouldn't be an easy adjustment to make. He had worked during the winter months over the years—once at a clothing store in Owensboro, for example—but going to the same job day after day would be a whole new experience.

First, in early '67, Charlie Grote, a former teammate at Georgetown College, helped Corky acquire a job with Ashland Oil. As an asphalt salesman for Ashland, there was considerable travel required. Soon tiring from this travel, Corky, with Barbara and the kids, moved to Canton, Ohio, to be closer to his work. They kept their house in Central City, choosing to rent in Canton. Their stay in Canton would last only six months, however.

Corky's opportunity to leave Ashland Oil came when he accepted a job selling high school and college yearbooks for Jostens, an Atlanta-based ring and yearbook company. This position came with a sales region in western Kentucky, and with this, allowed Corky and his family the opportunity to return to their house in Central City. For the next three years, Corky traveled to schools in the counties near their home.

With their return to Muhlenberg County, Keith was enrolled at Central City Graded School in the fall of 1969, but, again, the stay wouldn't last long. "Barbara didn't like living in Central City and wanted to be closer to her mother," Corky explains. Selling their house in Central City, the Withrows purchased one with two acres of land about ten miles south of Owensboro in the Pleasant Ridge community of Daviess County.

Although his job with Jostens had been "mostly good," Corky's restless nature again prevailed. In 1974, after three years of selling yearbooks for Jostens, he resigned to accept a position as an insurance salesman for All State in Owensboro. A desk job, especially one requiring a large amount of paperwork, was a new experience for him, and one that, he admits, "just wasn't for me. I didn't like it at all." So, once again, he turned to a former teammate for help.

This time the teammate was Ethan Blackaby. "Blackie," he explains, "was part-owner of the Phoenix Giants and worked in their front office." With his assistance, Corky was able to find work, but not any related to baseball. Instead, the work was in the construction field and involved driving a water truck for the purpose of—believe it or not—"watering down the desert." This involved moving to Arizona, of course, but Barbara opted to remain in Kentucky with the children.

Corky's stay in Arizona lasted only three months before another of his Georgetown teammates, Tom Cox, helped him find work as a "roustabout" on an Anderson-Barnett oil rig in the Gulf of Mexico. Cox lived in Lafayette, Louisiana, and was involved in the insurance business at the time. Since he handled insurance for Anderson-Barnett, Tom's connections proved productive.

Corky's work on the oil rig was twenty miles from the coastal port of Grand Chenier Island, Louisiana, and was an extremely dangerous job. Although it usually required 100 hours of work per week (40 regular and 60 overtime), the $1,000 per week pay check and "seven days on-seven days off" schedule made it worth a try. This did allow him to travel back to Kentucky to be with his family every other week, but the danger and stress proved more than he could deal with. As a result, after only one month as a roustabout, he sought work elsewhere.

Leaving Anderson-Barnett, Corky next accepted a job with Timco, another Lafayette-based company. As a sales rep for Timco, he would be selling oil field jobs and equipment, but the position would require a move to Houston, Texas. Here, he would be earning a handsome $30,000 annual salary, an amount exceeding any salaried job he had previously held. This would provide an opportunity for Barbara to move to Houston with him, and since Keith and Kelly Lynn had graduated from Owensboro Apollo High by this time, they made the move to Texas as well. Keith, it might be added, had been an All-Third Region basketball performer for Apollo, as well as later excelling as an amateur boxer.

Corky's stay with Timco lasted about two years, until political events in Kentucky in the fall of '83 provided him an opportunity to return to Owensboro, something that both he and Barbara were yearning to do. As before, this opportunity came by way of a former Georgetown College classmate. Corky explains:

> When I was in the fraternity at Georgetown, my "big brother" had been Bill Collins, the husband of Martha Layne, who was elected Governor in '83. Barbara and I wanted to come back to Kentucky by this time, so I called Bill in hopes that he could use his influence to get me a job around Owensboro. He did, and it was a state job as an oil well inspector with the Oil and Gas Division of the Kentucky Department for Mines and Minerals. This gave us the opportunity to move back to Owensboro.

Corky's stay with this state job lasted only a few years, however, as he soon learned there was more money to be made capping wells than inspecting them. "I saw how much money there was in the oil business, so I started my own well-capping business," he explains. "I had my own trucks and equipment and capped wells for about twenty years, maybe ten or twelve a year. I did okay with my company and sold it in 1994 for a fair amount. I guess you could say I retired then, but now I work for my son with his plumbing business in Owensboro, but it doesn't pay much!"

Today, at age seventy-eight, Corky looks back on his life with mixed feelings. His high school and college basketball careers were ones equaled by few others, even though his college years were bittersweet. And although his stint at baseball's highest level was short, he did make it there. Maintaining a long minor league career is certainly an accomplishment of some note as well.

On Saturday night, July 12, 2014, Corky walked to center stage at the Historic State Theatre in Elizabethtown, Kentucky. Here, in only the third class to be inducted into the Kentucky High School Basketball Hall of Fame, Corky shared center stage with Frank Ramsey, one of his boyhood heroes. This honor, like several others in recent years, came long after his playing days had ended, but the fact that Barbara, his children and grandchildren, and many of his dearest friends were there to celebrate the evening with him truly made it well worth the long and wait.

As Corky looks back on his life and reflects on his many accomplishments, he does so with a sense of pride, but also with a twinge of aborting an unfulfilled mission. "I've been really blessed," says Corky, "so I wouldn't want anyone to think I'm not thankful for all the things I've experienced in my life. But it's like a man who climbs Mt. Everest. He gets to the pinnacle, puts one foot at the peak, but never gets to stand at the top with both feet. When I think of my short stay with St. Louis, I had more in me—a lot more—but I never got another chance to show it."

And while the kid from Central City made the majors, befriended a childhood hero, and packed a lifetime of seeing places and doing things that now, looking back, seems to have taken place at warp speed, Corky still has that George Bailey quality about him, one allowing him to smile as he remembers that, after all is said and done, it's been a "Wonderful Life!"

Epilogue

If you meet Raymond Withrow today, you'll find a mild-mannered, grandfatherly figure, one that friends and colleagues still know affectionately only as "Corky".

Gone is the brash, cocky, headstrong young man, one who frequently locked horns with reputable minor league managers and other baseball officials, rejecting their advice and suggestions, some of which may have catapulted him onto baseball's biggest stage for an extended stay. Bending rules simply because he could, Corky, more than once, it seems, proved to be his own worst enemy.

The strong and massive hands once ripping a Louisville Slugger through the strike zone—in the process launching towering homeruns in minor league stadiums across the country—are now most likely to be found shaking hands, autographing photos taken decades ago, or, as most grandfathers seem content to do, holding and hugging precious grandchildren and great-grandchildren.

The speed and agility Corky displayed while roaming ballpark outfields and racing down hardwood courts on fast breaks decades ago is gone now, replaced by a lumbersome gait, one more like his contemporaries who, athletically, never performed at, or even near, his level.

Corky's life, in most ways at least, has come full circle. He confesses, unhesitatingly, to not being the same person he once was and has even been heard to explain to friends, "You might not have liked me back then," a concept hard for anyone who knows him now to imagine.

Out of the limelight for half a century now, and with a sports legacy mostly forgotten, he admits to having felt hurt when contemporaries—"King" Kelly Coleman, for example—still garnered statewide attention. Ironically, it was Bowling Green author Gary West's biography on Coleman that would shine some light back on Corky's career in the process.

In Gary's book, a chapter, or at least part of, is devoted to the '55 Christmas Eve game between Corky's Tide and Kelly's Wasps. West, in some detail, also writes about Corky's athletic talents, and by doing so, drew the attention of some Hardin County basketball enthusiasts who, in turn, made it their goal to see that Corky's legacy was not one lost to time.

Through their efforts, with interest and assistance from others, Corky's story took on a life of its own, and with this, other things resulted. The most significant result, although indirectly, was the creation of the Kentucky High School Basketball Hall of Fame in Elizabethtown in 2012.

About the Authors

Sherrill Williams, a native of Larue County, Kentucky, is a retired school teacher residing in Vine Grove, Hardin County, Kentucky. He holds degrees in Education and History from the University of Kentucky and Western Kentucky University. Since retiring from his teaching position at North Hardin High School, Sherrill has remained active as a musician, comedian, and artist, as well as an avid researcher of genealogy, Abraham Lincoln and his family, and Civil War history—the latter with a special interest in Central Kentucky's guerrilla warfare of 1864-65.

Charles Thurman was born and raised in Sonora, Hardin County, Kentucky. After earning a degrees in Mathematics from Western Kentucky University and a degree in Geology from the University of Kentucky, he resided in New Orleans, Louisiana, where he was in the oil and gas business. Returning to Sonora a decade ago, he now owns and manages the Thurman-Phillips Guest Home in his family's 1897 ancestral house. Along with his interest in Kentucky high school sports history, Charlie is a life-long student of American history and has built and maintained a personal library of over 1,500 books.

Index

Numerical

4th Region Tournament 29, 41, 57, 87
16th District Tournament 29, 39, 56, 84

A

Aaron, Hank 174, 214-215
Aaron, Tommy 182, 214, 216, 236
Ackley, Fritz 209, 213
Adair County Indians 52, 55, 139
Adair, Marion D. "Bill" 191-193, 195, 204, 230, 271
Adams, Ed 120
Adams Texaco 199
Adcock, Joe 176-177, 214
A. E. Staley Food Starch Company 202
Albuquerque Dukes 205
Albuquerque, New Mexico 266
Alexander, Claude 141
Alexander, Rex 112
Allison, Atlas 15
Allison, Maud Keeling 15
All State 278
Amarillo Gold Sox 193, 205
Amburgey, Warren 93, 96
American Legion Post 61 Team 141
Anderson-Barnett 278
Anderson, Bobby 36, 40, 141
Anderson, Sparky 203
Aparicio, Luis 209, 212, 234
Arkansas Travelers 268
Arnzen, Stan 48, 75
Arrington, Gene 158
Asheville Tourists 174
Ashland High 63
Ashland Oil 277
Atlanta Crackers 189, 271-272
Atlanta-Fulton County Stadium 272
Attles, Al 198
Auburn Yankees 172
Austin Senators 190-191, 193, 200, 204, 207, 209, 231
Autry, Gene 166

B

Baker, Tony 139
Baltimore Orioles 202
Barass, Don 58, 59
Barnett, Dick 123-125
Barnhill, John 123, 125
Bartow, Florida 216, 263
Batavia Indians 167
Bats 205
Baugh, Lyle 99
Baxter's 101
Bean, Ronnie 110
Beard, Ken 59
Bears Stadium 216, 218
Beasley's 101
Bellamy, Walt 197-198
Bellarmine Knights 115
Bell, Gus 215
Benson, Pascal 104, 156
Berea 127, 146
Berea Mountaineers 115
Berea Pirates 75
Berra, Yogi 216
Berry, Ken 209
Best, James 22
Bevars, Ron 8, 253
Bevars, Susan 8
Bickett, Leslie 42, 47
Bicknell, Darrell 75-76
Bird, Calvin 76
Birmingham Barons 189
Blackaby, Ethan 216, 220-221, 228, 236, 278
Blankenship, Orville 44-45
Blasingame, Wade 206-207, 215-216, 236
Bogota, Colombia 211
Boone County, West Virginia 13
Bosse Field 110, 225, 275
Boston Braves 161, 163, 189
Boston Celtics 196
Botz, Bob 175
Bowling Green 37
Bowling Green's Purples 27
Boyer, Clete 183
Boyer, Ken 221-222, 224, 257
Braden, Glenn 143, 155
Bragan, Bobby 215, 232
Brand, Eddie 141
Brandon, Marlon 65
Braves, Milwaukee 237
Bravo, Angel 209
Breckinridge County 29-30, 57-59
Bremen 26-27, 34, 38-40, 49, 54, 56-57, 67, 83
Brewers High 44
Brewers Redmen 37
Bridewell, Ron 75
Bridgeman, Jeff 9
Briggs Stadium 181
Brooklyn Dodgers 191, 203
Brown 159
Brown, Elleanor Durall 67
Brown, Hillery 125
Brown, Jimmy 204, 232
Brown, John Y. 67
Brown, William "Buster" 192-193
Broyles, Bobby 47
Buchanan, Gale 56-57, 87
Buering, Mrs. 166, 171
Buford, Don 209
Bunning, Jim 181
Burdette, Freddie 260
Burdette, Lew 214
Burgess, Forrest "Smoky" 223
Burgess, Tom 188
Burke, Alexa 250-251
Burke, Carl 250
Burke, Jackson 250
Burke, Kelly Lynn 250
Burke, Olivia 250
Burlington, Iowa 179
Burr, Ben 139
Burr, John 55, 139
Burton, Ellis 266
Busch, Gussie 224, 257, 260
Busch Stadium 257
Butcher, Donnis 61, 197
Butler, Cecil 175
Butler County 36, 41-42, 50-51, 57, 59, 76-77, 79-80, 88, 90
Butler County High School 81
Butler, Don "Quack" 72, 74
Butler Fieldhouse 105

C

Cairo Dodgers 192
Calhoun 27, 29, 34, 38-39, 50, 54, 68, 83
Calhoun, Jim 94, 96
California Angels 187
Calvert, Jerry 33, 48
Campbell, "Copper John" 70
Camp Leonard Wood 227
Canton, Ohio 277
Cantrell, Hayley 250
Cantrell, Lester 250
Cantrell, Logan 250
Caracas, Venezuela 210
Carlisle, Ralph 43, 48
Carlson, Richard 102
Carman, Tony 59
Carr Creek High 91, 93, 141, 146
Carrico, Johnny 93
Carroll, Clay 217, 236
Carroll, Dan 112
Carroll, George 127, 156
Carson, Johnny 175
Carswell, Frank 245, 274
Carter 159
Carter, Pusey 115
Carty, Rico 215
Carver, Carl 46-47
Cash, Johnny 64
Cash, Norm 181
Cassady, Billy Ray 44-45
Cassidy, "Hopalong" 166
Castro, Fidel 210
Cather, Alex 99
Catholic High 82
Caverna Colonels 27, 37
Cedar Rapids, Iowa 177-178, 180
Central City High School 7, 23, 27, 29-30, 32-33, 36-37, 39-44, 49-51, 54, 56-57, 60, 64-65, 68-71, 74-76, 81-82, 84, 91, 93, 98, 150

Central City Invitational Tournament (CCIT) 27, 36, 49, 69, 70, 143
Central City Jr. High 25
Central City, Kentucky 4, 17, 20-21, 36, 43, 76, 103, 110, 132-133, 168, 277-278
Central City Reds 193
Centre College 127
Centre Colonels 115
Chamberlain, Wilt 197-199
Chance, Dean 188
Chaney, Tom 116, 159
Chapman, Ray 111
Charleston Chasox 174
Charlotte Hornets 174
Chattanooga Lookouts 189
Cheatham, George 139
Chicago Bears 202
Chicago Colts 162
Chicago Packers 196
Chicago White Sox 209, 216, 219, 274
Chigger Club 101
Chile Bowl 103, 151
Christian County 88
Chuck Taylor North-South All-Star Classic 158
Cincinnati Reds 202, 205, 219
Cincinnati Royals 196
Clarkson High 87
Clarksville Cats 192
Cleveland Indians 28
Cloniger, Tony 215
Cloninger, Tony 178
Coates, Jim 169
Cobb, Murriel 141
Cobb, Ty 162, 262
Coin, Walter 42
Cole, Carl 197
Coleman, Bob 111, 225
Coleman, Kelly 7, 62, 66, 69-74, 91, 96-97, 104, 105-107, 113, 142, 144, 147-149, 156, 158, 255-256, 282
Coleman, Linda Carol 97, 148
Collins, Bill 279
Columbus, Ohio 272
Columbus Pirates 174
Combs, Billy Ray 73
Combs, Charles 36
Combs, Morton 91, 93
Como, Perry 24
Conover, Bill 139
Cooksey, Adrian 42
Cooper, Bill 186
Cooper, Walker 188, 230
Cope, Mason 37
Corbin 76
Cornelius, Kenny 156
Corning Red Sox 167
Cotrell, David 159
Couch, E.A. 93, 95-96, 104, 156
Cox, Bobby 271
Cox, Earl 75
Cox, Johnny 60-61
Cox, Tom 278
Craig 159
Crandall, Del 214
Creason, Coy 37
Crisler, Carney 158
Crittenden, Howard "Howie" 147
Cromwell 29
Crosley Field 239-240, 258
Cubs 257, 259
Cullinan, Jr., Craig F. 174

D

Dallas/Ft. Worth Rangers 187-188, 196, 217, 221
Dallas/Ft. Worth Spurs 265
Daugherty, Ray 139
Davenport, Bowman "Bo" 87-88
Daviess County 28, 37, 54, 83
Davis, Bob 114-122, 124, 125-126, 128, 159-160
Davis, Dr. 45
Davis, Melvin 125
Davis, Ralph 156
Davis, Terry 96
Dawhare, Serur 256
Day, Jack 51, 61, 93, 142
Daytona Beach, Florida 202
Dean, James 64
Dean, Jerome "Dizzy" 240, 259
Deavers, Richard 8
DeMerit, John 175
Dennis, Billy 193
Denton, David 104-105, 156
Denver Bears 206-207, 214, 217-218, 220, 235-236, 268
Denver, Colorado 216, 219
Detroit Pistons 196
Detroit Tigers 181, 217, 273
Diddle, Ed 53-54, 83, 89, 105
Dilce Combs 44
Dimaggio, Joe 191
Disch Field 205
Divine, Gerald 57
Divine, Joe 38
Domino, Fats 64
Doom, E. P. 136
Dorsey, Ralph 27
Drakesboro High 27, 29, 31, 34, 36, 39, 49, 54, 56-57, 69, 83
Drakesboro's Cardinals 29
Dressen, Charlie "Chuck" 202-203, 232
Dunmor 27, 29, 34, 39, 49, 56-57, 68, 86
Dunnivan 159
Durall, Ellie 67
Durocher, Leo 203
Duvall 159
Duvall, Billy Ray 48, 58-60, 66, 73, 75-76, 92-93, 96, 139, 141, 148
Duvall, Don 115
Dykes, Jimmy 182, 226
Dykstra, Lenny 171

E

Eagle, Dean 61
East (Kentucky) All-Stars 156
East-West Series 104-105
Edmonson County 88
Elizabethtown, Kentucky 280
Ellison, Albert 158
Elmira Pioneers 167
El Paso Sunkings 205
Encyclopedia of Kentucky High School Basketball 9
Erie Sailors 167
Evansville Braves 110, 112, 225
Evansville, Indiana 275
Evansville White Sox 225, 245, 274
Everly, Don 4, 22, 65
Everly, Ike 21, 65
Everly, Margaret Embry 21, 65
Everly, Phil 4, 22, 65

F

Fannin, Omar 45
Farmer, Richie 96
Farrell, "Doc" 72
Farris 159
Flaherty 41
Flood, Curt 221-223
Forbes Field 221, 224, 239
Ford, Whitey 6
Forsyth, Bob 99
Foster, Bobby Lee 181, 185
Foster, Jenny 99
Francis, Earl 224
Fregosi, Jim 188
Frick, Ford 260
Ft. Leonard Wood 180
Ft. Worth Cats 264
Fuller, Buddy 33, 139
Fulton Railroaders 192
Fultz, Billy Ray 73
Fultz, Jerry 8, 256
Fultz, King 256
Furman College 99

G

Gabrielson, Len 184, 215-216
Gager, Barry 104
Garner, Horace 174
Geneva Redlegs 172
Georgetown 118
Georgetown College 114, 122, 127
Georgetown College Tigers 115, 119, 125-126, 159
Gering 159
Gering, Gerry 115
Gibbon, Bob 224
Gibson, Bob 262
Gibson, 'Hoot' 117
Gilliam, Ralph 60
Gish, Delmas 23, 25-26, 28, 30, 33, 36, 39, 42, 46, 59, 66-68, 80-82, 89, 93-94, 136, 139-141, 158
Glasgow Scotties 60
Godwin, Jim 37
Goff, Lavon 64, 113
Golden Tide 23, 26-29, 34, 39-40, 42-43, 45, 48-50, 52, 54, 56-60, 67, 76, 83, 85, 95, 136-139
Goldstein, Al 123
Goode 159
Goode, Earl 141
Gooden, Dwight 171
Gottlieb, Eddie 197, 199
Graham 27, 34, 36, 39-41, 49, 56-57, 69-70
Grammas, Alex 244, 265-267
Grand Chenier Island, Louisiana 278
Gray, Charles 26, 33, 98, 136
Green, Bobby 36, 42
Green River 20
Greenville Blackhawks 27, 29, 35-36, 38-40, 49, 54, 56-59, 69, 82-83, 85, 137
Greenville, South Carolina 99
Groat, Dick 222, 224, 257
Grote 159
Grote, Charlie 115-117, 120, 122-123, 126, 128, 277
Guy, Margaret Everly 22

H

Haas, Eddie 216
Hack, Stan 243, 268-269
Halas, George 202
Haley, Bill 24
Hall, Charles 156
Hall, Elmond 73
Hall High School 63
Hall, Stewart 256
Hammers, Lowell 50
Hammers, Raydean 50, 58, 79, 80-81, 90
Hammond, Indiana 17
Hansford, Tyanna 256
Harper, Bernie Ray 101
Harper, "Fatty" 101
Harper, Jimmy 68
Harper, Robie 49, 54, 57, 68, 87
Hartford 41, 49, 58-59
Hartford Mustangs 36
Hartwell Field 189
Hatton, Vernon 43
Hawaiian Islanders 218, 268
Hawesville 29
Hayes, George "Gabby" 165-166
Hay, Jim 183-184
Hazard Bulldogs 60
Heath 54
Henry-Cisney Chevrolet 43
Henry, Ed 43
Herron, Allen 87-88, 90
Hershey, Pennsylvania 196
Hiatt, Jack 188
Hickman, Bernard "Peck" 53, 118, 123
Higgs, Ronnie 141
High, Ashland 62
Historic State Theatre 254, 280
History of Central City Basketball, The 9
Holland, Martin 156
Honolulu, Hawaii 269
Hope, H.L. "Hub" 31-32, 34, 36-38, 41-42, 44-46, 48
Hopkinsville Hoppers 192
Hornback, Ted 105
Hornell Redlegs 167
Horse Branch 41
Host, Jim 62
Houston, Eddie 26, 33, 48-49, 136, 139
Houston, Mac 92
Houston, Texas 278-279
Howerton, Junior 19, 26, 33, 136
Hudson, Willis 158
Hughes-Kirk 27, 34, 37, 39-40, 49-50, 56-57, 68-69, 76, 84, 86
Hughes, Lowell 104, 156
Huhn, Charles 158
Hunt, Howard 158
Hunt, Lamar 265

I

Indianapolis Indians 268
Inez High 138
Inez Indians 42-45, 52
Irvington 58-59
Irwin, Carlos 30

J

Jackson Generals 192-193
Jackson, "Shoeless Joe" 162
Jacksonville Braves 174
Jacksonville (Braves) Baseball Company 227
Jacksonville Suns 263
Jamestown Falcons 167
Jamison, Carl 48, 58-59, 66, 69, 73, 76, 79, 82, 87, 94-96, 139, 141
Javier, Julian 222-223, 257
Jeans, Jimmy 76
Jennings, Ned 197
Jerry Adkin's Florist Shop 41
Jimenez, Manny 175
Johnson, Lou 216
Johnson, Rossie 125
Johnson, Wally 36, 46, 50, 58-59, 77-79, 89-90
Johnson, Willard "Sprout" 93
Johnston, Ray 187
Jones 159
Jones, Deacon 209
Jones, Kennedy 21
Joseph, Ricardo 169
Jostens 277-278
Joyce, Lewis 209
Judd, Dr. 114
Judd, President 121

K

Kaline, Al 181
Kansas City Athletics 216
Keane, Johnny 223, 236, 259, 262
Keely, Dick 110, 182
Kelley, Dick 178, 216
Kelly, Harold 256
Kennedy, President 210
Kentucky All-Stars 105
Kentucky Colonels 83
Kentucky High School Basketball Hall of Fame 282
Kentucky High School State Baseball Tournament 62
Kentucky Intercollegiate Athletic Conference (KIAC) 115
Kentucky Wesleyan 62, 67, 113
Khrushchev, Soviet Premier 210
King Kelly Coleman: Kentucky's Greatest Basketball Legend 8
Knoxville Smokies 174
Knoxville, Tennessee 185
Koosman, Jerry 184
Koufax, Sandy 258
Kubek, Tony 191
Kuhn, Kenny 28, 61

L

LaCour, Fred 158
Lafayette 44
Lafayette, Louisiana 278
Lagrave Field 264
Lakeland, Florida 181
Lamb, Mrs. 101
Lamustus, Kenny 98
Lancaster, Harry 53
Lane, Alan "Rocky" 102
Lear, Buddy 33, 67, 98, 185
Leitchfield 29, 41, 58
Lemaster, Denny 175, 215
Lemastus, Chris 141
Lemastus, Jimmie 141
Lexington, KY 43, 96
Lexington Lafayette 34, 43
Lexington Lafayette Generals 48
Lickert, Billy Ray 197
Lile, Connie 141
Lile, Johnny 141
Lincoln, Nebraska 178
Lindbeck, Emerit "Em" 170, 206, 228
Litchfield, Terry 76
Litkenhous, Dr. 75
Litkenhous, Frank 34
Little Rock Travelers 189
London High 27
Long, Dale 263
Los Angeles Dodgers 258
Los Angeles Lakers 196
Louisville Atherton 27, 35, 52
Louisville Colonels 217
Louisville Courier-Journal 61
Louisville Invitational Tournament (LIT) 52, 146
Louisville, Kentucky 52, 105
Louisville Male 28, 44
Louisville Manual 63
Louisville Redbirds 205
Louisville Southern 75
Lowery, Bobby 42
Lozano, Wally 172
Luckenbill, Ted 197

M

Macon Dodgers 174
Macon Peaches 189
Madisonville 83
Madisonville Maroons 28, 37
Madisonville Miners 192
Maggard, Freddie 93, 95-97, 104, 146-147
Male High 38
Mantilla, Felix 174
Mantle, Mickey 216
Martin, Dean 24
Martin, J. C. 209
Mason, Billy 48-51, 56, 57-60, 66, 68, 73, 75-76, 82, 85, 90, 92, 94, 96, 98, 139, 141, 158
Mathis, Van 37
Matthews, Eddie 214
Matthews, Walt 184
Maxie, Larry 178
Maye, Lee 215
Mayer, Kenny 156
Mayfield Clothiers 192
Mays, Carl 111, 202
McAfoos, Bob 119
McAuliffe, Dick 181
McCann, Kevin 192-193
McCarver, Tim 222-223, 257, 262
McCutcheon, Arad 112
McDonald, Legon 35
McDowell High 71
McElwain, R.C. 87
McHenry 29
McKinney, "Bones" 55
McKnight, Jim 216, 235
McLendon, John 123-124
McMillan, Roy 214
McNeil, Bob 197
McPhail, Larry 203
McQuary, Ralph 139
McQuire, Frank 197, 199
Meade County 41-42
Medwick, Joe 203
Memorial Coliseum 44-45, 92
Memorial Gymnasium 25, 55, 83, 136, 142
Memphis Chicks 191
Menke, Denis 178, 214
Mercer, Bobby 26, 33, 136
Mercer, Tommy 265
Meriwether, Porter 125
Mesa, Arizona 267
Meschery, Tom 197
Mile-High Stadium 216
Millard, Bobby Don 26, 30, 32, 34, 37, 40, 42, 44-48, 61, 136, 141
Miller Field 191
Miller, Neal 42
Miller's Drugs 103
Mills, Claude 43
Mills, Don 61, 75-76, 104, 146, 156
Mills, Glenn 59
Milwaukee Braves 108, 110, 181, 202-203, 214,

216, 236, 238, 257, 259, 271-272
Minneapolis Millers 202
Minnesota Twins 216
Minor, Harry 171-172, 226
Mitchell 159
Mitchell, Jimmy 28
Mix, Tom 166
Mobile Bay, Alabama 188
Mobile Bears 188, 190
Mohon, Glen 141
Moline Plowboys 202
Monchak, Alex "Al" 165, 167-168, 171, 177-180, 193, 226
Monroe, Bill 22
Montgomery, Gordon "Goose" 115
Moore, Donnie 96, 139, 141, 146
Moore, Kayla 255-256
Morehead, Charles 20
Morehead's Horse Mill 20
Moreland, Jackie 106-107, 158
Morgantown 29
Morgantown, KY 29-30, 87
Morley, Leroy "Stix" 119
Morrison's Cafeteria 215
Moss, Les 209, 234
Muhlenberg Central 26, 27, 29, 34, 38-40, 48, 54, 56, 69, 83, 84
Murff, John Robert "Red" 183,-186, 193, 230, 263
Murray 37
Murray State 112-113
Musial, Stan 6-7, 199, 205, 221-222, 224, 238-241, 259

N

NAIA National Tournament 118, 127, 169
Naismith, James 123
Nashville Volunteers 189, 203
National Athletic Intercollegiate Association (NAIA) 115
Nen, Dick 258
Newcom, Charles 42, 58-59
Newman, Roger 29, 32, 35-36, 38, 40, 45, 47, 54-55, 57-59, 70, 83, 85-87, 93, 95, 104-107, 114, 137, 146, 156, 158, 197
Newman, T.R. 40, 114-115, 137
Newport Public 44, 75
Newport Wildcats 48, 52-53
New York City 99
New York Knicks 196
New York Mets 207
Niekro, Phil 175, 183-184
Noga, George 275
North-South Chuck Taylor Classic 104
Nuxhall, Joe 260

O

Ohio County, Kentucky 13
Oiler Park 205
Oilers 265
Oklahoma City 89ers 217, 268
Oldham, John 55
Olean Oilers 167
Olivo, Chi Chi 216
Olsen, Bud 123
O'Malley, Walter 258
O'Nan, Eugene 80-81
O'Nan, Norman 80-81
Osborne, Charlie 197
Otis 159
Otis, Bill 115, 122
Overstreet, Wynton 178
Owensboro 29, 37, 52, 56, 82
Owensboro Catholic 51
Owensboro Catholic Jr. High 25
Owensboro Catholic's Aces 27
Owensboro, Kentucky 28, 54, 103, 260, 271, 273, 279
Owensboro Oilers 191-192
Owensboro Red Devils 83
Owensboro Senior's Red Devils 27

P

Pacific Coast League 217
Pacific Lutheran 119
Paducah Tilghman 28, 37, 54
Page, Patti 24
Paintsville, KY 105
Pan-American Games 194
Panthers, Robert "Bullet" Wilson's 113
Papillon, Daniel 161
Pendleton, Louis 139
Peoria Tractors 202
Pepitone, Joe 172-173
Pepper, Hugh 188
Philadelphia Warriors 196
Phillips 159
Phillips 66ers 83
Phillips, Larry 115, 117, 122
Phillips, Sam 64
Phillips, Taylor "T-Bone" 209
Pickett, Roger 139
Pike, Harold 115
Pikeville Bulldogs 115
Pikeville College 127
Pikeville, Kentucky 105
Pikeville Panthers 60
Pinson, Byron 99, 104
Pirrie, Jack 158
Plain, Truman Layton "T.L." 30, 67, 104, 156
Podres, Johnny 258
Polley, Rex 156
Porter, J.W. "Jay" 216, 219-220, 228-229
Portland Beavers 218, 268
Presley, Elvis 64
Price, Lawrence 70
Prine, John 21
Pruitt, Joe 98, 185
Pryor, Chad 250
Pryor, Whitney 250

R

Rager, Mose 21
Rambler Rose Motel 71, 143
Ramsey, Frank 280
Ramsey, Jack 38
Randall, Terry 55, 139
Ranew, Merritt 169-170, 175, 178-179, 182, 228-229, 260
Rascoe, Bobby 83
Ray, Hayden 193
Ray, Larry 26, 33, 35, 40-41, 44-45, 48, 136, 185
Reds 260
Reese, Harold "Pee Wee" 6, 203, 259
Reiser, Pete 203
Reynolds, Tom 169
Ribant, Dennis 207-208, 216
Rice, Grantland 162
Richard, Little 64
Richardson, Ed 93, 96
Richardson, Joe 193
Richert 159
Richmond Braves 272
Rickey, Branch 203, 257
Rider College 119
Rigney, Bill 187
Rio Grande Giants 193
Risenhoover, Bob 172
Riverbats 205
Riverside, California 187
Rixey, Eppa 202
Robert C. Stedier Award 172
Robertson, Daryl 175
Robertson, Oscar 67, 105
Robinson 57
Robinson, Billy 26, 33, 35, 40, 48-49, 51, 59, 136, 139
Robinson, Frank 219
Robinson, Melvin 72, 73
Rodgers, Guy 198
Roger Newman 27
Rogers, Bob "Buck" 188
Rogers, Roy 166
Roof, Phil 216, 236
Roosevelt High 206
Rosario, Santiago 169-170
Rose, Pete 183, 260
Rous, Bob 188
Roush, Edd 202
Rowe, Haskin 55, 139
Ruby, Stan 35, 48-49, 139
Ruby, Stanley 26, 33, 136
Rupp, Adolph 4, 6, 53, 61, 107, 110, 112, 146
Ruth, Babe 6
Ryan, Nolan 184

S

Sadowski, Bob 215
Salem High 63
Salmon, Chico 216
Salt Lake City 243
Salt Lake City Bees 217, 264, 267
Salt Lake City, Utah 267
San Antonio Missions 193, 205
Sanders, Simon 141
San Diego Padres 217, 268
Sanford, Ted 31-32, 81, 91
Satterwhite, Jim 125
Savannah Reds 174
Sawatski, Carl 223, 232, 259
Sawyer, Fred 197
Schott, Marge 205
Seattle Angels 268
Seattle Rainiers 218
Sedalia 37, 51-52, 82
Sedalia Lions 48
Self, Jimmy 76
Settles, Roy 30
Shackelford, Ed 76
Shannon, Mike 222
Shaw, Bob 215
Shearer, Ralph 55-56, 61, 139
Sheffield, Jimmy 141
Shepherd, Bobby 92-96, 104, 156
Shields, Allan 50, 58, 89
Shively, Doug 43
Shreveport Sports 189
Shultz, Charles 47
Sidwell, Kenny 27, 37
Simmons, Carl 32
Simmons, Curt 222
Simone, Simone 43
Simpson, Lawrence 139
Sisti, Sebastian "Sibby" 175-176, 183, 226
Skelton, Red 43
Slone, Curtis Ray 71-72
Smith 159
Smith, A. Ray 205
Smith, Ootsie 64
Soergel, Dick 158

Southside Bar and Grill 199
Spahn, Warren 206, 214
Sparks, Larry 35, 57, 59, 141
Spokane Indians 218, 268
Sporting News 268
Sportsman Park 239-240
Stacy, Howard 197
State Legion Baseball Tournament 141
Stengel, Casey 111
Stitts, Mr. 14-15, 130
St. Louis Browns 219
St. Louis Cardinals 7, 18, 204, 221, 224, 236, 238-239, 257, 262
St. Louis Hawks 196
St. Louis, Missouri 257
Stone, Larry 141
Stone, Mark 8
Story, Rex 104, 156
St. Petersburg, Florida 262
Strawberry, Darrell 171
Stroud, John 21
St. Xavier Tigers 38, 49
Swainn, Bennie 120
Swann, Jimmy 48, 73, 93, 96, 139, 141
Swann, Johnny 33, 48
Sweet 16 42, 59, 89, 146
Sydnor, Buck 83
Syracuse Chiefs 245, 273
Syracuse Nationals 196

T

Tackett Jr., Ben 256
Tackett, Julian 252
Tacoma Giants 218, 268
Tarry, McCoy 48, 51
Taylor, Chuck 196
Taylor, George 23, 80
Taylor, Ron 223
Tebbetts, Birdie 176, 203
Temple Hill High 84
Tennessee A&I 119-120, 123-125, 127
Tennessee Tech 55
Texas League All-Star game 205
Texas Southern 119
Texas Southern Bobcats 120
Thompson, Glen 57
Thompson, Winfred 48, 51, 59-60, 63, 67, 73, 75-76, 83, 87-88, 92, 94, 96, 106, 139, 141
Thurman, Charles 283
Thurman, Charlie 66, 253, 255-256
Thweat, Barney 37
Tighe, Jack 217, 219, 221, 236
Timco 278-279
Times-Argus Messenger 45
Tim, Tiny 170
Todd County 69, 70
Todd, Robert "Bobby" 86
Toothman, Ken 188
Topmiller, Ben 50, 86
Toronto Maple Leafs 202, 203
Torre, Joe 214
Transylvania Pioneers 115
Travis, Merle 21
Triplett, Herbie 44-45, 61
Trivette, John Bill 60, 104, 117, 156
Tullar Field 166
Tulsa Oilers 193, 205
Turner, John 75-76, 123, 197
Turner, Johnny 52
Turner, Sandra 256
Tyra, Charlie 27, 35, 52

U

Uecker, Bob 175, 183, 215-216
Union Bulldogs 115
Union City Greyhounds 192
University of Kentucky 4, 6, 53-54, 61, 146
University of Louisville 118, 123

V

Vancouver, Canada 169
Vancouver Mounties 170, 268
VanHoose, J.R. 255-256
Varney, Everett 156
Veale, Bob 223
Veterans Memorial Stadium 178
Victoria Rosebuds 193
Vincent, Sue 99

W

Waggoner, Frank 51
Wake Forest University 55
Walker, Dennis 158
Walker, Dixie 203
Walker, Ewart "Dixie" 263
Walker, Fred "Dixie" 263
Walker, Harry "The Hat" 189, 244, 263-264
Wallace, Tom 9
Walls, Halford 17
Walls, Juanita Withrow 17
Ward, Lowell 141
Warley, Ben 125
Warren, William C. "Bill" 50, 77, 89
Watkins, Bob 147
Waycross Coastliners 162
Waycross, Georgia 161-162, 169, 174
Wayland High School 7, 70, 73-74
Wayland Wasps 69-70, 143
Wayne, John 166
Weaver, Earl 210
Wellsville Braves 165, 167, 170
Wellsville, New York 165-166, 171
Werts, Eugene 125
Wester, Denny 47
Westerfield 159
Western Illinois 119-120
Western Kentucky Hilltoppers 83
Western Raptors 209, 212
West, Gary 5, 8, 72, 282
West, Jerry 67, 105
West (Kentucky) All Stars 156
West Palm Beach, Florida 214
West Palm Beach Municipal Stadium 214
West Virginia Wesleyan 119
White, Bill 257
White, Bob 141
White, Ernest Daniel "Ernie" 189-190, 193, 230
Whitesburg, KY 105
Whobrey, Kim 8
Whobrey, Rick 7-8, 255-256
Wilkins, Lynn 141
Willard Vincent's Central 101
Will, Bob 264
Williams 159
Williams, Hank 24
Williams, Jack 115
Williams, Jim 42, 87
Williams, Jimmy 47
Williamson, Jimmy 76
Williamson, West Virginia 104
Williams, Sherrill 4, 253, 255-256, 283
Wilson 159
Wilson, Art 192-193
Wilson, Bob 51
Wilson, Mookie 171
Wilson, Robert "Bullet" 67
Wilson, Shirley 47
Winchester, Roy 42
Wingo 51, 82
Wisconsin Reserve Unit 227
Withrow, Barbara 134, 204, 210, 213-214, 216, 218-219, 248-250, 262, 267-268, 271-273, 277, 279-280
Withrow, Betty 134
Withrow, Chad 134
Withrow, Cleopatra Brown 13, 131
Withrow, Duane 134
Withrow, Etsel Lee 13, 131
Withrow, Flo Eva Allison 13-15, 17, 20, 34, 68, 76, 98, 122, 129, 133-134, 168, 171
Withrow, Frank "Kid" 110
Withrow, Keith 134, 249-250, 252, 257, 262, 267-268, 271-272, 279
Withrow, Kelly Lynn 134, 249, 273, 279
Withrow, Kim 250
Withrow, Otis Earl 13-17, 20, 62, 129-134, 168
Withrow, Peggy Sue 14, 19-20, 131
Withrow, Raymond Wallace "Corky" 4, 6, 8, 13-15, 18-20, 23, 25-26, 29-30, 32, 34-38, 40-42, 44-65, 67-73, 75-83, 85-90, 92-108, 110, 116-126, 128-129, 131-134, 136-137, 139-144, 146-151, 154-168, 170-172, 174-178, 180-186, 188, 190-196, 198-200, 203-206, 208-210, 212-220, 222-223, 227, 229, 231, 235-242, 245, 247-250, 252-257, 260, 262, 264-268, 270-281
Withrow, Roy Duane "D.D." 13, 18-20, 26, 29, 33-36, 40, 42, 44-45, 48, 50, 62, 68-69, 84, 86, 98, 113, 129, 131-132, 134, 136-138
Wolfe, Dick 26-27, 29, 31, 136
Wolfson Park 174
Woodall, Rondall 57
Woodward, Woody 216
Wrather, M.O. 106
Wray, Ken 51
Wrigley Field 17, 18, 242, 259

Y

Yewell, Barbara 199-200
Yewell, Frank Lloyd 199
Yewell, Gladie V. Flener 199
Young, Bill 161
Young, Bobby 141
Young, Loretta 43